D0583804

Between Brown and Black

Between Brown and Black

Anti-Racist Activism in Brazil

ANTONIO JOSÉ BACELAR DA SILVA

Rutgers University Press

New Brunswick, Camden, and Newark, New Jersey, and London

Library of Congress Cataloging-in-Publication Data
Names: Silva, Antonio José Bacelar da, author.
Title: Between brown and black: anti-racist activism in Brazil / Antonio José Bacelar da Silva.
Description: New Brunswick, NJ: Rutgers University Press, 2022. | Includes bibliographical
    references and index.
Identifiers: LCCN 2021032968 | ISBN 9781978808522 (paperback) | ISBN 9781978808539
    (hardback) | ISBN 9781978808546 (epub) | ISBN 9781978808553 (mobi) |
    ISBN 9781978808560 (pdf)
Subjects: LCSH: Blacks—Race identity—Brazil. | Blacks—Political activity—Brazil. |
    Anti-racism—Brazil. | Brazil—Social conditions—21st century.
Classification: LCC F2659.B53 S54 2022 | DDC 305.896/081—dc23
LC record available at https://lccn.loc.gov/2021032968

A British Cataloging-in-Publication record for this book is available from the British Library.

Copyright © 2022 by Antonio José Bacelar da Silva
All rights reserved

No part of this book may be reproduced or utilized in any form or by any means, electronic or
mechanical, or by any information storage and retrieval system, without written permission
from the publisher. Please contact Rutgers University Press, 106 Somerset Street, New
Brunswick, NJ 08901. The only exception to this prohibition is "fair use" as defined by U.S.
copyright law.

References to internet websites (URLs) were accurate at the time of writing. Neither the author
nor Rutgers University Press is responsible for URLs that may have expired or changed since the
manuscript was prepared.

♾ The paper used in this publication meets the requirements of the American National
Standard for Information Sciences—Permanence of Paper for Printed Library Materials, ANSI
Z39.48-1992.

www.rutgersuniversitypress.org

Manufactured in the United States of America

For my mother, Yêda.

Note: Unless otherwise indicated, all translations are the author's own.

Contents

Contents

Between Brown and Black

1

Black into Brown,
Brown into Black

Afro-Brazilians Grapple with
Racial Categorization

Brazil's national culture and identity hinge on its history of racial mixture and the mythology that there are no racial divisions in the country. In an interview with Robert Darnton of the *New York Review of Books*, the Brazilian historian and anthropologist Lilia Schwarcz offers insight into this phenomenon:

> That is the most common image of our country, and it was, in a way, actually an artificial construct created by Getúlio Vargas, the populist president of the 1930s. He "nationalized," so to speak, Capoeira, Candomblé, samba, and soccer. He even construed "feijoada" (a food derived from slave cooking) as a symbol of Brazil. The white of the rice, he said, stood for the white population. The black of the beans represented the Africans. The red of the pepper corresponded to the indigenous people. The yellow of the manioc symbolized the Japanese and Chinese who had poured into the country in the beginning of the twentieth century. And the green of the vegetables was the forest. You could call it political marketing, but it was very clever, and today we see Brazil

as a country of one culture, even though we have many different subcultures. (Darnton 2010)

Miscegenation, or racial mixing, provides the ideological basis for this Brazilian national discourse. Growing up in Brazil, I recall the absence of racial difference, racial conflict, and legal segregation being recurring themes in conversations about what it meant to be Brazilian. To this day the notion of *brasilidade* (Brazilianness)—the idea that all Brazilians are a blend of African, European, and Indigenous peoples, and that there are no racial divisions or distinct racial identities in Brazil—is at the core of Brazilian lore. Even Brazil's 2014 soccer World Cup opening ceremonies became a celebration of *brasilidade* with the synchronized, slick cultural presentation of three children (Black, Indigenous, and White) releasing white doves. Highlighting Brazil's supposed racial harmony, the white dove release represented what Roberto DaMatta (1990) has called the "fable of three races." The opening ceremony of the 2016 Summer Olympics in Rio de Janeiro was likewise steeped in Brazilian racial ideology, depicting migration and miscegenation as central to what it means to be Brazilian. The ceremony portrayed the country's mix of cultures as contributing to make Brazil the harmonic mosaic it is today.

A good example of reinforcing Brazil's racial exceptionalism can be seen in a remark by Jair Bolsonaro, the current president. In November 2020, during a speech at the summit of the Group of Twenty (G20), Bolsonaro emphatically stated that there was no racism in Brazil and that some people wanted to "import racial tensions." He was referring to the wave of public demonstrations occurring across Brazil at the time. Echoing the marches against racial injustice across the United States after the gruesome death of George Floyd on May 25, 2020, at the hands of the Minneapolis police, Brazilians were taking to the streets to protest the death of João Alberto, beaten to death by security guards at a grocery store in the city of Porto Alegre on November 20, 2020. Bolsonaro began his speech by addressing the social unrest but without directly mentioning Alberto's death that provoked it: "Brazil has a diverse culture, unique among nations. We are a miscegenated people. Whites, blacks, and Indians built the body and spirit of a rich and wonderful people. In a single Brazilian family we can contemplate a greater diversity than whole countries" (quoted in Drumond 2020).

All these examples point to Brazilians' enduring allegiance to the idea of race mixing and racial harmony. Racial mixture and racial integration also emerge in conversations with outside observers visiting Brazil who note the ways in which Brazilians cross racial divides and come together in public spaces. During the 2014 World Cup, I was in Brazil conducting fieldwork, and my husband, Ed, came to visit during the games. Turning to me with an expression of admiration, he said, "I feel there is less racial tension in Brazil. Look at all this mingling of people of all colors, many at the same table." In his perception, Brazilians lived race differently, meaning they had achieved a level of racial integration that appeared nonexistent in the United States. His comment echoed the widespread perspective that Brazil is genuinely a mixed-race culture.

Miscegenation is central to Brazilians' concept of race, and it has long been a defining feature of how Brazilians understand racial categorization. Unlike the United States, where racial separation is often understood in terms of concrete biological (hypodescent) and cultural boundaries,[1] racial difference in Brazil is not viewed primarily as a matter of ancestry but of phenotype. To categorize someone as Black, more or less Black or more or less White (Brown), or White, Brazilians focus on bodily characteristics (skin color, hair texture, and facial features). As sociologist Denise Ferreira da Silva notes, the Brazilian soul "is 'undivided'; it is Brazilian (national)" (1998, 228). Brazilians are accustomed to being racially identified in different ways over time, across contexts, or even in a single daily encounter. Without a sense of belonging to a racial community, Brazilians' understandings of race are flexible. Brazilians have a non-exhaustive list of racial/color terms: *branco* (white), *moreno* (brown), *pardo* (brown), *escuro* (dark), *preto* (black), and over one hundred others. The Instituto Brasileiro de Geografia e Estatística (Brazilian Institute of Geography and Statistics), which administers censuses in Brazil, uses five categories: *branco, pardo, preto, amarelo* (yellow), and *indígena* (indigenous). In my English translations, I try to be as faithful as possible to the descriptors Brazilians typically use. I recognize, however, that they are not always perfect—especially not *pardo* and *moreno*, as there is not an equivalent intermediate category in the U.S. ("multiracial," maybe, but that does not foreground phenotype).

Herein lies the paradox of Brazilian race relations: Despite widespread cohabitation of Black, Brown, and White people—along with superficial tolerance and lack of racial conflict—Brazilians are no less racist than are

Americans or anyone else. Groundbreaking Brazilianist scholars have pointed out the fundamental contradiction that racism in fact exists in Brazil, not merely in isolated and individual manifestations of racist behavior but in widespread structural and institutional racism. As João Costa Vargas notes, "The simultaneous negation of the relevance of race in general, and Blackness in particular, and the hyperconsciousness of race, and Blackness specifically [are] normative parameters from which behavior, representations, and institutional arrangements draw" (2012, 6). In other words, the denial of racism and the invisibilization of Blackness go hand in hand with the virulent, excessive consciousness of racial difference affecting the everyday and institutional lives of Black Brazilians.

The patterns of socioeconomic disparity across racial categories have challenged Brazil's dominant narrative. The starkest divides occur in measures of education, employment, income, and infant mortality. Blacks represent 68 percent of Brazilians in poverty (Paixão et al. 2011; Paixão and Rossetto 2019), reflecting centuries of White privilege that have made it particularly difficult for Black Brazilians to achieve economic security. When it comes to Black homicide, analyses have revealed a national crisis. According to Daniel Cerqueira and colleagues (2019, 49), in 2017, 75.5 percent of homicide victims were Black or Brown, as defined in the Brazilian census, and the homicide rate per 100,000 Blacks was 43.1, compared to 16.0 for non-Blacks (Indigenous, White, and Asian). Put another way, for each non-Black individual who was murdered in 2017, approximately 2.7 Blacks were killed (Muñoz Acebes 2016; also see C. Smith 2016). In sum, "pobreza no Brazil tem cor" (poverty in Brazil has color; Carneiro 2011, 57) and it is Black; or, as Jennifer Roth-Gordon notes, there are "ubiquitous signs of blackness and whiteness within a context that discourages them from describing what they see in racial terms" (2017, 7). This book is informed by this fundamental problem: Systemic racism has always been a major issue in Brazil, yet at the same time, most Brazilians tend to believe that they live in a country where race no longer determines exclusion and they therefore ignore racism and accept the social order as established by other factors such as class and individual limitations. In particular, I explore how the facts of Brazilian miscegenation circumscribe the ways Afro-Brazilians in Salvador (Bahia state) negotiate the boundaries of Blackness in contemporary Brazilian society. In their current approach to anti-racist activism, Afro-Brazilians employ various linguistic resources to critically engage individual and collective experiences of race and Blackness.

Rendering Blackness Invisible in the Tropical Democracy

In "Tropical Democracy," Silva provides insight into how the history of miscegenation has shaped Brazilians' relationship with Blackness. Based on a discursive study of statements on the Brazilian nation published between 1880 and the 1930s, Silva describes how changes in the meaning of miscegenation over time have been integrated and internalized into the Brazilian identity. She identifies two moments when the meaning of miscegenation significantly changed. Common to both moments was the construction of new modes of being Brazilian that sought to obliterate via the concept of racial mixture: Brazil's racial subalterns, Africans and Indians. The first references to miscegenation, meaning the interbreeding of races, to describe Brazil's racial situation and the majority of its people, occurred sometime in the mid- to late nineteenth century. Race mixing was associated with the ideology of eugenics to connote "moral degeneration," which was deeply entrenched in the United States racial discourse at the time (D. F. Silva 2007, 222–223). Eugenicists believe a human population can be improved by increasing the occurrence of desirable, heritable (White) characteristics through controlled breeding. During the late nineteenth century, Brazilian intellectuals, politicians, and scientists would promote the perceptions and beliefs that mixed-race people were contributing to racial decline by introducing harmful, objectionable, or unpleasant African and Indigenous traits in Brazilian people.

Thinking and writing between 1870 and 1930, anthropologists Raimundo Nina Rodrigues and Artur Ramos applied racial degeneration to Brazilian conceptions of race. Describing Black people as the lower strata of Brazilian society, they warned of the danger of miscegenation, specifically that the growing presence of Black people would eventually cause the disappearance of superior races and cultures. As Silva notes, their word formalized this eugenic ideology within Brazil: "Miscegenation would continuously threaten Brazil's future, as the discussion of deployments of the arsenal of race relations indicates, for it is always available as a global (racial and cultural) signifier to explain why Brazil has been condemned to remain on the outskirts of capitalist globality" (2007, 231). But the ideology of miscegenation, and sentiment toward it, continued to evolve significantly as part of Brazil's nation-building project. The most significant changes stemmed from arguments related to "whitening" and racial democracy, which led to the two important moments of change in the meaning of miscegenation.

In the first instance—a repudiation of the idea of racial degeneration that had spread through Brazilian society during the nationalist movement from 1870 to the 1930s—some members of the intelligentsia and political elites, such as João Baptista de Lacerda and Sílvio Romero, challenged the idea of Brazilian society as doomed. They struggled to project the notion of the Mestiço as a pathway toward civilization instead of ruin. Their views altered in significant ways the narrative that Brazilian people were destined to fail because of their degenerate racial composition. Instead they argued that Brazilian society mirrored European society and that through immigration and miscegenation, European traits would, in due course, come to dominate African and Indian physical traits in the Brazilian population. This whitening thesis reworked miscegenation and offered Brazilians a path toward replicating White European culture in their country. As Silva reminds us, the whitening thesis enabled Brazilians to see miscegenation as leading not to the degeneration of Europeans but to the eventual "obliteration of the Indian and the African from Brazilian bodies and minds" (2007, 238). The whitening process would cleanse the stains off Brazilian Blacks whose African heritage tainted their bodies and muddled their minds.

The next modification to the trope of miscegenation happened with the publication of Gilberto Freyre's *Casa-Grande & Senzala* (*The Masters and the Slaves*; 1933). At this point, a new self-definition of Brazilian society as a racial democracy emerged in parallel to the whitening ideal. Merging the ideologies of whitening and racial democracy, Brazilians found a way to live without racism and in racial harmony, but the cost was suppressing racial difference. In yet another revision of miscegenation as a representation of Brazilian culture, the racial democracy identity oriented itself toward Portuguese influence while seeking to eliminate the Black component. Here, "the method of de-Africanizing the 'new' negro was to mix them with a mass of 'ladinos' or veterans, so as the slave quarters became the practical school of brazilianization" (Freyre [1933] 1987, 357).

In both transformations of the meaning of miscegenation (whitening and racial democracy), the central strategy was not only to cast the Brazilian people as of mixed race but also, and simultaneously, to vanish (or erase) inferior races (especially Blacks) through assimilation (D. F. Silva 2007, 234, 238–239). This perspective on the history of miscegenation offers important insight into the complexity of any project to promote racial equity among Brazilians. Engaging critically with the many iterations of Brazilian miscegenation, I explore current changes in Brazil's racial ideologies as a foundation for analyzing the dynamics among miscegenation, racism against dark-skinned individuals, and anti-racist activism among Afro-Brazilians. Afro-Brazilian's linguistic approach to anti-racism is a focal point for articulating my analysis throughout the book.

"Miscegenation Is Also Genocide"

Novembro Negro (Black November) is an annual celebration of Black consciousness throughout Brazil. The monthlong event grew out of a meeting of Black activists in Porto Alegre, Rio Grande do Sul, on November 20, 1971. November 20 was the death date of Zumbi dos Palmares, leader of the iconic Quilombo dos Palmares (a community of African escapees from enslavement) who led the resistance against slavery in the Serra da Barriga in Alagoas.[2] On that day in 1695, Zumbi was ambushed and assassinated, and his head was displayed in the public square as a warning against resistance. When the Movimento Negro Unificado (MNU; Unified Black Movement) was founded in 1978, it designated November 20 as a national day of commemoration, and in 2003, it was officially recognized as a school holiday. In the decades since the founding of the MNU, Black Consciousness Day celebrations spread throughout Brazil as a national campaign to denounce racism and raise Black pride. In 2011 President Dilma Rousseff named November 20 as Dia Nacional de Zumbi and Consciência Negra (Zumbi and Black Consciousness Day). Legislation to make the day a national holiday has been introduced in the National Congress twice, in 2015 and 2017, but as of 2021 neither bill has come up for a vote (Projeto de lei senado 482/2017). For supporters of these bills, November 20 is a symbol of struggle, resistance, and affirmation that Blackness is not inferior and that Black people have value and a place in Brazilian society (Porfírio 2020).

In November 2009, I visited a public library in Salvador to join a group of about thirty attendees for a talk on the life and work of the Black scholar and activist Abdias do Nascimento as part of the Black November events. I had met the speaker, activist, and scholar I will call Jussara Nogueira,[3] at the Centro de Estudos Afro-Orientais (CEAO; Center for Afro-Oriental Studies) days earlier, and she invited me to attend the talk. Having recently received her master's degree in language studies from the Universidade do Estado da Bahia (State University of Bahia), Nogueira was an instructor of racial and gender equality at CEAO and an MNU member.

She began by greeting the audience and thanking them for taking interest in Novembro Negro events and Abdias do Nascimento in particular. She continued by asking who in the audience had heard of Nascimento, an important figure in the Brazilian Black movement, and pointing out that other important Black Brazilians are also largely unknown. She then explained that the topic of her master's thesis was one of Nascimento's books of poetry, but that to really understand and analyze the poems, she needed to learn about his life. Born in 1914, Nascimento was at this time ninety-five (he would die in 2011, at age ninety-seven), so he had lived through the twentieth century and into the twenty-first. Brazilian abolition occurred in 1888, less than three decades before Nascimento's birth, so he experienced Brazil's century-old history of anti-Black racism. Nogueira argued that Black Brazilians, even brilliant people like Nascimento, continued to struggle for validity and visibility not only in their outstanding work but in their very existence.

Early on Nascimento struggled to find a balance between the euphoria of Brazilians celebrating a pronationalist government and mobilization against their racist assumptions. Particularly interesting in this regard is the fact that those early twentieth-century leaders of Brazil's emerging modern Black movement who expressed allegiance to the national project failed to engage in honest and critical discussions about racism (Davis 1999, 188–189). Reading between the lines of Nogueira's speech, I realized she was preparing her audience for an open discussion of the interplay of race, nation, and Black consciousness. As she talked about Nascimento's role in fighting for Black inclusion in White-dominated spaces such as theater, Nogueira invited her listeners to reflect on issues—both old and new—pertaining to Brazil's national family, miscegenation, and the ostensible racial democracy. At that time, the thinking was that Blacks and Whites in Brazil lived in perfect harmony, even though inequality was very high, a point that Nogueira stated indignantly. But the specifics of this historical moment were actually a rhetorical strategy to provide a backdrop against which she would address contemporary issues of Black consciousness.

Moving on to a major theme of her speech, Nogueira cited important Black figures such as Edson Carneiro and Guerreiro Ramos who worked to raise awareness of inequality, emphasizing that their Black (*negro*) identity had been erased from public discourse. She acknowledged that her emphasis on this *negro* identity might strike some people as odd, though the term is being used more frequently, she added. As she continued to speak,

Nogueira's voice was hardened by sarcasm and a tinge of resentment. Admiration for Nascimento's intellectual and political accomplishments vied with sarcasm over the intricacies of what appeared in the accepted history of Brazil and what was erased as incompatible with the dominant ideology. She told of Nascimento's trip to Lagos, Nigeria, in 1977, to attend a colloquium at the Second World Black and African Festival of Arts and Culture, or FESTAC 77, where he spoke at length about the need to dispute the narrative of Brazil's racial harmony, which was propagated not only in Brazil but worldwide. Nogueira's voice became louder and more intense as she recited a portion of Nascimento's poem "Padê de Exu libertador":

> Zumbi Luiza Mahin Luiz Gama
> Cosme Isidoro João Cândido
> sabes que em cada coração de negro
> há um quilombo pulsando
> . . . .
> outro palmares crepita
>
> Zumbi, Luiza Mahin, Luiz Gama
> Cosme Isidoro, João Cândido
> you know that in every black heart, there is a pulsating quilombo,
> . . . .
> another palmares can light up

(Nascimento 1983, 35)

Nogueira's choice of this excerpt from Nascimento's poem was very much in tune with Novembro Negro and Brazilian Blacks' strategies for demanding full belonging in the nation. Even if the majority of listeners did not recognize the names recited, that did not matter. Those people, whose Black identities and stories of Black resistance remained obscured from public view, would become known to her audience that day. During the question-and-answer segment, I asked Nogueira to talk about the Black movement's critique of miscegenation. She explained,

> Quanto mais negro você é nessa cidade, nesse país, e isso envolve desde a cor da pele até a forma como você se veste, mais fora do esquema você está, mais agredido você é, mais violentado você é, então nesse sentido, pra mim a mestiçagem não interessa.

> The more Black you are in this city, in this country, and this goes from the
> color of your skin to the clothes you wear, the more excluded you are from the
> system, the more harmed you are, the more you are victimized by violence, so
> in this sense, mestiçagem [*mestizaje*] doesn't interest me.

A priority for Nogueira and the other Black activists I met in Brazil was to reveal that thinking of race relations in terms of race mixing allows racial discrimination and racial exclusion to go unchallenged. These activists' interactions with the state and society as a whole are thus part of a larger shift in the ways that Afro-Brazilians engage with Brazil's racialized ideology about race mixing. The novelty of this shift surrounds the ways in which they complicate the interrelatedness of race mixing and Blackness.

Nascimento's *Brazil, Mixture or Massacre?*, which addresses Brazil's racial contradiction, largely shapes the dissatisfaction with the "never-too-celebrated miscegenation syndrome" (Nascimento 1989, vii) among activists and scholars, and increasingly among members of Brazil's Black community. A compilation of some of his previous works, the book includes the text of his 1977 speech, "Genocide: XX," at the FESTAC 77 colloquium. In it Nascimento notes how the whitening imperative was infused with the idea of integration and justified by the notion of racial democracy: "In the face of the racist, genocidal character of the ideology of so-called 'racial democracy,' it would be irresponsible to fail to expose and roundly denounce the social structure supposedly based on it. To be silent would be to give tacit approval to the exploitation and destruction of one race by another through dissimulated but systematic oppression and racial arrogance. It would be to condone genocide: a criminal act which perpetuates an unjust society totally iniquitous to Blacks and native Indians in Brazil" (Nascimento 1989, 90).

Nascimento's speech and Silva's "Tropical Democracy" take a similar approach to miscegenation as a historic signifier that silenced Brazil's racial underclass by obliterating them or placing them outside the national subject (D. F. Silva 2017, 224–225). When demonstrators in São Paulo at the Fourteenth Black Consciousness March on November 20, 2017, carried a large banner with the words "Miscigenàção Também É Genocídio" (Miscegenation Is Also Genocide), it caused a stir on mainstream and social media, as many interpreted it as a statement against the union of people of different racial backgrounds. Writing for Alma Preta (Black Soul), an independent news outlet, Lia Vainer Schucman and Mônica Mendes Gonçalves argued the banner instead echoed Nascimento's words. The activists display-ing the banner meant to counter the discourse of race mixing and racial democracy that say "that we are all equal, because we are all mestizos . . . this equality that operates on the genetic plane has never operated on the social plane" (Schucman and Gonçalves 2017) At the same time, we can liken both Nascimento's "Genocide: XX" and Silva's "Tropical Democracy" to more current scholarship that digs into how the social structures in multiracial societies perpetuate anti-Blackness. As Vargas notes, "Racial democracy—the concept, its proponents and revisionists, and the institutional and cor-porate apparatuses that sustain it—is nothing but the denial of antiblackness masqueraded as an elegy to the country's fictional inclusive multiraciality" (Vargas 2018, 44). These writings and this scholarship have shifted the terms of discussion about research and mobilization that address both racial dis-crimination and exclusion.

Anti-Blackness, so understood, emerges not only from obvious forms, such as overt racism, but also—and most important—from the systematic marginalization of Black people due to invisible (unconscious) systems of thinking. Scholars theorizing anti-Blackness generally agree on several prop-ositions (Vargas 2018). First, anti-Blackness is understood as the asymmet-rical relationship between Blacks and non-Blacks in a racial hierarchy that makes full humanity something impossible for Blacks to achieve. Second, because they are viewed as not fully human in nature or character, Black people need to be persistently policed. Regardless of whether or not they believe in equality and social justice, people are culturally duped into believ-ing that Blacks are inhuman. The last proposition holds that although Black people have made huge strides toward racial justice, they face constant threats to their humanity in their daily lives, as anti-Blackness continues to oppress Black people based on a slavery mindset.[4]

To engage with these questions requires cutting through the layers of a fundamental and problematic issue: the interaction of the long-standing idea of racial mixture with widespread anti-Black racism. Afro-Brazilians I have worked with in my research are currently collectively reevaluating these contradictions long taken for granted. Their approaches to the issue reveal an unspoken lack of convergence as to the extent of freedom in self-identification as Black—that is, who is and is not allowed to self-identify as Black. Some are trying to inculcate, through Black consciousness-raising programs, the idea that Afro-Brazilians have an ethical obligation to embrace their Black identities. Meanwhile, other Black activists are focusing on affirmative action programs, such as racial quotas, to increase the number of Black people within institutions of higher education, civil service jobs, and other prestigious areas of society. Their criteria for racial quotas, for example, target demographic groups whom, they argue, have been under-represented in positions of leadership, professional roles, and academics.

Anti-racist Consciousness among Afro-Brazilians

Questions of miscegenation and Black mobilization in Brazil have long fascinated not only scholars of Brazilian race relations but also activists, because these issues almost instantly raise questions of racial identity among people who inhabit a landscape in which racial group boundaries are flexible and race is continuous and fluid. Several scholars of race relations in Brazil have discussed, theorized, and analyzed the ways in which this flexibility permeates Afro-Brazilians' engagement with Black consciousness movements. Tianna Paschel insightfully illustrates how the process of forging and politicizing a collective Black identity can be achieved through what she refers to as "political field alignments": "I have taken seriously the idea of becoming black—rather than being black—by examining its political articulation. In so doing, I trace monumental transformations in politics in Colombia and Brazil at the same time that I show the many limitations and ambiguities of this shift" (2016, 238).

Arguing for an antiessentialist way of thinking about identity and political struggle, Paschel demonstrates that "people are never exclusively or singularly black, but rather inhabit many social locations simultaneously" (2016, 13). Yet it seems the jury is still out on the validity of the notion of "identity" as a category of analysis.[5] With that said, a short word about identity is in order. We should never treat identity as a given, an established fact. We should think of identity "as a discourse or truth claim available to certain groups or individuals, and not to others" (Weinstein 2015, 23). In addition, the function of identity is molded to communicative purpose, social context, and the user's way of thinking about the world. It can be the cause of a movement or simply a marker of difference. In this sense, the notion of identity remains pivotal to an understanding of anti-racist activism among Afro-Brazilians. The aim of this book is to find a way of analyzing Afro-Brazilians' relationship with Blackness without making totalizing claims about their Black identities. Instead, I pay careful attention to the ways in which they repeatedly position their own identities between Brown and Black, self-identifying as "Black" in the box when applying for racial quotas and responding to Black activists' racially targeted political messages. I am particularly interested in how Afro-Brazilians frame their relationship with Blackness and to what ends.

Research that theorizes Black identity and politics in Brazil is critical and necessary for a general analysis of anti-racist activism among Afro-Brazilians. Early studies were concerned with examining the paradox that anti-racist organizations fail to generate grassroots support for anti-racist programs even in the face of pervasive racial inequality. They sought to explain the alleged weakness of anti-racist mobilization among Afro-Brazilians (Degler 1971; Hanchard 1994; Twine 1998). Grounded in a comparison of racial politics between Brazil and the United States, these scholars were particularly interested in the relationship between Brazilians' strongly held belief in Brazil's racial mixture and Afro-Brazilians' comparative difficulty in organizing around being Black. In *Orpheus and Power* (1994), a study about the Black movement in the cities of Rio de Janeiro and São Paulo, Michael George Hanchard attempts to explain how the ideology of race mixing and false premises of racial equality in Brazil have neutralized Black mobilization among Afro-Brazilians. Hanchard characterizes the racial consciousness of Afro-Brazilians in terms of its minimal resemblance to the strong racial consciousness of African Americans. In early studies, Black political mobilization was largely seen as the end product of an individual's process of coming to terms with a Black identity. Black consciousness was thus described in terms of a realization of oneself as Black and a collective fight against the oppression of Blacks (Moura 1994; Twine 1997, 1998). John Burdick's (1998) study of Afro-Brazilian followers of popular Christianity shows that the Black movement's approach to collective action fails to resonate with this group, whose members otherwise identify as Black. In a nutshell, members of the Black movement establish close relationships with communities of cultural significance, such as the houses of Candomblé (an Afro-Brazilian religion), while failing to create a message that resonated with evangelist beliefs. Followers of popular Christianity felt excluded from the Black movement. Burdick's work ultimately challenged the thesis that the weakness of Brazil's Black consciousness movement correlates to a weakness of Black identity among Brazilians of African descent.

The gradual increase in the visibility of Brazilian Black movement discourse has motivated scholars to continue this line of research (Sheriff 2001).

Several scholars have taken identity as a key category of description and analysis to explain Afro-Brazilians' process of gaining racial awareness and mobilizing against the exclusion of Black Brazilians (Caldwell 2007; French 2009; Perry 2013). Jan Hoffman French's *Legalizing Identities* (2009) offers one of the most detailed discussions of the process of creating new ethnoracial identities (identity shift) that was triggered by Brazil's race-conscious laws and policies. She documents how members of the *quilombo* community of Mocambo in the Sergipe-Alagoas region revised (changed) their ethnoracial identities from mixed-race rural people to *negro* (Black) in the context of legal recognition of their rights to *quilombo* lands based on Black ancestry. According to French, the revival or reinvention of their ethnoracial identities is mediated by state intervention that has provided the legal language with which the new identities are constructed with the goal of securing rights and resources. Elizabeth Farfán-Santos (2016) has challenged the premise that Afro-Brazilians strategically perform Black identities as a "tactic" for obtaining rights. She critiques, for example, French's focus on performative identity construction (as in cultural practices such as festivals, rituals, and plays) as a response to bureaucratic requirements. Instead, through an ethnography of the *quilombo* community of Grande Paraguaçu, Farfán-Santos explores how the *quilombo* habitus, or "internalized structures" and "schemes of perception" (Bourdieu 1977, 86), draws community members into their everyday experiences of Blackness and their stories of precarious situations and sufferings. Overall, this literature is useful in showing how Black activists mobilizing in Brazil have attempted to challenge the myth of racial democracy. More important, these researchers have engaged in nuanced theorizations of how anti-racist activism can capitalize on Brazil's shared ideal of racial inclusiveness, presenting it as a goal yet to be achieved. While there is some skepticism about the possibility of constructing Blackness in a society used to changes in how they are racially identified overtime, across contexts, or even within a single daily encounter (e.g., Sansone 2003), I foreground how the self-reflexive nature of the proliferation of Afro-Brazilian anti-racist activism has turned vulnerability into political strength.

Celebrated, vilified, yet seemingly inescapable, miscegenation in Brazil has always fascinated laypeople and scholars alike. And, as Silva (1998, 222) points out, Brazil's specific racial configuration, which defines both the country's modes of racial subordination and strategies of opposition to it, should be a point of departure for any study of racial politics in the country.

Between Brown and Black addresses the intricate aspects of miscegenation through a multilayered analysis of several contexts in which Afro-Brazilians are presented with a range of identity choices, from how they classify themselves to how they vote. These contexts include neglected dimensions of Afro-Brazilians' mobilizing strategies, including anti-racist socialization by which they implicitly or explicitly pass on the meaning of one's race, knowledge about one's heritage and cultural traditions, racial pride, awareness of how anti-Blackness feeds into racial discrimination, and strategies to resist discrimination. I also delve into the affirmative action racial quota system that seeks to remedy racial exclusion of Brazilian Blacks from higher education and civil service jobs. Then I probe the limits and possibilities of the electoral politics of race as a site for anti-racist activism. Throughout I highlight Afro-Brazilians' ability to interactively align each other's anti-racist actions at different levels of discourse. My main argument is that Afro-Brazilians' relationship with Blackness should no longer be characterized by the old premise of miscegenation as an obstacle to racial consciousness among Afro-Brazilians but instead by new ideas about the critical force of anti-racism for negotiations around their racial positions with respect to Blackness.

More on Identity and Voice

As I have noted, the long-standing idea of miscegenation came to represent Brazilian society as a harmonious whole of mixed-race people with a common culture. I use the notions of monologism and dialogism to parse changes in the meanings of miscegenation over time. Mikhail Bakhtin (1981) used *monologism* to refer to the process of inhibiting the flow of dialogue and all of its potentials. The counterpart to monologism is *dialogism*, referring to exchanges in which there is room for debate over different and often competing points of view or voices. I posit that the idea of "people of different races merging together" through miscegenation became monologized as universal truth in the formation of the Brazilian nation. Although Brazilians recognize the stark racial disparities in the country, the ideas of *brasilidade* and the benefits of racial mixing still resonate for most of them. As Brazilian president Jair Bolsonaro's speech during the G20 summit in 2020 reveals, to this date there are forces (voices) that perpetuate the idea that racism is not a problem in Brazil. Reacting on Twitter to protests against the death of João Alberto, Bolsonaro wrote that miscegenation eliminated racism in Brazil, accusing protesters of threatening the Brazilian family with "conflict, resentment, hatred, and class division" (M. Andrade 2020). Meanwhile, the growing anti-racist movements in Brazil are challenging the miscegenation monologue of Brazilian society. Beginning in the 1970s, they gained force in the 1980s and 1990s and since then have taken center stage through ethnoracial reforms in education, employment, and politics, enacted as a large contingent of citizens started calling out structural racism in Brazilian society (Paschel 2016). It can be argued that Afro-Brazilians' understanding of their society has become increasingly decentered and multivoiced, and thereby dialogized. Brazilians' different ideological positions currently operate as a myriad of imbricated voices. Inspired by Bakhtin's dialogic approach, my goal in *Between Brown and Black* is to cut through the thick, deep layers of the many voices speaking both between and within individuals.

Returning to the concept of identity, it is a long-standing theme in studies of Brazilian race relations that social scientists today, no less than in the earliest research, continue to apply in their studies of emerging forms of Afro-Brazilian political action. The concept gained currency in the 1990s as scholars across many disciplines sought to account for Black politics, or the lack thereof, in Brazil. It is therefore appropriate to examine identity as a category of description and analysis in order to better understand Afro-Brazilians' ways of thinking about their racial positionalities and their engagement in anti-racist activism. Scholars today recognize that identity (race, gender, nationality) is not essentially a given and that group identities are more than a matter of essential commonality among people (Kroskrity 2000; Mendoza-Denton 2002). Though it might seem that so-called sociodemographic categories are relatively stable, a significant body of research on race and language, for example, has demonstrated that identities are fluid, unstable, multidimensional, and intersectional. In fact, racial identities are "the product of a continuous axis of difference (race/ethnicity, class, sexuality, age, status, profession, momentary stance), none of which is solely determinative (Mendoza-Denton 2002, 492). Yet the conception of identity as completely fluid and free flowing has also been problematized. As Barbara Weinstein (2015, 23) notes, identity may or may not harden boundaries of difference and reinforce hierarchies and divisions. Further, while identity can be a matter of individual choice—that is, deliberately produced—at the same time it can be pressed on people by ascription within social relationships and particular social spaces, not merely in the abstract but in the concrete variety of its ways of life (Calhoun 2003a). Thus, although there are some freedoms in identity making in the context of ongoing social interactions, macrolevel processes constrain the choices we make.

Sociolinguists and linguistic anthropologists have emphasized the role of communicative practices in the construction of identities, both exterior (how others see me) and interior (how I perceive myself). Linguistic anthropologists have explored how speech can be characterized by a multiplicity of voices (polyphony). Following Bakhtin, they define voice as the linguistic embodiment of points of views, subject positions, and consciousness (e.g., particular instances of speech habits, lexical choices, and speech reporting). With respect to Afro-Brazilians' use of language, Jane Hill's pioneering work embraces "voice" as a unit of analysis to demonstrate how language becomes a site of struggle in which voices—which may be juxtaposed even within a single word spoken by a single speaker—compete with one another to project a point of view. In a famous study (1995), Hill laid out a brilliant ethnographic analysis of a story she heard from Don Gabriel, a resident of a subsistence-farming village in central Mexico. Don Gabriel spoke both Mexicano, a Native American language, and Spanish. His story was about the murder of his adult son caused by envy. According to Hill's analysis, Don Gabriel used different linguistic strategies (language switching, choice of words, intonation, etc.) to implicitly convey a variety of voices in his narrative, each voice connected to a competing way of life and value system (peasant reciprocity versus capitalist profit). Hill identified not only different voices belonging to different people but also different voices inhabiting a single person in Don Gabriel's story. For example, when reporting his own speech, Don Gabriel switched back and forth between Mexicano and Spanish. Though he spoke both languages, he struggled with the Spanish lexicon of transactions for profit and became disfluent when using it in his narrative. In juggling between the two languages, Don Gabriel represented "fundamentally opposed ideological positions of peasant communitarianism and the economics of reciprocity in the Mexicano-speaking community on the one hand, and the pursuit of individual profit in the Spanish-speaking world of the marketplace on the other" (Hill 1995, 116).

My approach to discourse analysis builds on previous linguistic anthropological work on multivocality, adding a new dimension to the analysis of the interplay of voices, or dialogism. For example, in chapter 2, I move the analytical focus of Black activists' linguistic strategies beyond identifying the variety of voices (from family, friends, teachers, the media, and society at large) woven into their speech to explore how they socialize one another into taking an active role in scrutinizing the ideological and practical significance of the fusion of voices in their own and others' speech. At stake in anti-racist activism among Afro-Brazilians, I argue, is a dialogic interplay of dominant and subversive voices. Weighted with competing racial ideologies, all of these voices amount to recasting the foundational narrative of Brazilian race relations. Using the Bakhtinian concept of voice allows a more nuanced understanding of ideology, consciousness, and political resistance. I argue that Black activists' adoption of voice, polyphony, and dialogism in their communicative practices is part of a larger political project to critically re-create and reproject their relationship with miscegenation and Blackness.

Methods

Between Brown and Black draws from ethnographic fieldwork conducted primarily in the city of Salvador (Bahia, Brazil) spanning eleven years from 2009 to 2020. Part of that fieldwork included gathering materials from online and print mass media sources, including social media. The initial phase of research occurred in 2009–2010 with fieldwork in nonprofit, community-based nongovernmental organizations (NGOs) in the Black movement in Salvador. Since the 1990s, about a decade into the redemocratization process after military rule in Brazil, a vast array of Black NGOs have emerged that deploy race as a strategy to press their claims for resources and rights for Afro-Brazilians. At this time, I spent about a year researching consciousness-raising strategies at three Black NGOs as well as the experiences of Afro-Brazilians who were directly or indirectly part of these organizations, with particular interest in individuals who normally would not be viewed as Black in Salvador. Differences in age, socioeconomic background, gender, and education also provided for different experiences. I have given the pseudonyms Centro Cultural Palmares (Palmares Cultural Center), Grupo Engenho de Salvador (Engenho de Salvador Group), and Instituto Lutas de Zumbi (Zumbi Struggles Institute) to the organizations I worked with. All three concentrated on building collective capacity within the local Black population through supplemental instruction and Black consciousness-raising. Each organization operated different programs aligned with its specific goals, such as college admissions preparatory classes, tutoring support in math and sciences for high school youth, vocational classes, and teacher development courses. All three organized their instruction around notions of the social construction of race and the reality of discrimination, always putting race front and center. The core of their pedagogy revolved around aspects of critical race theory to prepare the mostly Black youth to think critically about their personal struggles over the acceptance and negation of Blackness and, ultimately, to fight against racial inequality. I conducted participant observations of countless activities at the three organizations. In addition, I conducted around forty interviews and numerous informal conversations during which I collected personal stories of how people (of various ages) in these organizations became involved in anti-racist activism, noting their perceptions about the Brazilian Black movement in general and the organizations they were affiliated with in particular. During semistructured interviews, I gathered interviewees' demographic information as well as information about the Black NGOs. Formal interviews and observations were audio- and video-recorded, then later transcribed and translated, while informal conversations were documented in retrospective field notes.

Following the initial study, I expanded the scope of investigation beyond anti-racist socialization within educational settings. Since 2014, I have been researching Black activists' electoral politics in Salvador to explore the degree to which Black mobilization has impacted voting patterns among Afro-Brazilians. In 2014–2015, I spent about ten months conducting ethnographic fieldwork in three mostly Black neighborhoods of Salvador, which I will call Bora, Oliveiras, and Pontal. These areas of the city are consistently targeted for anti-racist outreach. Historically, Brazilian Blacks have been at a huge disadvantage in the electoral process, even in the state of Bahia, where people of African descent are a large voting bloc (80 percent). The persistence of Brazil's dominant ideology of racial mixture and harmony has forced Black candidates to confront questions of whether and how they can effectively utilize racial consciousness as an electoral strategy. Besides living in different areas of the city, the people included in this study differed in socioeconomic classes, gender, levels of education, and professions. I collected the majority of the data from both traditional and social media campaigning during the 2014 election cycle. For the 2018 and 2020 election cycles, I followed media participation and collected campaign materials by some of the same candidates. In 2020 a group of graduate and undergraduate

Afro-Brazilian students, the majority living in Salvador, joined me as coresearchers on this project.

Because enormous social change came with the implementation of affirmative action laws and policies across Brazil, and particularly racial quotas in university admissions and higher education and government hiring, I began to explore the application to and experiences of racial quotas among Afro-Brazilians. In most instances the racial quotas require only self-identification, but in other cases they also require racial identification by a verification committee (known in Brazil as *heteroidentificação* (heteroidentification, or identification by others). Unlike the hypodescent rule in the United States, unequal social and economic status in Brazil is partly a function of how others perceive you. Dark-skinned Brazilians with visible African features are the ones most severely affected by anti-Black racism. The verification committees were established to counter racial fraud in which non-Black Brazilians claimed Blackness based on ancestry to further their careers through the quota system. Both government officials and Black movement activists have been influential in the implementation of the committees that determine the eligibility of affirmative action applicants, based on whether they are Black enough to qualify for a quota spot. As Sales Augusto dos Santos (2021a) demonstrates, these committees have indeed helped guard against fraud. Clearly there has been a notable shift in the ways anti-racist activists and policy makers approach racial identification, from challenging all Afro-Brazilians to organize around being Black to scrutinizing, based on phenotype, who is Black enough to qualify for Black quotas. In 2018, I set out to study the ways in which the Brazilian quota system and verification committees caused renegotiation of long-held racial categories in Brazil. To draw on data from regions with different racial makeups, I carried out interviews and personal correspondence with people in three major cities: Brasília, Florianópolis, and Salvador. There are significant differences, as well as striking similarities, between these stories.

Discussion of the changes in anti-racist discourse emerging in Brazil is linked to broader consideration of language (content, form, and tone) as it pertains to voice in Bakhtinian terms. Afro-Brazilians are increasingly engaged with a social world made up of multiple voices competing to express their everyday experiences. Black activist and politician Sílvio Humberto often told his students in a consciousness-raising class that, in order to be an active advocate against racial injustice, they needed to use their critical voice to constantly dialogue with their own implicit biases and preconceived notions about race (Sílvio Humberto, personal communication, February 28, 2010). Humberto's approach to racial awareness could be best framed as dialogics of resistance. Similarly, in *Black Bodies, Black Rights*, Farfán-Santos (2016) reveals, without using the concept of voice, how *quilombolas* describe being transformed through dialogue, fusing with parts of the other's discourse (legal language of labor, land, and culture) modeled and described by friends and neighbors, using this language to make connections between their labor and themselves as bearers of land rights. Analysis using the dialogic conception of anti-racism exposes how in their anti-racist discourses, Afro-Brazilians make racism a "voice" to which they can respond in an ongoing interrogation of Brazil's dominant racial ideologies and negotiations of the boundaries of Blackness. Language is crucial to anti-racist activism. It serves both as a primary means of foregrounding and making interpretable the meanings of miscegenation, race, Blackness, and so forth in Brazil and as a vehicle for anti-racist socialization. An examination of Afro-Brazilian anti-racist politics should consider more than just references to identity as strategies for contestation. It must also look at the dialogic processes of the production of Black political subjects within the ubiquitous existence of racial mixture. As the following chapters variously aim to show, voicing becomes a site of consciousness, subjectivity, struggle, and resistance. For Afro-Brazilians, to gain critical consciousness is to be able to claim political positions among competing ways of speaking, voices, and ideologies. Positing the idea of anti-racism as a discursive struggle, this book challenges the established theorization of Afro-Brazilian mobilization and contributes to the larger inquiry about racial politics in Brazil and beyond.

An Overview of This Book

Between Brown and Black is a multifaceted study of Afro-Brazilian anti-racist activism. Having kept my ear close to the ground since 2009 has allowed me to understand origins, be aware of persistence, and notice change. And things have changed considerably, most compellingly through the implementation of nationwide racial quotas. But more than anti-racist laws and policies have changed; so have understandings of race, racism, and Blackness. This appreciation for change in anti-racist activism among Afro-Brazilians and its multiple perspectives on Blackness forms the basis of the chapters that follow.

Chapter 2 begins with a study of the complex and unexplored world of anti-racist socializing practices among Afro-Brazilians and the effects of those practices, including adoption of *negro* as an affirmative term to describe Blackness. "When you start self-identifying as *negro*, what is it exactly to be *negro*"? Luiza asked on her first day at a race consciousness-raising workshop. Her classmate Carlos responded, "A person who is conscious, one who knows what her goal is, what she wants to accomplish in life." Afro-Brazilian activists have always faced the difficult task of juggling anti-racism with public promotion and pride in miscegenation. What kind of movement against anti-Black racism is possible in this context? I argue that it is crucial to look into the interactive process through which Afro-Brazilian community organizers engage one another in critical examinations of specific views of race, Blackness, and anti-racism. Using the lens of Bakhtinian voice and dialogism. I position Black activists' work of anti-racist socialization on a dialogic battlefield in which experienced activists guide neophytes to see why, by whom, and for whom competing worldviews of Brazilian society have been built. Anti-racist socialization highlights for newcomers how these worldviews have shaped the everyday lives of Black Brazilians for centuries. Most important, through the process of anti-racist socialization, they have acquired the intellectual tools to act on their society.

In chapter 3, I focus on the narrative and memory practices Afro-Brazilians use to explore different accounts of Afro-Brazilian history and culture. Specifically, one Black NGO had students narrate in first person the life stories of famous Black people who have been whitened over time. The goal of this activity was to teach youth about the erasure of the Blackness of (famous people) and its possible implications for social memory in Brazil. I focus on specific examples of the strategies used to revise the terms of Blacks' relationship with Brazil's nationalist narrative. What binds the examples in this chapter is the crucial role that time and space (real or imagined) play not only in allowing anti-racist activists to create multiple modes with which to insert themselves into the public discourses on race and national identity but also in building competing perspectives on historical figures. In doing so they claimed something of broader social significance. By rearranging what they identified as the distorted pattern of narrative and memory to the proper historical facts, Afro-Brazilians' critical identity politics sought to expose the power of ideology that both racialized and avoided Blackness in the forging of Brazil's national culture.

In chapter 4, I examine excerpts from Afro-Brazilians' responses to my request to hear the stories of how they became involved in struggles against racism. This chapter investigates the ways that Afro-Brazilians' anti-racist consciousness shape their individual encounters with Blackness and how such encounters often entails locating it beyond self-identification as Black and within discourses of racial mixture, pressing racial problems for Black Brazilians' advancement, and racial justice prioritization. The key point that emerged from these personal stories is that anti-racist consciousness emerges as an ideological critique in and through language that crosses racial identifications. This is primarily a form of reflexive engagement between oneself and multiple and different racial notions, narratives, and images available in society. Chapter 4 shows how racial categorization is problematized by Afro-Brazilians' anti-racist activism. I argue that in their individual enactments of anti-racist consciousness, Afro-Brazilians are fully aware of more nuanced notions of how one should engage with Blackness.

Chapter 5 centers on the dynamics of redistributive and reparatory measures to offset racial stratification, such as racial quotas in higher education and government hiring. Unequal social and economic status in Brazil is mainly a function of how others view a person's physical features. The people viewed as *negro* or *preto* are individuals whose skin color, hair, and other physical features are indicators of "pure" African ancestry. Both government officials and Black movement activists have been influential in the implementation of committees to inspect the racial phenotype of affirmative action applicants. The fundamental points I explore in this chapter are the ways in which redistributive and reparatory measures (1) intertwine and interweave with the Brazilian discourse of race and identity and (2) have changed what it means to be Black in Brazil.

Chapter 6 explores the increasing use of race as an electoral strategy and its role in shaping the politics of Blackness in Salvadorean elections. Given the deeply entrenched racism and ideology of miscegenation in Brazil, Black activists have historically avoided race-specific messages in their electoral campaigns, framing political agendas as aimed at benefiting Brazilians of all backgrounds. How is the new racial climate affecting politics from campaign strategies to voter patterns? How much weight do Afro-Brazilian-targeted racial messages lend to Black candidates' campaigns? This chapter analyzes the verbal and nonverbal messages Black candidates use in order to articulate the issues that affect their constituencies and market themselves to voters. It examines the interpretive perspectives that voters contend with in interpreting communications—specifically, how receptive they are to these messages and how their votes are influenced. Afro-Brazilians do not vote along racial lines, so campaigns based on race have been stymied in obstacles located in the intersection of liberal citizenship and racial politics. The complexity of racially targeted political campaigning in Salvador lies in the voters' struggle to reconcile conflicting viewpoints of Brazil's dominant ideology of race mixing with the obligations of liberal citizenship (to treat people as equal citizens) and federal affirmative action policies. Facing competing forms of democratic participation—minority rights versus nondiscriminatory liberal rights—Afro-Brazilians lean toward the liberal perspective. In this chapter, I work to untangle the interacting variables in the complex calculus of race and politics in Brazil through describing several Black candidates' campaigns. I provide nuanced understandings of identity construction within both campaign messages and voters' reactions, with an eye to the political relevance of an approach to race in electoral politics in Salvador. I argue that Black activists running for office in Salvador must constantly adjust how they speak about race to accommodate the evolving ways in which Afro-Brazilian relate to Blackness in contemporary Brazil.

In the conclusion I muse on understanding anti-racist activism in the larger context of racial identity formation. First, I share an image that updates the trope of Brazilian miscegenation. I step back and reflect on how Afro-Brazilians situate Blackness in relation to Brazil's reality of racial mixture and racial integration, Black Brazilians' everyday lived experiences of anti-Black racism and anti-racist consciousness. I close by reflecting on the conflicting ways in which Afro-Brazilians' lives have been impacted by the complex succession of their anti-racist struggles and affirmative action programs. As they find themselves caught between the racially political and the racially descriptive aspects of being Black, Afro-Brazilians critically explore their own Blackness and articulate a vision of anti-racist consciousness and a call to action—at both individual and collective levels.

2
The Language of Afro-Brazilian Anti-racist Socialization

Chapter 1 provided context for understanding the ideological struggles inherent in anti-racist activism among Afro-Brazilians. This chapter and chapter 3 cover in detail their process of anti-racist socialization: how Blacks teach one another to recognize racism, understand its origins and functions, and work to oppose it.[1] I scrutinize the ways in which Afro-Brazilians weave an understanding of language with racial justice in order to renegotiate the heteroglossia of race in Brazil—the presence of various voices or expressed viewpoints through which Brazilians understand racial differences. On both individual and community levels, Afro-Brazilians are reimagining their relationship with Blackness in a landscape in which race mixture has long been on display. In the process, they find themselves exploring the limits and possibilities of being Black in Brazil. Nowhere is this process more evident than in the context of socialization through the language used in race consciousness-raising activities, the road less traveled by other researchers in the study of anti-racism in Brazil. A study of the role that language plays in various anti-racist activities is crucial for probing deeply into how Afro-Brazilians deploy race to formulate an anti-racist approach to social justice in Brazil.

Some leading researchers in the social sciences have sought to explain the relationship between individual consciousness and diverse mechanisms of power and oppression (Althusser 1971; Day 2004; Gramsci 1972; Seidler 1994). Others have explored the ways in which individual actors incorporate social and cultural formations into their ways of speaking and acting (Bakhtin 1986; Bourdieu 1977; Spivak 1988). My analysis of anti-racist socialization generally follows a dialogic framework (Bakhtin 1984; Hill 1995; Volosinov 1986). Central to dialogism is the idea that words, utterances, and discourse, even of a single speaker, are always filled with a multiplicity of viewpoints linguistically embodied as voice. Instances of speech always exist in relationship to other instances, mutually influencing and being influenced by one another (Bakhtin 1986). Thus speech, even by a single person, entails polyphony—that is, multiple voices with unique ideological positions. In this chapter, I pay careful attention to the patterns of discourse and interactions that take place as Afro-Brazilians are socialized to identify cultural values and positions in their own and others' speech, analyzing their potential not only to reproduce dominant racial ideologies but also to effect social change. This analysis also builds on other approaches within linguistic anthropology, including John Gumperz and Dell Hymes's (1972) ethnography of communication and Erving Goffman's (1981) analysis of framing. All of this leads to an examination of the methods and practices Black movement activists use to teach anti-racism in the context of social and political changes in Brazil. My analysis shows how anti-racist voices are formed as these activists engage with Brazil's competing racial ideologies.

As an example of this development, Black activists' utterances gave rise to intricate oral exchanges focused on the many ways dominant Brazilian discourses of race were fused with their own words and those of their fellow community members. Seasoned and inexperienced activists alike regularly engaged in oral exchanges through which they worked diligently to unravel the discourses of race that were intricately woven in their own words and the words of others. As they sought to tease out and identify the sources of particular statements of race in their own and others' speech, they exposed long-standing notions of race that were constructed from a collection of quotations, citations, and repetitions from other sources. Afro-Brazilian activists' consciousness-raising strategies not only invoked and explored contrasts among ideologies of race in their own and others' speech but also communicated them in particular ways so as to encourage one interpretation over another. Facing both familiar and new ways of thinking about race and

Blackness, Afro-Brazilians grappled with the idea that they could be both Brown (mixed) and Black. Ultimately, the anti-racist tone they adopted framed their task as a broader struggle of locating racism within competing principles, visions, and viewpoints. This chapter offers a fresh look at Afro-Brazilian political and social movements. Through an innovative focus on the interactive process of anti-racist socialization, we can reinterpret the anti-racist project and expand our understanding of Afro-Brazilians' quest for social justice.

Afro-Brazilian History and Culture: Teaching and Learning about Racism

In 2003, as part of an unprecedented turn toward affirmative action, the Brazilian government enacted Law 10.639/03 (Government of Brazil 2003), requiring that education about African and Afro-Brazilian people be incorporated into existing school subjects like Portuguese language, literature, history, and geography. This law was followed by other ethnoracial reforms that illuminated recent social and political changes in racial discourse in Brazil. A secondary goal of the 2003 law was to create opportunities for students to learn about race and racism. Such statutes sent a strong message to the nation about the importance of questioning basic assumptions regarding the popular myth of racial mixture—the idea that Brazilians are a blend of African, European, and Indigenous peoples who are not divided along racial lines—that has historically been a foundation of Brazilian national culture and identity. Given that Brazil has long prided itself on its racial mixture and absence of racial divisions, the law was a remarkable development that established the Brazilian Black movement's policy-making influence for years to come. Since initiating fieldwork in the city of Salvador in the state of Bahia in 2009–2010, I have observed that implementation of the law has triggered struggles in the classroom among competing racial ideologies. Over four months in 2009–2010, I became a participant observer in a course on Afro-Brazilian history and culture organized by a Black nongovernmental organization that I was studying—which I have given the pseudonym Grupo Engenho de Salvador (Engenho de Salvador Group)—and whose members I have kept in touch with for a decade. I dedicated my weekdays (at least six hours a day) to observations of socialization activities and to informal conversations and interviews with organization members. Created in 2003 to serve mostly Black communities, Grupo Engenho de Salvador describes its mission as developing social and cultural projects with an emphasis on issues of gender and race. It works with public agencies to address social inequities and to promote equality for practitioners of the Afro-Brazilian religion Candomblé, of which the group's leaders are themselves practitioners. Grupo Engenho de Salvador's main goal is to educate the public about the values of Candomblé as a component of African and Afro-Brazilian history and culture. At the heart of its organizing strategy was a course aimed at preparing teachers to implement the 2003 law mandating the teaching of African and Afro-Brazilian history and culture.

My focus in this chapter is on this course. During the course, I listened to several schoolteachers who were attending explain why it was difficult to put the 2003 law into practice. They faced the thorny task of reconciling the shifting legal status of Blackness with Brazil's historically celebrated ideologies of racial integration and racial democracy. Even though many Brazilians supported anti-racist education—the teaching of issues regarding race and racism—they also supported the belief in Brazil as a racial democracy (see Sheriff 2001). For Brazilian Black movement activists, the 2003 law opened a space in the heart of White hegemony and also situated itself in one of the centers that generated opinion, ideas, and knowledge—the school.

The first two course meetings, lasting about three hours each, took place at a local school on the outskirts of Salvador. We were told the third class would meet at a different location: Pelourinho, in the historic center of Salvador. "There is no better site," one of the lead instructors told us; since colonial times, the word *pelourinho* (whipping post) has developed an iconic association with the place where criminals in general, and particularly slaves, were whipped and punished. One of the tall vertical stone columns remains as a monument at the site, which was also the place where enslaved Africans were auctioned during the slave trade period. That evening I was the first to arrive at the designated address, a restored colonial-era townhouse in Pelourinho, and the classroom was still locked. Three other people arrived shortly after me. I greeted the two I recognized, and we cheerfully reintroduced ourselves. The third, Luiza Costa, whom we had not met before, seemed rather reserved. Unlike most of the other attendees, who wore either everyday clothes (jeans, T-shirts, and sneakers) or colorful African-inspired clothing and accessories, she wore modest, conservative business attire, a grayish dress and jacket. Luiza's straightened hair was tied back with a band, which also contrasted with the hairstyles of all the other attendees, who wore some form of braided hair or a loose-textured Afro. After our extended greetings, Luiza said she had seen an advertisement for the course in the Afro-Brazilian insert in the city newspaper. She asked what else we knew and what we could tell her about the course. We began trying to describe what we witnessed, and another attendee, Júlia, offered a more comprehensive description:

> Eu posso ver dois objetivos. Eles nos ensinam o assunto, nossa história. Eles também aumentam a conscientização sobre questões de raça, discriminação racial e exclusão racial. Tivemos discussões com a classe inteira e em pequenos grupos. Todos tiveram a oportunidade de participar ativamente. Conversamos sobre miscigenação, branqueamento e democracia racial, tudo relacionado à ideologia racial do Brasil.

> I can see two goals. They teach us the subject, our history. They also raise awareness of issues of race, racial discrimination, and racial exclusion. We have whole-class and small-group discussions. Everyone had the opportunity to participate actively. We have talked about miscegenation, whitening, and racial democracy, everything related to Brazil's racial ideology.

Júlia quickly added that to this day these themes "still influence" social relations at all levels of Brazilian society. She continued, "Como você sabe, atualmente eles acendem debates acalorados na sociedade brasileira e os instrutores apresentaram esses tópicos de múltiplas perspectivas e por meio de uma variedade de textos e mídias." (As you know, currently they ignite heated debates in Brazilian society, and the instructors have presented these topics from multiple perspectives and through a variety of texts and media). Júlia's intervention prompted us to review everything we had talked about in the previous course meetings, such as the fact that Brazilian racial mixture is a key component of the notion of racial democracy. As we became more relaxed and comfortable with one another, we began bantering back and forth. Because those who attended the first meeting knew I was living in the United States, they asked me to comment on the one-drop rule that defines Blackness there. I explained that the one-drop rule referred to the concept of hypodescent, which unlike in Brazil, relegated mixed-blood children to the non-White category and that, in contrast, Brazilian racial mixing inspired various intermediate categories to describe people who were neither wholly Black nor White. Something about my explanation made everyone start chuckling. I had in mind Carl Degler's (1971) words, which have historically provided a moral ground for the Brazilian state to claim racial neutrality while also constituting an effective strategy to defuse conflict (see also Cunha 1998; and Racusen 2004). As João Costa Vargas notes, Brazil's founding logic, rendered commonsensical, negates the relevance of racial identification because most Brazilians are neither Black, Indigenous, nor White but rather a combination of the "original" three races (Vargas 2004, 449). The widespread view of Brazil as a harmonious, multiracial society, however, has not generally translated into Blacks faring well socioeconomically. This theme had emerged several times during the first class meeting.

Even though the course targeted practicing teachers, community members at large were also invited to participate. Forty-seven people enrolled in the course, about two-thirds of whom were practicing teachers. Some described themselves as *educadores sociais* (social educators) or *mestres da sala de aula, no dia a dia* (noncertified teachers—literally, teachers in everyday classrooms). According to one participant, they expected that "learning about Afro-Brazilian history and culture would give [them] passage into the empowering world of Black community organizing." Others just wanted to learn more about the subject. Most of the attendees had learned about the course through friends, coworkers, internet discussion lists, local newspapers, or flyers sent out to local community organizations. (The same was true for me: I was actively looking for information about Black mobilization in local papers when I saw the course announcement.) The course participants ranged in age from their mid-twenties to their seventies. About thirty regularly attended all six hours of class each weekday evening, even though they had full-time jobs during the day, had families of their own, or engaged in community work during their spare time. Some took the same bus as me to get there; some even took two buses. Except for three participants who were light-skinned and self-identified as White, all the other participants had dark skin and were visibly of African descent. All of them held some type of professional employment, though most did not have a college degree. A few held bachelor's degrees in history, liberal arts, education, or psychology, or were pursuing their undergraduate degree at the time of the study. Eight participants were certified elementary or middle-school teachers. The others were self-described social educators, teachers in vocational and recreational areas such as hair styling, fashion design, handicrafts, music, dance, and the like. At the first meeting, the instructors asked us to introduce ourselves and explain what motivated us to enroll in the course. The most common reason offered was to learn ways of implementing the 2003 law. In addition, participants hoped that networking with other educators would help them feel more prepared to explore strategies for teaching about the complexity of race and racism in their classrooms.

Each lesson incorporated activities to raise participants' consciousness of various issues—for instance, how individual behaviors both influence broader social structures and are influenced by them. In line with the anti-racist mission of the organization, the instructors consistently challenged participants to critically reflect on and analyze the cultural and historical specificity of racism, citizenship rights, and public policies. Considerable time was devoted to sharing new ideas and challenging peers to construct new ways of taking a stance against anti-Black racism within the context of Brazilian discourses on race and national culture and identity. Participants were often encouraged to identify ways to use and apply what they learned in their own classrooms or in the outside world. I audio- and video-recorded all of the course meetings. I also collected field notes from my informal conversations with students and teachers before and after class and during coffee breaks.

Two activist history teachers, a man and woman in their thirties, led the course with the help of several community experts who were invited to talk about topics in their areas of expertise, such as politics and religion. These activists stated that they learned about the history and critical theory of race and racism from more seasoned activists in Black movement nongovernmental organizations and through formal education. More community leaders, however, were self-taught. Like the Black activists in Robin Sheriff's study (2001), many were well read in the history, ethnography, and critical theory of race and racism in Brazil. All of them, including the ones who knew next to nothing about critical race theory, reported that their heightened consciousness resulted in part from widely circulating public discourse on racial equality in contemporary Brazil. Ana, a Black movement activist, was one of the two instructors. One of her lessons is the focus of this chapter. Ana had a bachelor's degree in history and was pursuing her master's in gender studies. When asked to talk about the goals of the course, she noted that in the beginning the course attendees were frequently unable to recognize or describe many of the significant everyday aspects of racism, such as systemic discrimination in hiring and employment practices, racially motivated police harassment, and racially constructed patterns of authority and deference. My impression was that the group of students in the course was very heterogeneous in terms of critical knowledge about such issues. Much in line with Paulo Freire's proposal for the development of social consciousness through education (e.g., Freire 2004), Ana focused her lessons on leading participants to form a more critical picture of the hierarchy of Brazilian society by raising their awareness of racial stigmas, stereotypes, discrimination, and inequalities. The themes of miscegenation (racial mixing), whitening, and racial democracy—which have historically been central features of Brazil's racial ideology—ran through the class sessions. As was mentioned in chapter 1, these themes still influence social relations at all levels of Brazilian society, igniting heated debates over racially conscious laws and reforms (especially affirmative action) to this day.

Whole-class and small-group discussions were very common during Ana's classes, and she often switched between one and the other. The room was never silent, and I recall a few times when people were so immersed in discussions that Ana had to resort to hushing them to return their attention to her. These classes can be conceptualized as discourse-centered socialization, where during their social interactions participants taught one another about how everyday speech has the potential for both racist and anti-racist sentiments. I did hear explicit talk about the notion of a multiplicity of dynamic, interacting voices ("multivoicedness" in the Baktinian sense), but instructors and students also used a number of linguistic strategies, defined here as *affirmative language practices*. These linguistic practices consisted of dialogic engagements with the landscape of Brazilian ideologies of race. They explored the interrelations among racial ideologies, language, and individual points of view. Students were challenged to pay attention to how issues of race emerged as voices in speech. They were constantly challenged to probe their own and others' speech for the dominant racial ideologies that had been passed on to them and were unconsciously embodied in such speech. This was an important way in which community organizers imparted their understanding of anti-racism to others. For instance, Ana often directed her students' attention to the ways in which dominant voices have imperceptibly influenced the voices of people who uncritically repeat their words. Initially, Ana regularly drew students' attention to the many ways in which everyday speech expressed contradictory racial ideologies.

Racial Ideologies in Conflict: Polyphony and Dialogism

The complexity of ideological interactions in present-day Brazil clearly emerged several times during the course on Afro-Brazilian history and culture. The give-and-take during the class session in Pelourinho is one example. It was driven in part by a debate about one of the readings for the class, written by Miriam Leitão (2002), a well-known economic and business commentator who worked for Brazil's most popular TV network, about racism among Brazil's business elite. She urged the business elite to work to end racial discrimination, arguing that racial inequality ultimately erected barriers to the expansion of the Brazilian consumer market. The class session lasted about two hours and bore a major emphasis on activities that encouraged students to pay close attention to how race played a role in their access to social influence and power. Ana used the reading to teach critical thinking skills. She strategically picked an article by a well-known TV personality. Rather than asking students to simply agree or disagree, she focused on helping them uncover assumptions and biases within the text, introducing them to the concept of ideology. As one example, Ana spoke about the ideology of *brasilidade* (Brazilianness)—that is, the narrative of national culture and identity rooted in race mixing promulgated in textbooks and in common lore. Ana framed her critique of *brasilidade* in terms of lexical choices, contrasting two voices: one that said Blacks "contributed" to nation formation versus another that said Blacks "built" the nation. Looking at speech through the lens of dialogism allows us to see how voices may collide within a single word, revealing the conflicting perspectives of those who use it (Bakhtin 1984, 184). As Ana explained,

> Nós não *contribuímos*, nós *construímos* esse país, né? "Nós *influenciamos*. As populações negras influenciaram." Não *influenciamos*. *Construímos*. E construímos a partir de conhecimento secularmente trabalhado, né? . . . Não viemos do processo de escravida——, escravização, nem de diáspora, *a passeio*, né?

> We didn't *contribute*, we *built* this country, right? [They say,] "We *influenced*. The Black populations *influenced*." We didn't *influence*. We *built* it. And we built it based on knowledge that we gained over the centuries, right? . . . We didn't come here during slaver——, enslavement, or during the diaspora, *on holiday*, right?

Ana illustrated the types of discursive processes through which the critical role of Blacks in Brazilian history has been minimized in Brazil's nation-building rhetoric. Invoking a distinction between lexical choices, she also gave voice to an alternative perspective. Ana simultaneously represented, evaluated, and contested the dominant voice that said Blacks "contributed" to the building of the Brazilian nation. She contrasted "contribuímos" (we contributed) with "construímos" (we built) to draw students' attention to the power of words to invoke ideologically weighted positions on the history of Brazil and the portrayals of Blacks. Ana strategically framed her argument in terms of embodied lexical choices representing competing voices: when she said "Nós não *contribuímos*" (We didn't *contribute*), she used double voicing (with negation and a pinch of irony) to locate the dominant voice from the nation-building rhetoric behind the verb *contribuir* as far as possible from the voice she identified with most closely: the one that used *construir* instead, as in "*Construímos*" (We *built* it). She further highlighted this contrast by comparing "Nós *influenciamos*" (We *influenced*) with "*Construímos*" (We *built* it).

During the course, Ana often highlighted the difference between *escravo* (slave) and *escravizado* (enslaved), explaining that built into *escravo* is the idea that a natural category of slave exists. *Escravizado* is more accurate because Africans were forcibly enslaved, rather than natural slaves. Notably, during this exchange with her students, Ana inadvertently began to say "escravidão" (slavery), which like *escravo* is considered inaccurate because it fails to capture the forceful condition of enslavement. She immediately corrected herself and said "escravização" (enslavement). What struck me about this self-correction was that, in struggling to interrupt the dominant voice, Ana's correction epitomized the clash of voices battling for domination within a single word (Keane 2011, 173–174). The behavior of contrasting these two words circulated widely among activists, especially in the context of repairs suggested or made by a speaker, addressee, or even audience in order to disavow the use of *escravo*.[2] I often observed overt examples of this kind of repair by Ana and others during the course.

The interaction that is the focus of my analysis emerged during a discussion about Miriam Leitão's article. Ana had challenged participants to scrutinize everything they read or heard in terms of Brazilian race relations: "Vocês sempre vão encontrar uma história mais complicada." (You'll always find a more complicated story.) I often heard her say this. Like Ana, other activists I have met in Salvador work diligently to challenge the racial discourse in Brazil and unravel its multiple and competing perspectives. On this occasion, Ana also helped the students make connections between the current text and the content of previous lessons. As the class discussion evolved, Luiza, the newcomer attending the course for first time, spoke up. Luiza identified herself as a Brazilian of African descent in her mid-thirties. Most people in Salvador would view her as Black, but she struggled with the idea that a person could be both mixed (Brown) and Black. Much like the other participants, Luiza was attracted to the course because of its focus on African and Afro-Brazilian history and culture, which had become a topic of national interest and concern after the far-reaching curricular changes. In terms of race consciousness, participants harbored similar views about the existence of racism in Brazil, but they took various positions about using Africanness and Blackness as an overt political strategy. In spite of the huge changes in Brazil, people like Luiza still lived in a country that fully embraced its founding ideals of racial democracy. In a bold move for a newcomer—but one that exemplified popular opinion in Brazil—Luiza volunteered to speak and criticized Black politics and Black activists for contesting the ideology of *brasilidade* and driving a wedge between Blacks and the rest of the Brazilian population. This is a familiar pattern of argument from critics of race-based affirmative action in Brazil, who frequently characterize race relations in the United States as based on rigid racial lines and, in comparison, describe the situation in Brazil as the polar opposite, lacking racial division and—most important— more benign. They accuse defenders of Brazilian affirmative action of trying to Americanize Brazilian race relations. As Roth Gordon and I point out, "this discursive strategy has the effect of portraying particular voices as less 'authentic' than others" (Roth-Gordon and Silva, 2013, 382). Moreover, as the work of Laura Davenport (2013) and Kerry Ann Rockquemore (2002) on biracial Americans has shown, as the numbers of multiracial people in the United States continue to rise, mixed-race individuals whose identification was traditionally constrained by the one-drop rule are increasingly blurring racial boundaries. These scholars show how complex race can be regarding Black and White categorization and identification in the United States going beyond the one-drop rule. Thus, the United States versus Brazil logic in the argument of critics of Brazilian racial politics has become outdated. Yet, far from abating, this kind of comparison against racial politics in Brazil proves surprisingly durable. As other participants later told me, Luiza's view was the norm, not the exception, and it highlighted the degree to which Brazilians are divided over the best approach to achieving social justice.

In what follows, I carefully examine several excerpts from the course that include Luiza's initial comments and portions of the lengthy collective responses from her classmates. Interpreting Luiza's reaction as a critique of Black activism, her classmates diligently scrutinized the dominant discourses on race used by opponents of race-based affirmative action in Brazil, which were infused with similar terminology as Luiza's comments. In the first excerpt, Luiza explains her concern over the idea of self-identifying as Black and voices disapproval of Afro-Brazilian activists' use of race as a marker of political consciousness. Critics of Black politics in Brazil condemn Black activists for opposing the ideology of miscegenation and dividing the nation along racial lines. Black activists, in turn, are quick to argue that race consciousness unites Brazilians of visible African descent in a common struggle against racial discrimination. Fundamental to this debate is the political significance of race as a category of identity in its contested relation to racism. Picking up at this crucial point in the debate, where other scholars leave off, I argue that dialogical work was occurring as class members engaged with and were informed by different perspectives on race and racism in Brazil while they sought to play the different perspectives off one another. The social role of this dialogical work is crucial to the understanding of anti-racist activism among Afro-Brazilians. It is even more crucial in Afro-Brazilians' encounter with their own Blackness as it occurred in the era of affirmative action in Brazil. As Luiza said,

> Na verdade, quando a gente para para refletir, a gente pode perceber muito pensamento envolvendo o povo *negro*. Eu geralmente não gosto de usar muito esse termo negro. . . . Teve um evento que eu participei que falava sobre poder para o povo negro. . . . Mas como fazer com que o povo negro tenha esse poder e use muito bem, a seu próprio favor e a favor da sua própria raça, da sua própria geração, da sua nação, não apenas mobilizando a favor de um único grupo?

> The truth is, when we take time to think seriously, we can notice a lot of ideas about Black people. Normally, I don't really like to use the term *black*. . . . There was an event I participated in where people talked about power for Black people. . . . But how to make sure Black people have this power and

use it conscientiously, for their own benefit, and for the good of their own race, their own generation, their own nation, not mobilizing just for one single group?

In this excerpt, Luiza demonstrated her awareness of contemporary Black mobilization in Brazil by stating that she had participated in other events sponsored by the Black movement. These events left her with some concerns about the use of *negro* as a term of identification. The use of the term is crucial in understanding anti-racist activism in Brazil today. Besides meaning "black" in the literal sense, *negro* suggests an anti-racist stance and ideological distinction between the meanings of color versus race. It frequently reveals a voice of Black awareness and pride. Luiza's concerns also appeared related to the Black movement's deployment of race as a political strategy. A preliminary examination suggests that Luiza's voice was in dialogue with the voices of the anti-affirmative-action campaigners who have received widespread coverage in the mainstream media. Media critics have often expressed concerns that racial politics is polarizing the nation along racial lines, which could potentially undermine Brazil's long-cherished mixed-race identity (see, e.g., Kaufmann 2008; and Zakabi and Camargo 2007). Black movement activists have been quick to respond that race has been an unwavering artifact of oppression in Brazil and is central to their arguments and struggles for equity and opportunity, especially when it comes to fighting for spaces of power, such as in public higher education and other state sectors.

As Luiza expressed her perception of the Black movement in the preceding excerpt and the next two examples, she relied on different voices to construct what she saw as the complexity of racial politics. Initially she did not clearly demarcate the various voices in her speech through, for example, metadiscursive devices indicating quotation (e.g., reportive verbs like *say* or *tell*). Yet voices can come forth as identifiable, "a potential or postulated resemblance involving some more durable or systematized imagery" (Keane 2011, 168). Nonetheless, Luiza did use various linguistic resources—for example, lexical choices, register use, and syntax—to indicate that her words did convey two or more speaking voices. Gradually she more overtly marked the various voices in her utterances, as when she worked to establish her authoritative stance. For example, in the first excerpt, Luiza used *negro* in reporting that she had attended a Black movement event where she heard "a lot of ideas involving Black people." In Brazil both *negro* and *preto* mean Black in a racial sense, though *negro* has acquired an assertive meaning among Black activists, and even outside Black movement circles, its use as an identification term indexes critical consciousness. My research considers the centrality of *negro* as a criterion of membership in Black organizing, even among Brazilians whose physical features would not place them in the Black category in Brazil. People are now using *negro* (an affirmative term) to describe themselves and others in everyday exchanges as a marker of Black consciousness. People with dark skin generally identify as *preto*, whereas Black activists with Brown skin typically self-identify as *negro* rather than *preto* (as I do). When asked directly, people who do not have black skin and kinky hair and do not identity as *preto* explain that neither they nor society in general views them as *preto* but as *moreno* (brown). When speaking the word *negro*, Luiza used a slower tempo, a common prosodic strategy for double-voicing the word with a hint of doubt, signaling the "dialogic angle" from which she spoke (Keane 2011, 174) and thus avoiding a complete fusion of the two voices. In using a slower tempo, Luiza rendered audible the voices of the Black movement and its opposition.

As Luiza's second (opposing) voice sounded forth, her classmates became restless, eager to jump into the discussion. The split in her use of negro became even clearer in her following remark: "Eu geralmente não gosto de usar muito esse termo *negro*." (Normally, I don't really like to use that term *black*.) Here she clarified her stance on the counterposed voices in her discourse: her voice was at variance with the voice of Black movement activists who embraced the use of *negro*. Predictably, Luiza's distancing herself from *negro*—a term embraced by most in the room—triggered an oral exchange of different points of view on the issue. In Brazil, *negro* may convey both a plurality of voices and the clashes among them, revealing their dialogic angles (Roth-Gordon and Silva 2013). Luiza's classmates understood that there was more than one voice in her use of the word *negro*, and they used this as an opening to practice what they were learning: to take a critical stance on dominant views of racism through dialogue.

Luiza continued her critique of Black mobilization, pondering over the implications of the Black movement's politicization of race to the collective national self. In the next excerpt, note the layers of citations she used to establish the position from which she constructed her thoughts about Black mobilization. In response to a question from Júlia, who asked her to elaborate on her ideas about the word *negro*, Luiza stated,

Quando eu falei sobre a palavra *negro*, eu não disse que me incomodava, mas que eu não gostava de usar. Eu não gosto de usar pela seguinte razão. Existem diversas pesquisas, comprovadamente, . . . recentemente passou até na TVE, um documentário sobre essa situação, dizendo, "Nós nos consideramos como o quê? Somos negros, brancos, mestiços, índios, amarelos? Somos pardos? O que somos realmente?" Então a partir do momento que você começa a se intitular como negro, o que é ser negro exatamente? . . . Mas é necessário que a gente se veja como seres humanos.

When I talked about the word *black*, I didn't say that it bothered me, but that I didn't like to use it. I don't like to use it for the following reason. There are several proven studies . . . recently even TVE aired a documentary about this situation, saying "What do we consider ourselves? Are we black, white, mixed, Indian, yellow? Are we brown? What are we really?" So the moment you start to self-identify as Black, what is it exactly to be Black? . . . But it is necessary that we see ourselves as human beings.

Luiza's speech can be viewed as an example of the many ubiquitous voices of ordinary commonsense racism that Luiza herself had to navigate in her everyday life and that Brazilian critics of anti-racist reforms also repeatedly used. In this excerpt, Luiza expressed her thoughts about the collective self-identity of Black movement activists using interrogatively framed quotations and assessments filled with intertextual links to a television documentary and to the fable of the three races that portrays Brazil as the fusion of Black, Indigenous, and White races (DaMatta 1981).

As I mentioned, this interaction took place on Luiza's first day in the course. Her classmates had been taught to recognize, mark, and discuss tokens of dominant discourses on race in their own and others' speech. Luiza's speech was filled with voices that she used not only to construct herself and others as intricately connected to the broader sociopolitical context but also to strategically assert her stance toward others' words. Luiza's classmates seized the opportunity to show off their newly acquired skills. For most of the class period, they collectively engaged in a critical analysis of the layers of voices infused with racial ideologies that inhabited her discourse. Next I examine the interpersonal, linguistic, and citational strategies that her classmates used not only to represent, evaluate, and contest the many voices lurking beneath Luiza's speech but also to project voices that embodied alternative, anti-racist ideologies.

The Multiple Voices of Anti-racist Socialization

> In real life as [when perceiving prose] we very keenly and subtly hear all these
> nuances in the speech of people surrounding us, and we ourselves work very
> skillfully with all these colors on the verbal palette.
>
> —Mikhail Bakhtin, *Problems of Dostoevsky's Poetics*

Luiza's classmates interpreted her utterances as sites of potential racial
consciousness-raising and anti-racist subjectivity, dialogue, and conflict,
realized through a complex construction of embedded voices. They challenged her to focus upon the ways in which her words were in fact also
someone else's, and on how they contributed to the sorting and stratification process affecting the Brazilian Black population. As Kathryn Woolard
(2004, 87) reminds us, voice is the social intention with which discourse is
infused. This became evident as participants engaged dialogically with
Luiza's system of voices, or the linguistic expression of multiple coexisting
viewpoints within her individual speech. Carlos responded to Luiza's statement that she did not really like to use the term *black* with, "Então nós
temos ainda muita dificuldade com relação a isso. Às vezes fico até com pena
de determinadas pessoas que ainda tem pensamento muito retrógrado.
Quando acham que falar a palavra *negro* é—uma coisa que não deve ser
dita." (So we still struggle a lot with this. At times I feel sorry for certain
people who still think in the old ways. When they think that using the word
black is—something one shouldn't use).

Here citational moves, such as referring to the words of generic others,
allowed Carlos to reconstruct in Luiza's discourse the embedded voices at
the heart of the struggles that Afro-Brazilians faced within the movement
for a new consciousness. He worked to show connections between the voices
that Luiza took on and the ideologies, or "doxa" (Bourdieu 1977), through
which race relations in Brazil were constructed and interpreted. Carlos
alluded to what these anonymous voices said about the use of the term *negro*:
that Blacks should not use it to embrace Blackness. He argued that if change
were going to come, it would need to begin at the level of the individual consciousness that questioned this dominant voice. Like Carlos, other participants pursued citational traces to address Luiza's polyphonic words and
stances. Early on, Ana, the instructor, attempted to show that Luiza was ani-
mating words that derived from other sources or principals (Goffman 1981)

and to uncover how Luiza's racial attitudes laid bare Brazil's dominant racial ideology: "Nós falamos na segunda aula quando nós trabalhamos um pouquinho de mídia. Vimos algumas imagens estereotipadas de homens e mulheres negras, nas telenovelas brasileiras sobre a escravidão. Imagens do escravo sujeitado, coitadinho, subalterno, infeliz, triste, suicida." (We talked about [this] in our second class when we worked a little bit on media. We saw some stereotypical images of Black men and women in the Brazilian soap operas about slavery. Images of a slave who was defeated, poor, subaltern, unhappy, sad, suicidal.)

In the two previous classes, Ana had challenged the students to critically examine the role of Brazilian soap operas in inculcating negative ideas about Blacks in the general public. In this excerpt, after briefly reviewing what the class had discussed before, Ana used a series of citational devices to refer to the sources of misconceptions and stereotypes that had formed stereotypical images of the Black population in Brazil. For example, she imitated certain vocal mannerisms when giving examples of deprecating words or roles that Brazilian soap operas commonly used to depict Blacks: *escravo sujeitado, coitadinho, subalterno, infeliz, triste, suicida* (defeated, poor, subaltern, unhappy, sad, suicidal slave). In a typical double voice with parodic intention, and without adding much more information, Ana showed how each word on that list was filled with multiple voices in dialogic relationships with one another. Ana spoke each word from at least two points of view simultaneously. As she uttered each word, she parodied the Brazilian soap opera voice, whose force she periodically sought to counteract with ridicule and accusations of racism. She also polemically exaggerated the deprecating words to cast a glancing blow at Luiza's speech, in which Ana identified mainstream media voices. In a close examination of these practices (e.g., their critique of Luiza), one sees the role of dialogism (the struggles of competing voices) in the activists' affirmative language practices, which diligently sought to expose and cope with the dominant voices as embodied dispositions (habitus) actualized in speech, rendered interpretable within a framework of social and cultural knowledge about race relations in Brazil. Rather than being grounded in an assertion of homogeneous collective Black identity, activists' anti-racist socialization reflected the broader understanding of multiple voices that had become embedded in Afro-Brazilians' lived experiences of a racial self. The same dialogism can be seen in the following excerpt, where André followed up on Luiza's argument that Blacks should not see themselves as a distinct race but as human beings. Tracing the history of the discourses embedded in Luiza's utterances, André opined that there was a notable familiarity in her argument:

> A gente às vezes fica andando em círculos tipo—eu entendo o quê a colega falou sobre o lance de você se achar ser humano, mas assim você voltar a esse tipo de—a esse tipo de discussão, é uma discussão do século retrasado. Negro era visto como inferior, era considerado inferior ao humano. Então, você ser humano era um ganho. Hoje em dia a gente já tem introjetado na nossa realidade. . . . Se a gente entrar nessa nessa discussão, que é alimentada pela elite branca, que nós somos todos iguais.

> And we sometimes keep going around in circles, like—I understand what our colleague is talking about—that we consider ourselves as human beings but, you know, to go back to this kind of argument, this is an argument from two centuries ago. Blacks were seen as inferior; Blacks were considered less than human. So to be recognized as human was a victory. Today, we already have that as part of our reality. . . . If we participate in this discussion, put forward by the White elite, that we are all the same.

To André, Luiza's words were repeating outdated reasoning. He used his historical knowledge of the nineteenth-century abolition campaigns in Brazil to show that Luiza's words were not simply the product of a lone contemporary speaker's voice but dated back to a time when Blacks fought against the dehumanization of enslaved bodies. André pointed out that, when Luiza stated everyone should be entitled to the same rights regardless of race, she spoke through and merged with the two-century-old argument against the enslavement of Blacks. He noted that although this logic was empowering at that time, currently it worked against anti-racist mobilization. André further identified an intertextual link between Luiza's claim and the voice of the *elite branca* (White elite), which, according to him, infiltrated her utterances. Through his deconstruction of Luiza's layers of voices, André worked to show the prong of Brazilian "folk theories of race and racism"—to use Jane Hill's (2008, 4) words—in the arguments of opponents of the race consciousness movement, who often based their claims against race-based policies on the idea that Blacks should see themselves as human beings (Morris 1992, 368). By means of this intervention into Luiza's argument, André argued that the dismantling of "cultured discourse"—discourse refracted through dominant ideologies (Bakhtin 1984, 203)—should be a goal of the struggle against anti-Black racism in contemporary Brazil. In line with the goals and nature of anti-racist socialization among people in the Black movement, André's stance toward the belief that racial differences are inconsequential (which is common to both liberal and conservative ideology) emerged as a critical strategy to expose the absence of racial neutrality in a regime of White supremacy. Júlia, who earlier challenged Luiza about her dislike of the term *negro*, also addressed Luiza's polyphonic speech. Following André, Júlia got up and recited a rhyme of her own invention, in which she dialogued with the multiple voices in Luiza's utterances.

> Negro acorda e cante o samba na universidade, e verás que o teu filho será príncipe de verdade. Daí então jamais tu voltarás ao barracão. Fala negão. Então essa é minha resposta pra essa questão toda aí de negro, negritude, o porquê nós não podemos negar nossa raça, entende?

> Blacks wake up and [*starts samba dancing*] sing samba in the university [*stops dancing*], and you'll see that your son will be a real prince. And you'll never go back to the shacks. Speak up, dear Black [*stands by her seat and faces Luiza*]. So this is my response [*looks around at others*] to this question about Blacks, Blackness, why we cannot deny our race, understand?

Júlia walked around the big circle of students, facing various classmates, as she recited her short rhyme. She then turned to Luiza as she switched from reciting to speaking. Júlia's persuasive rhetoric not only allowed her to speak to Luiza and the group simultaneously but also added considerable dialogic force to her critique of Luiza's stance toward racial politics. For example, Júlia dug into Luiza's speech and responded to the embedded voice of miscegenation that lurked beneath Luiza's words when she cited Roberto's DaMatta's (1981) "fable of three races," which tells Blacks that they are not Blacks but instead a mixture of three races. Júlia used the directive "sing samba at the university" as she danced the samba, rendering ironic Blacks' adoption of samba as a marker of their identity in popular culture while failing to embrace Black identity as a form of mobilization.

Júlia echoed other activists who criticized Brazilian Blacks for opposing affirmative action in college admissions while adopting manifestations of Black culture (such as music and dance) as part of their identity. Júlia's speech touched on the systemic dilemma at the heart of the controversy over affirmative action in Brazil today, which was constantly addressed during the consciousness-raising classes I observed: What is the stance of oppositional consciousness toward Brazil's hegemonic racial ideologies? What strikes me most in the preceding exchanges is that Afro-Brazilians now inhabit a vastly different landscape in which the contradictions between racial mixture and Black consciousness are being intensively reevaluated.

Anti-racist Activism: Challenges and Possibilities

This chapter has examined Afro-Brazilians' engagement in the twofold goal of developing their knowledge about African and Afro-Brazilian history and culture and putting this knowledge to work to promote anti-racism. The interactions analyzed herein illustrate several different linguistic strategies that juxtaposed Brazil's long-held racial ideologies with discourses and knowledge about race legitimized by race-conscious legislations and policies. Through these linguistic strategies, Black movement activists adopted various voices to frame different (and often competing) ideological positions on race in order to drive the debate over race and racism in Brazil toward an anti-racist vision of change in which they could negotiate their own identities between Brown and Black while critically questioning whether there are better or worse choices they could make.

Brazil has historically prided itself on being a racial democracy, meaning that, in contrast with the state-sponsored segregation in South Africa and the United States, Brazilian society has celebrated racial mixing. Yet Brazil is profoundly stratified by color. The contestation over race-based social justice activism in Brazil is part of a larger struggle over a long-held belief in the racial exceptionalism of Brazilian society: that there are no clear racial divisions. Black activists' contemporary linguistic and social challenges create ideological tensions with supporters of Brazil's mixed-race ideology, who accuse the Black movement of dividing Brazilian society along racial lines.

Affirmative action laws have been implemented across the country, via local, state, and federal government agencies, as well as individual educators, activists, and private institutions. Activists often describe the process of enacting the law as a mixed bag of opportunities and challenges. As my analysis shows, activists recognize the ideological diversity that divides groups according to their stances on issues of race and racism, which are in turn tied to different ways of talking about them. Embedded in Black activists' training on African and Afro-Brazilian history and culture is the goal of imparting knowledge about race and racism that teachers could use in their classrooms to hone students' critical thinking about those issues. In the process, these activists challenged students in the course I observed to critically reflect on their own racial experiences, revisit what they had been taught about race and racism, and relate their own experiences and ideas to contemporary ideological shifts in Brazil.

These are complex pedagogical challenges. Through socializing peers to recognize and critique commonsense notions of race and racism as voices, students became more attentive to the interconnectedness between everyday grassroots experiences of race and dominant ideologies, processes, and institutions. They distanced themselves from conventional notions and beliefs about race and racism. In doing so they branded these "folk theories" of race and racism (Hill 2008, 4) as inescapably audible voices that they could respond to and position themselves in relation to. As Mikhail Bakhtin argues, "Consciousness finds itself inevitably facing the necessity of having to choose a language. With each literary-verbal performance, consciousness must actively orient itself amidst heteroglossia" (1981, 295). This was manifested in the attempts of Luiza's classmates to socialize her into recognizing and taking a stance against the many voices that make up her own and others' speech. For Luiza and her fellow classmates, recognizing that one could be at the same time Black and Brown painted a nuanced picture that was equally staggering and illuminating.

3

Performing Ancestors, Claiming Blackness

Decades before 2003, when the Brazilian Black movement racked up several victories, including the passage of legislation that requires schools across the country to teach Afro-Brazilian history and culture, Black political organizers in Salvador devoted their free time after work to preparing Afro-Brazilians of all ages for college entrance exams. This outreach project evolved into Instituto Lutas de Zumbi (Zumbi Struggles Institute), or simply Zumbi, a community organizing dynamo in Salvador serving the *população negra* (Black population) who could not afford the ever-increasing cost of college preparation. Since the early 1990s Zumbi has served as a model in providing a combination of college preparatory classes and Black consciousness-raising education. While I was conducting fieldwork at Zumbi in 2010, I had the opportunity to interview César Silva, one of the organization's cofounders.[1] Emphasizing the consciousness-raising mission of the school, César repeated a common refrain within the organization, "Zumbi não é um pré-vestibular que oferece aula de consciência negra, mas uma escola de consciência negra que oferece aula de pré-vestibular." (Zumbi is not a college preparatory school that offers Black conscious-raising classes, but a Black consciousness-raising school that offers college preparatory classes.") Zumbi offered two college admissions prep classes: a yearlong evening course for working adults and a three-year after-school program for high school students. These students did not have to pay tuition, and they were provided with lunch and transportation support so that they could come directly to the institute from their public schools. The adults were required to pay tuition monthly at a nominal rate. Zumbi also offered a limited number of scholarships made available by community supporters. During an interview with Mariana, a former student, she told me she was allowed to attend classes even though she could not afford to pay the tuition because she had lost her job. She felt that the education she received was so valuable to her that later, after she graduated and got a job, she went back and proudly repaid what she owed for tuition.

I had the opportunity to witness Zumbi's decades-long organizing effort to provide anti-racist socialization to Afro-Brazilian youth and adults. For example, I was a participant observer in Jamile's language arts (Portuguese) class for a cohort of high school students. When the topic was Modern Art Week—a landmark festival of Brazil's modernist movement that took place in São Paulo in 1922—Jamile adapted the textbook lesson in order to help her students see the event through an anti-racist lens. Jamile's approach to teaching about Modern Art Week, the focus of this chapter, encapsulates Zumbi's educational project and political vision.

Anthropophagy during Modern Art Week

Modern Art Week became enshrined in Brazilian history as an oppositional event and landmark of Brazil's modernist movement. For a whole week, February 11–18, 1922, São Paulo became a hub for music, dance, poetry, and fine arts, thus changing Brazilian cultural history. The counterculture arts festival challenged traditional forms of art, art appreciation, and beauty; it also permanently reoriented politics and cultural life in Brazil in important ways (Camargos 2002). Writers Guilherme de Almeida, Oswald de Andrade, and Manuel Bandeira; painters Emiliano Di Cavalcanti and Anita Malfatti; composer Heitor Villa Lobos, and others came together hoping to ignite a cultural revolution against the traditional conservative art that prevailed in Brazil since the nineteenth century. Combining the ferment of European experimental literatures and arts at that time with the roots of Brazil's African, Indigenous, and traditional backland culture, the Semana de 22 (Week of 22), as it became known, highlighted narratives about Brazil that until then were unknown or stigmatized. The event also immortalized its participants in Brazilian cultural history, from nationally adored icons to promising local talents.

Central to the movement was a metaphor of anthropophagy to describe the process of Brazilian identity construction through the act of cannibalizing existing cultural expressions (foreign and Indigenous) to create new ones more attuned to the country's changing social and economic reality of the time. Oswald de Andrade's *Manifesto antropófago (or antropofágico)* (Anthropophagic Manifesto) of 1928, which defines the Brazilian movement of the 1920s and 1930s, encapsulates the ideological landscape in which the event happened: "Antes dos portugueses descobrirem o Brasil, o Brasil tinha descoberto a felicidade." (Before the Portuguese discovered Brazil, Brazil had discovered happiness; O. de Andrade [1928] 1973, 231.) Thereby Andrade developed a critique of oppressive colonial relations, calling for the critical absorption of foreign cultures and ideas, with the goal of converting those ideas into locally reusable cultural material.

This pivotal moment in the development of modern art in Brazil became a focal point of Jamile's language arts class. Instead of the usual lesson about the significance of the 1922 event, Jamile decided that her group of students should create an adaptation that captured the Brazilian Black experience. Students' adaptations are suggestive of the discursive weight of multivocality in their relationship with Blackness.

Performing Predecessors, Reclaiming Blackness

In one activity students learned about biased memory practices that "whitewashed" influential Black figures in Brazilian history. Through a series of monologues, students challenged the erasure of the Blackness of famous people in the nation's collective memory. These monologues featured biographical information and a chance for the students to show off their talent. I use this activity as a lens into how they reconfigured what they saw as a history of injustice in White-dominated, Eurocentric narratives of Brazilian cultural production. Writing about the presence of Blackness in Brazil's national imaginary, João Costa Vargas notes, "It ensures that the gendered Black subject is an impossible subject, one whose impossible gender, impossible Blackness, impossible being, inhabits the very impossible coordinates of time and space that make the nation possible. The nation is possible because the gendered Black subject, qua subject, qua citizen, is an oxymoron. Always already, thus timeless, thus outside of the linearity of time, the impossible Black subject occupies the zones of death" (2012, 5).

As the biographical details of the famous figures emerged from the depths of the dominant stories to the surface of students' monologues, the deeply whitewashed Brown identities were placed in a dialogue with their restored Black versions. Thus, the students questioned the place of Blacks and Blackness in Brazilian culture.

On one day in October, Jamile signaled that it was time to rehearse the monologues in front of the class. From the corner of the room, I followed the students with my video camera and audio recorder. The instructor took her place at the front of the room to my right. Rising from their seats, about ten of the thirty students stood clustered in the middle of the room. The other students remained seated in a semicircle around the perimeter. As the standing students flexed their muscles, the audience of seated students talked quietly among themselves. At one point, Jamile intervened, asking them to be quiet out of respect for those who were trying to remember their lines. A few minutes later she asked who would like to present their monologue first. Ricardo raised his hand and, after clearing his throat, started speaking. In a biographical sketch in which he portrayed the renowned author Afonso Henriques de Lima Barreto, he recounted the most important events, qualities, contributions, and connections in Lima Barreto's life. Speaking in the present tense—"Meu nome é Lima Barreto" (My name is Lima Barreto)—Ricardo brought the voice of this historical figure into the world of the living. He had composed his monologue to represent Lima Barreto as a Black person, capturing "a figura de Lima Barreto em carne e osso para além da versão enbraqueada que aparece nos livros, o senhor sabe" (the flesh-and-blood historical figure beyond the whitewashed version that appears in the textbooks, you know). At one point, for example, Ricardo talked about what it was like for Lima Barreto to be a Black man in Brazil. Further affirming Lima Barreto's Blackness, Ricardo emphasized how the author would put the interests of poor and Black people first. With details like these, he also foregrounded an affirmative version of Blackness. As he loudly recited his monologue, the others listened quietly.

Thus evolved a unique activity that was simultaneously a theatrical performance of a historical figure and an immersion in contemporary debates about race and racism in Brazil. Blurring the distinctions between the present and past, the Black personalities and themselves, the students' monologues "clarified the past by infusing it with present purposes" (Lowenthal 1998, xv). After Ricardo finished, one by one the other students in the center of the room presented their own historical figures. Whenever students forgot their lines, they would pull out a piece of paper from their pocket, check the words, and resume their monologues. As the centerpiece of this chapter, the students' reanimation and reinterpretation of the past provides "a critical reading of slavery's afterlife [which] means bringing social structures of the past, not as an unchanging same, but as symbolic reservoir whose energy dissipates into contemporary formations of race and gender" (Vargas 2012, 7). Moreover, by restoring Blackness to the whitewashed images of historical figures, the students' monologues addressed one of the most pressing questions of contemporary anti-racist activism in Brazil: What happens when their counternarratives of Blackness meet the master narratives of miscegenation?

I suggest that we consider the relationship between their different versions of what has taken place not as incompatible, where the two perspectives are so opposed in character as to be incapable of coexisting, but as dialogic, where the two perspectives constantly engage with and are informed by each other. In *Multidirectional Memory*, Michael Rothberg (2009) explored how the relationship between collective memories—for example, between Holocaust versus colonial memories—is not a zero-sum situation in which more public attention to one historical event results in less attention to another. According to Rothberg, rather than being in competition, the sense of awareness of one event can be heightened by a sense of awareness of the other, a process he described as "multidirectional memory." Rothberg's theorization offers important insight into the possibility of synergy between different collective memories, where the interaction of two or more (competing) memories can produce a combined effect greater than the sum of their separate effects.

In focusing on the interaction of separate, unrelated collective memories, Rothberg leaves open the question of how to analyze conflicting versions of the same spatial, temporal, and cultural event. In some respects, the relationship between the memory of the historical Black figures that emerged in the monologue exercise versus the dominant memory of the same figures could be characterized as dramatically different versions of the same event. Building on Rothberg's concept of multidirectional memory, one of the principal premises of this study is that there is not necessarily competition between the distinct, competing versions. I would argue that the interaction of the two versions produces a combined effect greater than the sum of their separate effects. In writing about anti-racism, Vargas notes that anti-racist projects "perform counter-narratives that, although not always effective in negating the imposed norms, nevertheless suggest possibilities beyond the material and symbolic confines of gendered antiblackness" (2012, 8). Along the same lines, Keisha-Khan Perry (2005) shows how Brazilian Black women use social memory as a political tool to bring attention to dominant narratives that support practices of exclusion. Alexandre Emboaba da Costa (2016) similarly explores how Afro-Brazilian artists practice decoloniality in their discourse of *ancestralidade* (ancestry) in order to challenge Brazil's assimilationist narratives. As they gained knowledge about Afro-Brazilian history and culture, people in Costa's study began to subvert Eurocentric thinking, which devalues African and Black thought.

Jamile's students' awareness of the different versions—the whitewashed versus the blackened identities of achievers in Brazilian history—allowed them to recognize how anti-Blackness manifests in collective memory. Jamile's approach was grounded in a moral imperative to recognize the Black identity of these notable Brazilian citizens. Evaluating their own position between Brown and Black, her students shared a similar ethical obligation to identify as Black.

Rendering Blackness Invisible in Brazilian History

The contestation of narratives of the Afro-Brazilian past is at the heart of the Brazilian Black movement's efforts to challenge dominant interpretations of Blackness itself. These challenges resound in interactions that socialize less experienced members of community-based organizations into an anti-racist stance toward Afro-Brazilian history and culture. This chapter builds on chapter 2, analyzing the role of anti-racist pedagogy in rediscovering Afro-Brazilian history and culture. In the monologue exercise, Zumbi instructors and students stood up against the erasure from Brazilian collective memory of the skin color of people whom Black movement activists view as inspirational figures that played a key role in Brazilian history. Most important, as Jamile often repeated, they learned "sobre a história de negros Brasileiros cujas notáveis conquistas foram coisas que seus pais, avós, e bisavós nunca imaginaram saber" (about the history of Black Brazilians whose remarkable accomplishments were something their parents, grandparents, and great-grandparents never thought they would see in their lifetimes). The roots of the memory practices I analyze in this chapter run deeply into the complex history of the relationship between Black Brazilians and Brazil's dominant discourse on race mixing and national identity. Kim Butler nicely describes this history as an "artful contest of position that often seems to avoid the violence and hatred of racial politics elsewhere. Yet surface appearances belie the intensity and high stakes of the underlying struggle" (Butler 1998, 160). In this section, I focus on relevant aspects of this history before moving on to an analysis of Jamile's students' experiences of stepping inside historical achievers and finding their Black voices.

Mediating the narrative about remarkable individuals in a world that was constructed to blot out their Black identities, Brazil's ideologies of miscegenation and racial democracy take us all the way back to Giberto Freyre's masterwork about Brazilian society, *Casa-grande & senzala* (Freyre [1933] 1987). First published in 1933, Freyre's idealized study of Brazilian society as a harmonious fusion of races and cultures set the foundation of Brazil's national identity and historical narratives. As Barbara Celarent notes, "for the rest of the twentieth and into the twenty-first century, Freyre's 'hymn to miscegenation' was parlayed by Brazilian conservatives into an image of nonracialism that, while masking Brazil's ongoing racial issues," undermined the specificity of the Black Brazilian experience (2010, 334). In line with Freyre's ideas, the regime of Getúlio Vargas (1930–1945) promoted the notion of "a racially harmonious Brazilian national family." Under Vargas, Brazilian nationalists successfully forged and institutionalized a dominant national identity based on the notion of *brasilidade*, a sense of Brazilianness free of racial discrimination, while avoiding or downplaying Blackness as a viable component of national identity (Davis 1999, 8, 28). As Darién Davis (1999, 218) notes, this was evident in popular culture, such as samba, Brazilian popular music, and soccer, all of which were considered manifestations of *brasilidade*. It is in this ideological context that Brazilian society obscured the Blackness of Brazil's historical figures.

After the end of the Vargas regime in 1945, Brazil's democratic government adopted Freyre's ideas about Brazil's exceptional race relations, which by then had become nationally and internationally known as racial democracy. In spite of the facts of ongoing racial exclusion and discrimination, the military regime that came to power in 1964 adhered completely to the ideology of racial democracy and suppressed the work of those seeking to call attention to racial discrimination. After the military took control of the country, Black organizations lay dormant or disbanded. Seeking a hegemonic culture, the military government exerted control over all cultural processes, including education, national history, and national identity, while imposing severe restrictions on civil liberties, democratic institutions, and political expression of social movements (J. Santos 2005, 78). The regime mandated that school curricula include content explicitly aimed at forming a national consciousness characterized by mixed-race ideology and the idea of Brazil as a nonracialized nation. This amounted to an unprecedented assault against enormous symbols of Afro-Brazilian history and culture.

Notably, the military regime also sought to affirm its cultural and historical ties to the African continent, driven by political and economic interests in Africa. In the 1960s and 1970s, Brazil increasingly focused on redefining Afro-Brazilian heritage. Among other things, it invested heavily in the Black tourism industry (Butler 1998, 168; see also Dzidzienyo and Oboler 2005).[2] Afro-Brazilian culture was advertised as Brazil's *alma brasileira* (Brazilian soul) (J. Santos 2005, 82). But, as Jocélio dos Santos reminds us, the idea took on a cultural rather than a political meaning. Acknowledgment of Afro-Brazilian presence in the nation took the form of "preservation of the Brazilian culture" (J. Santos, 2005, 34) in the context of an economic interest in turismo cultural (cultural tourism). In fact, there were "glaring contradictions between Brazil's renewed interest in Africa and the country's failure to include black Brazilians in the very operation of this interest" (Dzidzienyo 1985, 138; see also Jones–de Oliveira, 2003). This phenomenon demonstrates Brazilian ruling elites' refusal to recognize racism in spite of the dire condition of the Black population (J. Santos 2005, 79). During this period Blacks in the United States could publicly engage in the Black Power movement, even though it was viewed as un-American and a threat to the established order; Afro-Brazilians in Brazil, however, were forced to live the new national motto promulgated by the military government, "Brazil: Love It or Leave It" (Davis 1999, 225). The development of nationalism through what Davis describes as "avoidance of the dark" in Brazilian society is a foundational moment in Brazilian history.

Beginning in the mid-1970s, the Brazilian state underwent significant changes, culminating with the fall of the military dictatorship in 1985. With the implementation of a participatory democracy at the federal, state, and municipal levels, a number of Black movement organizations sprang up in the late 1970s to address racial discrimination. Since the mid-1990s, Brazil has advanced anti-racist policies that include racial quotas at Brazilian public universities and in civil service, scholarships for Black undergraduates to study at private institutions, and a federal law that requires all schools to teach African and Afro-Brazilian history and culture. Signaling the government's improved receptivity to the demands of the Black movement, government officials publicly acknowledged the existence of racial discrimination for the first time in 1996 (Paschel 2016; Tavolaro 2006, 36). In the same year, the federal government created the first National Human Rights Program, which focused on using the weight of the law to reduce racial inequality. All of these changes meant new possibilities for collective political action. Black activism evolved into the politicization of race, changing the focus of mobilization from policies to protect people of African descent from discrimination toward combating institutional racism through measures like affirmative action (Treviño González 2005, 122). One of the features that clearly stands out in the last three decades of Black mobilization is the effort to create point-by-point contrasts with Brazil's master narrative of miscegenation. Increasingly under scrutiny, the dominant narrative of race mixing has had far-reaching consequences in the making of heroes among Afro-Brazilians. Through Afro-Brazilian activists' scrutiny of dominant accounts of Afro-Brazilian history and culture they recognize or create the voices these accounts embody. They also point out the ways in which the dominant voices silence or oppose alternative voices.

In what follows, I focus on Jamile's students' theatrical monologues as one example of the practices that Black activists use to confront and shift established accounts of Afro-Brazilian history and culture, and more specifically the construction of Afro-Brazilians' heroic ancestors in educational media. I focus on the strategies that Black activists have used to juxtapose their own accounts against the dominant accounts of Afro-Brazilian history and culture on the one hand and between their own voices and those of their Black predecessors' on the other. Jamile's students found this experience invigorating because it was more engaging intellectually than anything they had experienced in their classes or textbooks. Their response reflects the extent to which such activities caused them to reflect deeply on the role of historical racisms in obliterating the Black identities of many outstanding Brazilians. By contrasting whitening and blackening in their response, the students found a juxtaposition that created an interesting and unique approach to anti-racism. I suggest that in juxtaposing their own monologues against the dominant accounts of Afro-Brazilian history and culture, they were claiming something of broader social significance. Jamile and her students were creating multiple modes of inserting themselves into the public discourses on race and national identity while building competing perspectives on what has taken place.

Black Art Week, Act I

From the initial lesson on the Modern Art Week, Jamile's classroom activity grew into Zumbi's Black Art Week, a public display of a variety of arts and cultural forms. Emulating the original 1922 event and its goal of ridding Brazilian society of Eurocentric ideology, Zumbi's Black Art Week took place at Praça das Artes (Arts Square) in Pelourinho, a historic area of downtown Salvador, on December 16–17, 2009. The festival staged musical, theatrical, and dance performances that explored alternative perspectives through which to understand Afro-Brazilian history, culture, and struggles. As noted by Danda, one of Jamile's colleagues who helped her organize the event, Zumbi's Black Art Week combined art and politics in order to fix the history of Black struggles in the consciousness of its students and the community at large. I directly observed and video-recorded most of the rehearsals for the different activities over an eight-week period. About a week before the festival began, rehearsals shifted into high gear.

The opening act was a manifesto, written by Zumbi instructors and students, to be recited on the first day by a group of six students, three women and three men. Zumbi's manifesto was inspired by Oswald de Andrade's *Manifesto Antropófago*, first published in May 1928. In it Andrade critiqued the Brazilian intellectual elite for seeking to copy European models. For example, he vehemently criticized the acculturation of Indigenous peoples by the White Christian agents of Western civilization. The allusion to Andrade's manifesto influenced the interpretation of Zumbi's manifesto in significant ways—particularly in the postcolonial attitudes apparent in both, which denounce and criticize the ideological work that has historically derided African and Indigenous ways of knowing and being. As Luciano Tosta points out, "long before the term 'postcolonial' was in fashion, Andrade's writings were already exploring some of the major theoretical postulates in postcolonial studies" (2011, 224–225). Here Tosta refers to the resistance against colonizing culture, the debunking of official historical discourses, the deconstruction of the images of the colonizing power, and most important, the struggle to reclaim a past that had been denied and an identity that had been prevented from being. Through the irreverence, defiance, and subversive power in their collective memory activities, members of Zumbi continuously framed the process of remembering as taking place through dialogic struggles to reevaluate and reshape the role of Blackness in Brazilian national identity. In the process, they made instrumental use of a multiplicity of perspectives and voices, seeking to alter and inform them.

Two excerpts of Zumbi's manifesto serve to introduce the reader to the dialogic aims of the memory practices that were the focus of the event as a whole. After a quick huddle to discuss the upcoming performances, the three women and three men stood in line, facing the rest of the class, which was seated in a semicircle. Jamile signaled them to start. The first student on the left pulled out a piece of paper and started what sounded like a dramatic reading of the manifesto: "Cambaleantes na sua própria escuridão onde foi colocado e esquecido pela sociedade e pelo mundo, a população negra vaga sem ter uma grande representação artística, literária e histórica, manifestando em nós, jovens negros, a inconformidade pela exclusão feita pela sociedade para com a nossa ancestralidade. . . ." (Swaying in its own darkness, where it was placed and forgotten by society and the world, the Black population drifts without strong artistic, literary, and historic representation, generating in us, Black youth, outrage at the exclusion of its ancestry by society. . . .)

The manifesto thus began by bemoaning the underrepresentation of Blacks in Brazilian art, literature, and historiography. Capturing the general theme of the week, the silence and lack of knowledge about Blacks in Brazilian historiography became a recurring theme of the manifesto. There was a poetic cadence in the compositional character of the piece, and as mentioned during the rehearsals, it was borrowed from Andrade's own manifesto: "Filhos do sol, mãe dos viventes. Encontrados e amados ferozmente, com toda a hipocrisia da saudade, pelos imigrados, pelos traficados e pelos turistas. No país da cobra grande." (Children of the sun, mother of living. Fiercely met and loved, with all the hypocrisy of longing: by the immigrated, by the trafficked, and by the tourists. In the country of the big snake. O. de Andrade [1928] 1973, 227).

Besides the rhythmic similarity and the likeness in terms between the two manifestos, the critical interpretation of colonial relations (past and present) is presented in Zumbi's manifesto through imitating images in Andrade's. It is crucial to understand the dynamics of the relationships between the authors, the texts, and their respective audiences. It could be said that the deliberate intertextual resemblance points to the fact that Zumbi teachers and students drew inspiration from Andrade, but beyond that, the appropriation enables Zumbi students to engage with Andrade's ideas as a (re)articulation of a self-reflexive, anti-racist intervention into the continued relevance of the foundational problem in the history of Brazilian race relations: anti-Blackness. Intended to be read as a broad statement of the views and aims of the organizers of the festival, parts of the Zumbi manifesto also read a bit like revisionist history in which the students reinterpreted an event, a person, an idea from the past.

The next student to speak talked about the African gods, which have been historically overlooked or misunderstood due to racism: "As histórias brasileiras devem ser contadas assim como os mitos gregos. Os deuses africanos devem ser venerados assim como os deuses do Olimpo. Deve-se acabar com as camufladas castas das expressões artísticas, com o falso moralismo ainda predominante, o mito da democracia racial. . . ." (The Brazilian stories must be told in the same way as the Greek myths. The African gods must be venerated in the same way as the gods of Olympus. We must end the camouflaged casts in the world of arts, with its false moralism, the myth of racial democracy. . . .)

As illustrated in this segment, the choice is never between Afrocentric or Eurocentric tendencies; rather, at stake, I suggest, is a subversive, anti-racist interpretation of the marginalized relationship between Black cultural production and elite White cultural production. The representational logic of the elite cultural production needs to be resisted in order for true inclusion of Brazilian Blacks to be accomplished. The students' critique of racial democracy highlights the ways in which their Zumbi classes have enlightened their understanding of the world around them, particularly the ways in which the ideas of nonracialism (not involving racial factors or racial discrimination) have worked. This was consistent with similar sentiments expressed by other Black activists I met during my fieldwork. As the dramatic presentation continued, the other students took their turns reading. Speaking with a forceful voice, the third student to speak added her own part: "Se a Bíblia diz que somos a imagem e a semelhança de Cristo, desejamos a imagem do Cristo negro em todas as entidades que seguem a doutrina." (If the Bible says that we are the mirror image and likeness of Christ, we wish the image [or statue] of a Black Christ to be present in all establishments that follow this doctrine."

Here she cites the biblical passage that says people have been molded in the image of Christ. The authors of Zumbi's manifesto alluded to Andrade's words in order to orchestrate points of comparison and the call for Brazilians—and Afro-Brazilians, in particular—to assert themselves against European postcolonial cultural domination. Consider Andrade's lines, "Se Deus é a consciência do Universo Incriado, Guaraci é a mãe dos viventes. Jaci é a mãe dos vegetais." (If God is the conscience of the Uncreated Universe, Guaraci is the mother of the living. Jaci is the mother of vegetables; O. Andrade [1928] 1973, 230). Andrade clearly exposes the differences in cosmovision, or worldview, between Christians and natives, posing opposition and confrontation between them (Tosta 2011, 223). Both manifestos express a need to establish specific conditions that set limits on religious and cultural Whiteness. Note how Andrade's use of the conjunction *if* (i.e., given that) establishes Guaraci and Jaci as part of God's universal conscience. Similarly, in the Zumbi manifesto, *if* (given that) is used to frame the assertion that all of us, including Blacks, were created in the image of Christ. By alluding to syntactic elements of Andrade's manifesto to surreptitiously bring about the desired intertextual effect, Zumbi teachers and students expressed their concerns and conflicts over Whiteness as the norm. The next segment of the Zumbi manifesto reads,

> Queremos apresentar e deslumbrar para o grande público as diversas manifestações que tiveram que permanecer em silêncio. . . . Vem dos jovens do Instituto Lutas de Zumbi a vontade de fazer uma transformação na sociedade em que vivemos, apresentando para a nação uma pluralidade de cultura, artes e pensamentos que estavam aprisionados dentro do seu próprio eu.

> We want to show for the fascination of the general public a variety of works that were kept in silence. . . . The youth at Zumbi Struggles Institute want to make transformations in our society, presenting to the nation a plurality of culture, arts, and thinking that were imprisoned inside their own selves.

There is a striking resemblance between this segment and Andrade's words, "Queremos a Revolução Caraíba. Maior que a Revolução Francesa. A unificação de todas as revoltas eficazes na direção do homem. Sem nós a Europa não teria sequer a sua pobre declaração dos direitos do homem." (We want the Caraíba Revolution. Bigger than the French Revolution. The uni-fication of all the efficient revolts for the sake of human beings. Without us, Europe would not even have had its poor declaration of the rights of men; O. de Andrade [1928] 1973, 227)

"Caraíba Revolution" is Andrade's term for the utopian transformation that would be driven by the natives of the Americas in their struggles against the degradations imposed by the colonizer. Further echoing between the two manifestos is accomplished through parallelisms (i.e., the use of succes-sive verbal constructions that correspond in grammatical structure and meaning) that throw into sharp relief existing adaptations in the kind of cultural work Zumbi teachers and students worked hard to present to their audience. In these excerpts and throughout the manifesto, the teachers and students introduced the key idea of Black Art Week: that their exclusion from established accounts has been a powerful tool of Black oppression and, at the same time, a staple for holding the racial democracy and mixed-race ideologies in place. The interrelationship between the two manifestos—and especially the way that Zumbi's updates Andrade's with a call to do away with the mentality of obliteration of Blackness from Brazilian history and culture—is striking. Of specific interest is how anti-racist pedagogy has created a space for Afro-Brazilians to reread narratives of race relations in Brazil that favored the racial mixture framework while downplaying Blackness as a vital component of national identity. By subverting racial identities as imposed categories keyed to the dominant racial ideology, Afro-Brazilians are reshaping their own self-identity as a critical and antag-onistic position against the obliteration of Blackness.

Following the manifesto, there was a choral performance, a play, a dance, and a series of first-person biographical monologues, which actively (re)con-structed and reconfigured dominant discourses on race and national iden-tity. These monologues, the focus of the rest of this chapter, invoked various beliefs and ideas underlying the accounts of the Afro-Brazilian past, hint-ing at the political and cultural factors behind what has historically been (mis)remembered in both official and vernacular memories. I argue that the force of these memory activities lies not in setting one account in direct opposition or competition with the other (pitting one account against the other) but through their interplay as a way to animate an anti-racist renarration of Afro-Brazilian history and culture in powerful and compel-ling ways.

Black Art Week, Act II

Zumbi's Black Art Week included a series of performances aimed at promoting public understanding of the obliteration of Blackness as part of the dynamics of Brazil's ideology of miscegenation. Teachers and students often talked about this task as being the most challenging. The belief that Brazilians have a long history of mixing across racial lines and thus are free of racial divisions has dominated Brazil's public discourses on race and national identity, leading Brazilians to avoid a discussion about the implications of racial difference for society (Davis 1999; Telles 2004). This is still true despite campaigns by the Black movement to expose the many ways Black Brazilians have been largely excluded from opportunities to pursue upward mobility (Roth-Gordon 2017; Sheriff 2001). The biographical monologues, by looking back at the Brazilian cultural and political past, (re)constructed and reconfigured the words and actions of outstanding Black citizens. Performers paid tribute to Black activists who had the courage to fight racism or stand up to social inequality. In each monologue one student played the role of a Black activist, telling that individual's personal story. The monologues focused on actual stories and events from the lives of the selected activists, with an emphasis on their contributions to the Black movement.

Regarding the pedagogical value of enacting the monologues, instructors repeatedly reminded students about the importance of recognizing the Black identity of these outstanding citizens, whose Blackness has been excluded from dominant memory. With this performance the instructors hoped to engage in an epistemic dispute by pushing to the forefront the idea that even though Brazilian society has honored these citizens to a greater or lesser extent, it has almost always redefined or quietly ignored their Black identities, and as a result Afro-Brazilians share a whitened version of the stories of their Black heroes. As one of the instructors responsible for the performance told me, in miscegenation-era Brazil these outstanding Black citizens were remembered mainly for the much-valued White traits and skills, the tactic by which Blacks were made all but invisible where it counts. One of their goals, she said, was to use these monologues as an educational practice to evoke remembrance among the students and the broader community, who know little and feel even less about the Black identities of these heroes.

In preparation for the presentation of the narratives on stage, each student was assigned to research the life of one Brazilian Black activist. Next, students were instructed to develop a first-person narrative from the activist's perspective, recounting the episodes in the activist's life and his or her thoughts, emotions, actions, speech, and reactions to those life experiences. They began each monologue with a long narrative section on the hero's life using biographical details selectively retrieved from the person's life experience. Feeding off the dominant texts from which they took their information, they digested them and produced something new, thereby taking control of what they believe is truth.

Individual performances paid homage to historical figures like Afonso Henriques de Lima Barreto, Chiquinha Gonzaga, Mario Gusmão, and others. Lima Barreto and Gonzaga provide interesting case studies: school textbooks tend to cover their accomplishments but omit discussions of how race and Blackness were intimately tied to who they were and their identities. Ultimately, students receive little substantial information about these important Brazilians' unique experiences of Blackness, a basic characteristic that determined their position in Brazilian society. For instance, Lima Barreto was a canonical author in Brazilian literature who wrote short stories, chronicles, and novels. He was also an incessantly loud voice in the struggle for equality of mostly Black minorities (Schwarcz 2017). Several school textbooks cover Lima Barreto's concern with social injustice and how his works described the hardships of people living on the margins of society, but these descriptions conspicuously omit Lima Barreto's Blackness, opting instead for a politically neutral skin tone, *pardo* (Brown). By portraying him as a *pardo* who suffered from color prejudice, they erase the fact that Lima Barreto often described himself as a poor Black man who lived in the ghetto. Collectively, textbook accounts read something like this:

> Filho de pais mestiços e pobres, Lima Barreto (1881–1992) carregou pelo resto da vida o fardo do preconceito de cor, que marcaria também sua obra literária. Foi jornalistas escreveu crônicas, contos e romances. Marginalizado, afastado das "elites" literárias, Lima Barreto escreveu, em sua própria linguagem, essa marginalidade. Seu estilo é simples e comunicativo, tendo sido considerado, por seus contemporâneos, um escritor desleixado. No entanto, foi valorizado pelos modernistas e hoje é visto como um dos importantes ficcionistas da nossa literatura.

> The son of mixed-race and poor parents, Lima Barreto (1881–1922) endured throughout his life the color prejudice of Brazilian society, which was a constant theme of his chronicles, short stories, and novels. Lima Barreto was

kept at the margins of Brazilian literary elites. His writing style was simple and communicative, which was held in contempt by some and was valorized by the modernists. Today Lima Barreto is regarded as one of the most important fiction writers in Brazilian literature.

Textbooks have a dominant role in school curricula in Brazil, and students' learning experience is mostly based on these readings. After surveying about a dozen textbooks with the help of middle school and high school teachers in Salvador, I concluded that the books keep students in the dark about the racism experienced by Brazil's historical Black figures like Lima Barreto, just as the teachers at Zumbi had told me. It could be claimed that those textbooks leave out any meaningful discussion of race, never using the word preto (Black) to describe Lima Barreto. When they address his appearance, they dilute, even dissolve, Lima Barreto's Blackness into a mixed-race ("mulatto") identity. They might acknowledge that he suffered color discrimination, but they avoid stating that he was viewed as too dark, and that is why he was discriminated against. The uniqueness of the Black experience in Brazil is not important information for textbook authors. They downplay Lima Barreto's Blackness in a type of admiration and respect for *brasilidade*, stifling any discussion of the racist experiences surrounding Lima Barreto's life (see D.F. Silva 1998; and Fanon 2008 chap. 5). It is no wonder that the students of Zumbi thought the dominant ideology informing the textbooks insulated them from the unique experiences of Black Brazilians who pioneered Black liberation struggles. For knowledge of their existence would have strengthened their resolve to build community and confront racism.

Delivered in a "key" (tone, manner, or spirit of utterance) that combined introspection and challenge, each monologue mounted an inventive memory construction of layers of Black history, engaging historical figures' oppositional stances on Black activists' own terms, and—most important—restating views of the past derived from each leader's biographical details. Ten students walked on stage. They took their places about five feet away from each other, some sitting in chairs while others stood. Again, Ricardo was the first presenter. Speaking at full volume, he traced the arc of Lima Barreto's life from a childhood of poverty to adulthood as novelist and journalist renowned for his social critiques:

Sou Afonso Henriques de Lima Barreto, mais conhecido como Lima Barreto. Nasci no dia 13 de maio de 1881 no Rio de Janeiro. Meu pai era tipógrafo, e minha mãe professora. Ambos eram escravos e por isso eu tive que viver na minha condição pobre em uma sociedade opressora. Sou um dos mais importantes jornalistas e escritores brasileiros.

I am Afonso Henriques de Lima Barreto, better known as Lima Barreto. I was born on May 13, 1881, in Rio de Janeiro. My father was a typographer, and my mother was a teacher. Both were slaves and because of this I was forced to live in poverty and oppression. I am one of the most important Brazilian journalists and writers.

The relationship between the dominant narratives and those of the Zumbi students is central to my interest in the study of anti-racist activism among Afro-Brazilians, and my primary concern here is to analyze what happens to both narratives when they are juxtaposed. There are important dimensions to the relationship between the two accounts as they interact in Zumbi students' reinterpretations, reconstructions, and negotiations. First, by saying that Lima Barreto's parents were enslaved—"Ambos eram escravos e por isso eu tive que viver na minha condição pobre em uma sociedade opressora" (Both were slaves and because of this I was forced to live in poverty and oppression)—Ricardo highlighted the status of Lima Barreto's parents. In contrast, textbooks omit that fact entirely, constructing him and his parents as racially mixed, and his literary work as being about class rather than racial struggles. Ricardo thus underscored the significance of Lima Barreto's Blackness to an open discussion of oppression. His process of reinterpretation had a combative quality (e.g., parody or polemic) to it. That is, he engaged with the monologic and monolithic textbook narratives (formed of a single, hegemonic and imposing thought) by inserting other information designed both to inform and alter them. In their struggle against unity, Zumbi students proposed alternative ways of operating within the constraints of the ideological environment of miscegenation.

The last section of each monologue was devoted to the Black figure's legacy, focusing on their role in the struggles for racial equality, as this continuation of the Lima Barreto monologue illustrates:

Minhas obras são vinculadas à realidade social urbana e suburbana do Rio de Janeiro, denotando por um lado a população pobre e oprimida e do outro o universo simbólico da classe dominante, e com isso refleti em minhas obras o preconceito racial, a pobreza, a truculência policial e a hipocrisia que cercava as relações sociais da sociedade opressora do último século. *Recordações do Escrivão Isaías Caminha, Triste Fim de Policarpo Quaresma* e *Clara dos Anjos* são algumas das minhas principais obras. Fui homenageado pela Escola da Samba Unidos da Tijuca no Ano de 1992 com o enredo Lima Barreto, Mulato Pobre mas Livre.

My works are linked to the social reality of urban and suburban Rio de Janeiro, noting on the one hand the poor and oppressed and on the other the symbolic universe of the dominant class, and this way in my works I reflected upon racial prejudice, poverty, police cruelty, and the hypocrisy surrounding the social relations of the oppressive society of the last century. *Recordações do Escrivão Isaías Caminha, Triste Fim de Policarpo Quaresma*, and *Clara dos Anjos* are some of my major works. I was honored with the carnival theme Lima Barreto, a Mulatto Who Was Poor but Free by the Unidos da Tijuca Samba School in the year 1992.

Again, opposing views on Lima Barreto's world were strikingly audible in Ricardo's speech. For example, Ricardo spoke confidently in reaction to the historical avoidance of race in discussions of oppression in Brazil, noting that "em minhas obras o preconceito racial, a pobreza, a truculência policial e a hipocrisia que cercava as relações sociais da sociedade opressora do último século" (in my works I reflected upon racial prejudice, poverty, police cruelty, and the hypocrisy surrounding the social relations of the oppressive society of the last century). The textbook accounts were thus treated as "opinions" or "prescribed narrative" that could be counterbalanced.

Also important to consider are the linguistic features that students chose when publicly conveying the ideas in the monologues. First is their use of the first person *I* instead of the third-person *he* or *she* used in textbooks, a choice that I argue is also a form of social action with ideological consequences. The use of the expressive form (*I* versus *he* or *she*) influences the way in which issues of authorship in ideological texts are brought forth. By using the first person, the Zumbi recastings displaced the centrality of the original "author" in the prescribed narrative, and in doing so, they focused attention not only toward reworking public misconceptions but also toward expressing an alternative voice, both of which give rise to potentially emancipatory discourses, as marginalized Black Brazilians subvert the dominant voice and reflect the times in which they are living.

The first-person voice that students used to publicly re-present the Black historical figures also reflects a shift that has been underway in Afro-Brazilians' orientation toward Blackness. Each monologue ended with a twist in which students attempted to integrate the experiences of their ancestors into their own lives. They stepped out of the voice of their historical figures and spoke in their own voice, introducing themselves as Black Brazilians: "No dia 1 de novembro de 1922, Lima Barreto falece de colapso cardíaco, e eu sou Ricardo, cidadão negro brasileiro." (On November 1, 1922, Lima Barreto dies of a heart attack, and I am Ricardo, a Brazilian Black citizen). This device added another layer of imbrication to the authorial manipulation, allowing the Zumbi students' identities to emerge. In this final shift, the students seemed focused on turning further inward as they expressed their own subjective changes. And in doing so they personalized their encounter with the Blackness of the historical figure they portrayed.

The key idea in these monologues was that prominent Black figures have not been portrayed in Brazilian historiography *as Black*. By veering off from Brazil's founding narratives that have erased or forgotten Black identity, the students reconstructed the biographies of these historical persons through selective emphasis on their Black identity and anti-racist stance. Through a reflexive revelation they pointed out the limits of what has been historically remembered and the possibility of other viewpoints, reflections, and resistance.

As the presentation of monologues continued, Adriana's turn to enact Chiquinha Gonzaga arrived. For Zumbi instructors and students, Chiquinha Gonzaga's story of flagrant memory distortion by Brazilian popular culture. For instance, TV Globo (Brazil's largest TV network) cast a well-known White actress to play the dark-skinned, African-descended Chinquinha Gonzaga in a biographical miniseries (Muniz et al [1999] 2008). Zumbi activists' argument has had great resonance with many other activists. In an online publication of *Revista raça* (*Race* magazine), Oswaldo Faustino noted, "Como a maioria de personagens negros brasileiros respeitados pela intelectualidade, Chiquinha Gonzaga também foi embranquecida e interpretada em novela, filme e teatro por atrizes brancas—Regina Duarte e sua filha Gabriela Duarte; Bete Mendes; Malu Galli e Rosamaria Murtinho—, apesar de ela, artisticamente, assumir sua negritude." (Like most Brazilian Black characters respected by the intelligentsia, Chiquinha Gonzaga was also whitened and played in a soap opera, film, and theater by White actresses—Regina Duarte and her daughter Gabriela Duarte, Bete Mendes, Malu Galli, and Rosamaria Murtinho—although Chiquinha artistically assumed her Blackness; 2016).

Adriana opened by swaying back and forth and from side to side while singing the first verse of Chiquinha Gonzaga's most famous song, "Abre Alas": "Ó abre alas que eu quero passar." (Open the way because I want to pass.) She then launched into her monologue:

> Sou Francisca Edwiges Neves Gonzaga, mais conhecida como Chiquinha Gonzaga. Nasci em 17 de outubro de 1849 no Rio de Janeiro. Sou a primeira mulher negra a reger uma orquestra sinfônica no Brasil. O Ó Abre Alas fui em que fundei em 1899. Sou também pianista e regente brasileira. Sou Adriana, cidadã negra Brasileira.

> I am Francisca Edwiges Neves Gonzaga, better known as Chiquinha Gonzaga. I was born on October 17, 1849, in Rio de Janeiro. I'm the first Black woman to direct a symphony orchestra in Brazil. I founded the Ó Abre Alas in 1899. I am also a Brazilian pianist and conductor. I am Adriana, a Brazilian Black citizen.

As in Ricardo's reinterpretation of Lima Barreto's person and elements of his daily life, Adriana engaged in a considerable amount of work to confront the veracity of established accounts, which were used as platforms to articulate a reinterpretation of Chiquinha Gonzaga's life story. As part of an ongoing dialogic negotiation between established and revised accounts, Zumbi students took control of the rewriting at various levels. Here, however, I would like to add another layer of analysis. As the biographical details are transformed into a text and then made relevant to the ongoing situation through a first-person recitation, a shift in spatiotemporal configurations also occurs. Although they represented speech belonging to Black figures who lived in the past—mostly in the distant past (the there and then)—they spoke in the present tense (the here and now) as if the historical figures were their contemporaries, existing in the same time as the students themselves: "Sou a primeira mulher negra a reger uma orquestra sinfônica no Brasil" (I'm the first Black woman to direct a symphony orchestra in Brazil). Mikhail Bakhtin's notion of chronotope (literally, time-space) in language and discourse can elucidate the strategic shift from the then and there to the here and now, and I suggest that there is something special about the way in which the students brought back to life Brazilians of significant historical importance.

Chronotopic constructions are central to the representations of others in theatrical pedagogy, the focus of Alaina Lemon's research. Lemon (2009) analyzes how configurations of time and space were represented as theater students performed the part of a person they had encountered in the past, thus shifting from representing their speech as belonging to others to speaking "their own" words (as if the words were theirs, as if they were the person they were portraying). This situation is in many ways similar to the Zumbi students' performances of historical Black figures. Lemon's analysis focuses on shifts between chronotopes within the theater students' lines as they put themselves into other people's shoes. Lemon examines, for instance, how students were required to build knowledge of the then-and-there lives of the people they were to portray as a way to craft understanding and empathy for their onstage portrayals in the here and now. According to Lemon, the theatrical strategy of imagining oneself in the situation of another person (their perspective, opinion, or point of view) prevented students from conveying quick judgments about the actions of the people being enacted. Lemon describes this as "chronotopic relativity," which takes the time-space circumstances of others into consideration. Understanding and empathizing with others requires transposing across chronotopes, understanding the there and then in contrast with the actor's here and now. She notes, "Scholars have detailed how historically contingent situations and relations *make* sentiments, how ideology, social expectations, or institutional possibilities can determine them" (Lemon 2009, 836–837). By placing people back in their original space and time, the theater students in Lemon's study could develop empathetic awareness of the feelings of another based on understandings of the other as a product of a different cultural framework that structured their social relations. The goal in the theatrical training was that students became able to produce an empathetic picture of the characters they performed.

The chronotopic strategy adopted at Zumbi was unique in that it went in the opposite direction from that of the theater students in Lemon's study. The performance activity at Zumbi involved removing the historical figures from the there and then and bringing them to the here and now. Zumbi narratives were in the present tense, suppressing explicit contextualization and centering the discourse deictically in the narrated events (rather than the narration of those events). For Zumbi members it was self-evident that understandings and representations of Blackness were historically grounded in colonialism and that Brazilians continued to associate Black people's existence with colonial times. The spatiotemporal shift presupposed the existence of a colonial chronotope of Blackness influencing attempts to represent Black life in society, and by focusing on the present, the students engaged in a project of extricating Black figures from the greater history of anti-Blackness in which they had been encased. In my conversations with them, Zumbi instructors explained that the shadow of colonial times continues to obstruct our vision of Blackness today. Their decision to ask students to portray their characters in the here and now was rooted in a desire to free Black historical figures from the there and then of colonialism—most notably, miscegenation based on anti-Black beliefs and values—and bring them back to life. In doing so they could be seen in the vista of the present moment of anti-racist activism.

By sweeping their characters out of the there and then into the here and now, the students' rewritings can be seen as juxtaposing representations and understandings of Blackness (textbook accounts versus their own) from different times and cultural spaces. Whereas mainstream narratives avoided Blackness as a viable component of Brazilian history and culture, the Zumbi students' current narratives chronicled the resilience, beauty, and values of Black people. It could be said, in sum, that the Zumbi monologues manifest the groundbreaking idea that these are different chronotopes of Blackness. As Michael Holquist (1990, 426) puts it, the chronotope is an "optic for reading texts as x-rays of the forces at work in the culture system." The expressive work of shifting spatiotemporal optics is another all-reflexive action that draws attention to artful ways of manipulating cultural meaning in a project intended to critique the life stories of Lima Barreto, Chiquinha Gonzaga, and others (see Wirtz 2011). In their preoccupation with space and time and the way in which Blackness relates to chronotope (i.e., Blackness as configured spatially and temporally) the Zumbi performances revealed the dialogic nature of their memory activity. For Rothberg, paying attention to the ways in which memory always and already works in relation to other stories and other histories helps us understand how seemingly incompatible memories can interact and thereby become "the very grounds on which people construct and act upon visions of justice" (2009, 19). In a form of symbolic revolution, the Zumbi students brought together past and present representations of Blackness and, dialogically, built new understandings based on resistance, rebuttal, and other forms of dialogic encounter with traditional understandings.

The idea of "cultural debt" plays an important role in Zumbi's Black Art Week, particularly in the monologues that captured the speech of influential Brazilians whose Black identities were rendered invisible in history. Textbooks have consistently failed to incorporate Blackness and Black identity in their narratives of influential Black Brazilians in history. While the textbooks do cover most of these individuals, they have systematically left out the ways in which race and Blackness mattered in their lives. Zumbi teachers and students often talked about how textbooks were supposed to teach them a common set of facts about who they were as Black Brazilians and how the stories of their ancestors were key to Brazil's history as a nation. The fact that these dominant narratives failed—through omissions, downright errors, and specious interpretations—to provide a documentary record of how race and Blackness mattered in the lives of notable Black Brazilians led to an exclusion of Afro-Brazilians from the perks of civic belonging and equitable opportunity or treatment in historical accounts.

As Denise Ferreira da Silva argues in her fierce critique of how miscegenation functioned as a strategy of power to obliterate Blackness in Brazil, "the Brazilian subject is the *mestiço*; the proportion of the markers of Blackness in his or her body will determine whether he or she belongs in the present and in the future of the nation" (2007, 248). The erasure of the Blackness of famous Afro-Brazilian people in history has denied Afro-Brazilians the truths of their collective past. In consequence, the Brazilian polity has an unpaid cultural debt to Afro-Brazilians. In "'Never Forget' the History of Racial Oppression," Nolan Cabrera talks about the contributions of people of color to the construction of higher education in the United States—how universities exist on land stolen from Native Americans and were built by slave labor, yet these groups are systematically excluded from those very institutions. "The past is never the past," Cabrera notes. "It contextualizes and informs the present"; thus, these institutions have an unpaid debt to communities of color " (2020, 38, 39). The instructors and students described in this chapter were participants in individual and collective remembering as a discursive process that aimed at the restitution of Blackness to their notable ancestors. In their redress efforts, they confronted the tasks of revisiting the foundational statement of Brazilian race relations, reflexively analyzing what it means to be Black in the era of anti-racism and redefining themselves between Brown and Black.

4

Becoming an Anti-racist, or "As Black as We Can Be"

"Você é feio." (You're ugly.)
"Seu cabelo não presta."
　(Your hair sucks.)
"Seu cabelo é duro."
　(Your hair is hard [kinky].)
"Você é negro." (You're Black.)
"Você é um preto que vem de periferia."
　(You're a Black person who comes
　from the periphery.)

Consciousness as Dialogue

This epigraph reproduces what Braga, a twenty-six-year-old member of one of the Black movement organizations in my study, told me about why he became involved in Black activism.[1] Braga used direct speech to recount a range of comments various people had made to him regarding his Black features. Braga's experience echoed statements I heard from many other self-identified *preto* (Black) Brazilians with noticeable African phenotype and skin color about why they decided to join the Black movement. Many told stories about childhood memories of being told Black people were ugly, marginalized, and lazy. What is striking about Braga's recollections is that societal attitudes are connected to the individual through a complex intermingling of voices—exemplifying Erving Goffman's analysis of the multiple participants that may be present in one speaker's talk.

According to Goffman (1981), a speaker (producer of an utterance), has three available roles: animator, author, and principal. In Braga's case, through a series of reference shifts, he uses *você* (you) to distinguish at least two voices in his speech: mainstream society's voice as "author" and/or "principal" versus his own as "animator" (Goffman 1981). He is the animator ("sounding box") of society, and society is both the actual author of the words he quotes and the principal (owner) of the beliefs and viewpoints he expresses. Braga's words simultaneously give expression to all kinds of voices embodied in various forms of reported speech, and these voices reveal anti-racist activists' sensitivity to the ways in which utterances can be constitutive of consciousness or self-knowledge. The phenomenon analyzed in this chapter is speech about speech, a strategy that allows the people like Braga not only to foreground what they see as predominating beliefs and attitudes about Blackness but also to carve out a position for themselves from which they can forge an ideological critique of those beliefs and points of view.

According to Mikhail Bakhtin, human consciousness is never grounded in a single individuality (unitary wholeness). Rather, Bakhtin emphasizes the social, or dialogic, nature of consciousness—in other words, one's tendency to assimilate others' discourses as part of one's "ideological becoming." Human consciousness always "orients itself amidst heteroglossia, it must move in and occupy a position for itself within it" (Bakhtin 1981, 295–296). The (re)orientation of consciousness hinges on the options available in the public space within which the voices circulate. For Bakhtin, voices compete to determine a speaker's relationship with the world (1981, 342). More concretely, and directly related to the analysis I present in this chapter, consciousness becomes embodied as a "voice" and is expressed through words and utterances. Further, Bakhtin conceived of people's lives as narratives, or framed dramaturgical presentations, in the sense that—like characters in a play, novel, or other artistic work—the individual consciousness is made whole by some exterior consciousness (i.e., the author or principal). The existence of the self thus depends on its being perceived by another through dialogue. As Craig Calhoun reminds us, "Nations and ethnic groups are internally differentiated in a variety of ways, overlap with, and are crosscut by, various other identities, and figure with greater or lesser salience when members are in different interpersonal situations and when different large-scale factors— say economic change—affect their overall positions" (2003a, 537). What we say, in one way or another, always hinges on these existing forces (voices). My conscious self exists only as a result of my interaction with another, whose gaze allows me to be the object of my own perception. Simply put, we see ourselves through another's eyes. Thinking about anti-racist consciousness in terms of voice and dialogism helps us understand the different ways anti-racist activists relate to Blackness. Bakhtin's notion of a dialogic self allows us to see anti-racist consciousness as a relationship of involvement (or argument) between selves (or voices). Through an analysis of Afro-Brazilians' personal stories of how they became involved in Black mobilization, this chapter explores their understandings of anti-racist consciousness and its place in contemporary anti-racism activism in Brazil. Their understandings of how to be anti-racists are based partly on existing institutional, cultural, and ideological power in Brazilian society and partly on new dialogical work. They gain anti-racist consciousness via a constant dialogue with different points of view/voices, which rarely reach consensus.

The immediate consequence of the Brazilian adherence to *brasilidade*, or the country's racial ideology of race mixing, is a widespread denial of racism as a serious problem in Brazilian society. Yet assumptions that racial and color differences correlate with a person's value in society in fact form the very basis for the degradation and rejection of Blackness in multiple contexts—such as employment, education, victimization by police, and criminal justice—that are crucial in determining the quality of that individual's life in Brazilian society. It has been noted, for instance, that the negative, racist messages that circulate in Brazilian society have historically shaped Afro-Brazilians' consciousness of race. Given that Whiteness enjoys great prestige, identifying oneself or others as *preto* or *negro* (Black) sounds extremist, putting interlocutors in a very awkward situation. In Brazil, no one is Black if they are perceived as having "enough" European ancestry to qualify as *moreno* (brown or light-skinned) or even White. Generally, only people who are *muito escuro* (very dark) would be described as *preto* or *negro*, and even then, *moreno* would be preferred as a more polite term for very-dark-skinned Afro-Brazilians (Sheriff 2001).

Over the past three decades, the Brazilian government has implemented sweeping policies to combat racial exclusion and racial discrimination against Black Brazilians, including the controversial implementation of racial quotas at all public universities, an ambitious slavery reparation program granting titles to occupied ancestral lands, and a law requiring schools throughout the country to teach African and Afro-Brazilian history and culture (see chapters 2 and 3). In this context, increasing numbers of nongovernmental organization have been pressuring officials at all levels of government for access to resources and rights on behalf of Brazil's marginalized populations. These organizations have had unprecedented national impact on public discourse about race. During the opening ceremony for the 2014 soccer World Cup in São Paulo, three children—one from each of Brazil's three distinct racial groups (Black, Indigenous, and White)— released white doves to celebrate peace and honor the country's racial integration. Unexpectedly, however, one of the children, an Indigenous Guarani boy, held up a banner reading "Demarcação" (Demarcation), demanding recognition of Indigenous land rights.

Black Consciousness among Afro-Brazilians

One of the great challenges in the study of racial identity among Afro-Brazilians over the past thirty years has been the fluidity of racial classifications, which scholars have foregrounded in a quest to understand the limits and possibilities of Black mobilization in Brazil. A large body of scholarly work addresses field-specific perspectives on racial identity among Brazilians of African descent, particularly relating to their motivations for mobilizing around being Black (e.g., Caldwell 2007; French 2009; Perry 2013). Nevertheless, scholars agree that racial identities are not immutable, but rather are undergoing constant (re)construction through active negotiations with larger social processes. They also agree that identities can be markers of difference that can serve to drive wedges between individuals or groups.

Early scholarship was intrigued by the fact that anti-racist organizations continually failed to generate grassroots support in Brazil, one of the most unequal countries in the world. The seemingly inevitable contrast of Black politics in Brazil versus the United States became intricately woven into the studies that sought to explain the alleged "weakness" of anti-racist mobilization among Afro-Brazilians (Degler 1971; Hanchard 1994; Twine 1998).

Michael George Hanchard (1994) attributes Afro-Brazilians' avoidance of the identification as Black and mobilization around being Black identity to Brazilians' strongly held belief in their country's racial mixture. Comparing Brazil with the United States, Hanchard argues that Black consciousness among Afro-Brazilians bears only a faint resemblance to the strong Black consciousness of African Americans. Later studies became greatly influenced by the work of Hanchard, with researchers theorizing Black consciousness among Afro-Brazilians in terms of a self-realization as Black (Moura 1994; Twine 1997, 1998). Thus, embracing the Brazilian Black movement was largely interpreted as the end product of a process of coming to terms with one's identity as Black.

John Burdick's (1998) work with Black Pentecostals broke new ground by challenging previous attempts to trace a direct correspondence between embracing a Black identity and supporting the Black movement. He argues that the Black movement's approach to collective action does not meet with the agreement of Black Pentecostals, who otherwise identify as Black. Burdick's book *Blessed Anastácia: Women, Race, and Christianity in Brazil* ultimately adds another layer of complexity to the study of race consciousness and Black identity among Brazilians of African descent.

Continuing this line of research, other scholars have documented a gradual increase in the visibility of Brazilian Black movement discourse. For example, they have shown that Black activists have sometimes sought to inspire collective action by focusing on how the myth of racial mixture has masked racial discrimination and stymied a civil rights movement in Brazil (Appelbaum, Macpherson, and Rosemblatt 2003, 8–9), and at other times have used Brazil's shared ideal of racial inclusiveness—racial democracy as a goal yet to be achieved—as an anti-racist strategy (Alberto 2011, 301–302). While there has been some skepticism about the possibility of constructing a Black identity in a society that lacks ethnic boundaries (Sansone 2003), there has also been some evidence that, through "Black radical becoming," vulnerability could become a political strength (Vargas 2006, 137).

Partially aligned with prevailing studies that define identity as a key analytical category, some scholarship has sought to understand Afro-Brazilians' significantly greater involvement in racial politics following the turn toward affirmative action in Brazil (Caldwell 2007; French 2009; Perry 2013). These scholars have concentrated on explaining Afro-Brazilians' process of identity change as they come to mobilize around being Black. Researchers typically approach Afro-Brazilians' engagement in oppositional movements with an eye to their use of identity politics—that is, organizing on the basis of a shared experience of injustice. A literature review of identity politics in Brazil shows that personal identity is a crucial foundation for collective action. One of the first discussions of this identity shift process is Jan French's (2009) work on Afro-Brazilians' struggles for ancestral land rights. By delving into the processes by which Afro-Brazilians conceive of and develop their social identities during negotiations with the national government, French sheds important light on how race-conscious laws and policies have triggered Afro-Brazilians' new ethnoracial identities.

Far from providing evidence of inauthenticity, the processes of identity construction based on legal negotiations with the Brazilian state have important consequences for social justice. Elizabeth Farfán-Santos (2016) tells a more complicated story about Afro-Brazilians' relationship with the state, focusing on their struggles for land rights in the context of the complexity of constructing a Black identity when violence against Blacks is normalized in Brazil. Critiquing studies that downplay Afro-Brazilians' construction of a Black identity as a "tactic" for obtaining rights, Farfán-Santos clearly demonstrates that self-identification as Afro-Brazilian to gain land rights is not linked to Black race or color per se but to the difficulties that Blacks have in gaining public recognition of their historical legacy of racial segregation. In doing so, she adds a dramatically different orientation and challenge to the study of Black mobilization in Brazil.

In *Afro-paradise*, Christen Smith (2016) similarly sheds important light on the complexity of defining racial identity among Afro-Brazilians. Smith toggles between an analysis of anti-Black violence perpetrated by the police in Salvador and an analysis of poor Afro-Brazilian street performers who denounce such violence. These street performers actively engage with neighborhood audiences to construct Blacks as being the targets of episodes of devastating violence during and following police and death squad raids. Specifically, Smith argues that the police performance of violence on Black bodies is one factor that produces Blackness.[2]

The scope of the previous review is limited to works that stand in direct dialogue with the content of this chapter. These scholars have made remarkable theoretical advances in what we know about Afro-Brazilians' relationship with Blackness. While there is widespread agreement about the legitimacy of political practices organized around a collective identity, scholars have pointed out the need for research that analyzes the internal differences often hidden under the umbrella of group identity (Bernstein 2005;

Calhoun 1994). "Brown" and "Black" cover a lot of ground in understanding the relationship between identity and political consciousness on the one hand and identity and affirmative action laws and policies on the other. People come to understand their racial position in complex and different ways, whether they decide to act upon racial discrimination and racial exclusion or to demand affirmative action. If one examines the striking range of racial identities that congregate under the umbrella of Black movements in Brazil, a far more complex reality of identity politics emerges. One of the problems in the study of racial identity of Afro-Brazilians in contemporary Brazil is what G. Reginald Daniel (2001, 2006) describes as the centrality of the Black/White divide in the understanding of how mixed-race people position themselves regarding anti-racism. More closely related with my own work presented in this book is Daniel's prominent study of the "new multiracial identity," in which he argues that mixed-raced people have come to the stage of pushing the boundaries between Black and White: "The new multiracial identity . . . can potentially forge more inclusive constructions of blackness (and whiteness). This in turn would provide the basis of new and varied forms of bonding and integration that would accommodate the varieties of African-derived subjectivity without at the same time negating a larger Africa-derived plurality" (Daniel 2001, 175; see also Daniel 2006). As he further points out, mixed-race people's understanding of racial consciousness "incorporate concepts of 'partly,' 'mostly,' or 'both/neither'" (2001, p. 180).

The most salient fact that emerged during my own studies of Black mobilization in Salvador (in the state of Bahia) was that Afro-Brazilians did not necessarily place identification as Black at the core of their understanding of what it means to be anti-racist. As they pressed their collective claims for access to resources and rights for Black Brazilians, they saw anti-racist consciousness as a voice defined in language according to its ideological stance on race and racism. In the next section, I explore how Afro-Brazilians have critically managed such differences, and particularly the entanglements between their own versus group identities, in order to focus in on Afro-Brazilians' understandings of anti-racist consciousness and their active participation in collective struggles. Language is crucial to this process. Black activists creatively juxtapose national narratives of racial mixture with race-conscious discourse unleashed by anti-racist legislation and policies. Examining the correspondence between anti-racist consciousness and Black identity in Afro-Brazilians' stories of their involvement in mobilization, I argue that, as Afro-Brazilians commit to a dialogic process of reorienting their anti-racist consciousness in relation to the dominant discourses of Blackness in Brazil, this consciousness emerges as an ideological critique through language that crosses racial identifications and articulates an oppositional stance toward racial categorization and racism in Brazil.

Voicing Anti-racist Consciousness

I collected the data analyzed here during ethnographic interviews with male and female members of the three organizations in which I conducted fieldwork: Centro Cultural Palmares (Palmares Cultural Center), Grupo Engenho de Salvador (Engenho de Salvador Group), and Instituto Lutas de Zumbi (Zumbi Struggles Institute). All self-identified as Afro-Brazilian and *negro*, and they ranged from sixteen to eighty years of age. Self-identification as *negro* has become increasingly common among Black movement activists. It originated as an insult used by the masters of the enslaved and overseers who were the employees who supervised the enslaved on behalf of the masters; in the 1930s, members of the Black organization Frente Negra Brasileira (Brazilian Black Front) used it in the context of Black activism. In later years Black movement activists have used it as an affirmative term (Garcia 2006, 24), whereas *preto* is often seen as a racially offensive term associated with low income, education, and status (Sansone 2003; Sheriff 2001). If asked, most Black movement activists would likely put *negro* at the top of their list of adjectives to describe themselves, as did all the individuals I interviewed. The Brazilian Census lists five racial/color terms (which do not include *negro*): *preto* (black), *pardo* (brown, or mixed race), *indígena* (Indigenous), *amarelo* (yellow), and *branco* (white). When asked to identify themselves according to the census categories most, but not all, Afro-Brazilians chose *preto*. Typically, those who did not chose *pardo* and were individuals whom society would label as *moreno* or *pardo* (brown or mixed race), or even *moreno claro* (light brown). When asked to elaborate, they explained that *pardo* was the only choice available to them since they did not see themselves as *preto* nor did the general public perceive them that way. They all, however, thought *negro* was a more accurate self-descriptor because it signaled their support for the Black cause. Afro-Brazilians' positions with regard to the racial/color categories defined in Brazil motivated me to investigate what self-identifying as *negro* and having *consciência racial* (racial consciousness) meant to them.

My analysis explores how a narrow notion of race consciousness among Afro-Brazilians may be reinvigorated by a focus on the heteroglossia of Blackness and race in Brazil. Mikhail Bakhtin's insights into heteroglossia show that a speaker's subjective world is constructed from a diversity of voices, assembled into a system that deals with difference in particular ways. Language plays a crucial role in this process. Afro-Brazilians construct an anti-racist consciousness through narratives that reflexively mobilize the many voices in Brazil's racial heteroglossia—from voices embodying dominant racial ideologies to voices criticizing those ideologies—so as to encourage critical forms of engagement with and reorientation toward them. The key point that became apparent from Afro-Brazilians' personal stories is that, by and large, they frame anti-racist consciousness as being independent of self-identifying as Black. Their self-narratives reveal that, for them, anti-racist consciousness is primarily a form of reflexive engagement between oneself and the multiple different racial notions, narratives, and images available in society. Language is fundamental in this process because it allows them to construct these notions, narratives, and images as keywords and strategic phrases, and ultimately to align themselves with or against them. In her pioneering work, Jane Hill applied Bakhtin's methods of literary analysis to conversational narratives. Her analyses revealed how a speaker "claims a moral position among conflicting ways of speaking, weighted with contradictory ideologies, by distributing these across a complex of 'voices'" (Hill 1995, 98; see also Du Bois 2009; Haviland 2005; Keane 2011; and Wortham 2001). In this section, I explore the nexus between race, voice, and consciousness in interviewees' accounts of their personal connection to the Black movement to show how they construct becoming *negro*. This is part of the process of becoming able to voice Brazilians' notions of race in order to engage with them in alternate ways. More specifically, the invocation of competing notions of race and Blackness through the process of voicing is a key part of Afro-Brazilians' construction of anti-racist consciousness.

What follows is a series of excerpts from people's responses to my request that they tell me their stories of how they became involved in anti-racism efforts. What is striking about their narratives is the differing trajectories of their coming to self-identify as Black. For some this identity emerged as intricately tied to an evolving awareness of their racial position in Brazilian society, whereas for others, their self-identification as Black emerged through their life experiences before they gained anti-racist consciousness and embraced Black movement ideals. More significant were the cases in which active support for anti-racism cut across racial and color lines; some light-skinned Afro-Brazilians never did self-identify as Black either before or after gaining anti-racist consciousness. These individuals reported that they decided to embrace Black movement ideology as they were developing a strong antipathy toward racism.

This book was written by an Afro-Brazilian with personal experience of living in Brazil through adult life and whose relationship with Blackness was influenced partly by the recent social and political transformations there and partly by living, studying, and working in the United States. I have added my own story to the case studies contained in this chapter. I begin with Deni and Catarina, whom I met during events sponsored by the Centro Cultural Palmares, one of the organizations in my study. Like the Instituto Lutas de Zumbi, Palmares was one of the pioneering Black community-based organizations that emerged in Salvador in the 1990s. From the onset, Palmares workers defined their mission as creating a cultural and educational center with a vocational focus, and they taught disenfranchised Afro-Brazilian youth job skills so that they could earn a living. They offered courses in video production and editing, fashion design and creation, hair styling, entrepreneurship, and other areas. Consciousness-raising activities were infused into the curricula. Also central to Palmares's vision of social change was that learners came to know about, understand, and appreciate their African heritage. For example, students had access to fabrics and materials imported from different parts of Africa. They participated in hands-on experiences of making and wearing various types of African-origin hair ties, headdresses, and wraparound dresses. I visited an exhibit where students taking fashion classes displayed their creations on mannequins in the foyer of the main public library.

The teachers were successful entrepreneurs in the Black community who were hired to be both instructors and role models. Some former students returned as staff (e.g., program coordinators, teaching assistants, or office personnel). The classes were held in underused classrooms at local public schools and community centers in the predominantly low-income Black neighborhoods where most of the students lived. The students were visibly of African descent, were mostly of high school age, and typically lived with their families. I visited many classes and observed two complete courses over a twelve-week period. One course met three hours daily and the other for two hours twice a week. The teachers consistently dedicated a significant amount of time to education surrounding issues of racial justice. In one

video production class, for example, the teacher started the lesson by asking students to share their impressions of a selection of acclaimed films she
had played for them in the previous class session. These videos, with such
titles as *A menina do cadaço amarrado* (The girl with tied shoelaces),
Mercado branco (White market), *Negação do Brasil* (Negation of Brazil), and
Ponto de interrogação (Interrogation mark), dealt with various issues related
to race, racism, and social inequality. As the teacher elicited the students'
perspectives about the films, she led the discussion to topics such as racial
inequality, racial prejudice and discrimination, and the typical representation of Blacks in Brazilian soap operas as servants, criminals, and gang members. She often taught students how to recognize and critically analyze
stereotypes, omissions, and misconceptions affecting social justice for Brazilian Blacks and how these relate to wider social inequalities. She also challenged the students to use that awareness to portray a different a type of
message in their own video projects.

In 2009–2010, Palmares sponsored an evening course on political communication for adults, during which I met Deni and Catarina. For them,
the processes of coming to describe themselves as Black and of gaining anti-
racist consciousness were interconnected. The first excerpt comes from
Deni. At the time of the interview, he was twenty-nine years old, had a college degree in history, and was working as a high school history teacher.
Deni stated he became a "militant" in the Black movement at age twenty-
one through the influence of one of his university professors who taught him
to think critically about race, racism, and society in general.

> Eu comecei a me inserir nesse pensamento, nesse discurso, nessa militância . . .
> com algum exemplo, né, que algum professor deu em sala de aula, e que eu
> tomei aquilo como exemplo, e a partir daí, eu comecei a pensar diferente, . . .
> desde quando eu comecei a pensar a sociedade, é que eu lembro, que me
> enquadrei nessa tipologia do IBGE; *negro*, né?

> I started to place myself within this way of thinking, in this discourse, this
> militancy . . . with this example that this teacher, you know, that some
> teacher gave in the classroom, and I took that as an example, and from that
> point on, I began to think differently . . . since I started to think about society,
> that I remember, that I fit into one of the boxes of the IBGE [Instituto
> Brasileiro de Geografia e Estatística, the Brazilian census bureau]; *negro*, you
> know?

Note that Deni substituted *negro* for *preto*, the actual term on the census form. He also used various linguistic strategies to narratively construct his evolving consciousness of race and racism as resulting from his reflections on the words of others. He spoke of a teacher who taught him to pay attention to issues of race, and whose critical attitude toward society Deni embraced as his own. He used linguistic features such as the reportive *deu* (gave) and the indexicals *nesse* (that) and *algum* (some) to indirectly invoke militants' words and examples given by one of his professors, which he later used to understand society. By saying that his self-knowledge of being Black developed as his view of society became more critical, Deni provided some clues as to the sources of meaning that dialogically shaped his view of himself both before and after his consciousness-raising experiences. Before gaining awareness, he refused to use the racial/color categories in the Brazilian census to describe himself, but "desde quando eu comecei a pensar a sociedade, é que eu lembro, que me enquadrei nessa tipologia do IBGE; *negro*, né? (since I started to think about society, that I remember, that I fit into one of the boxes of the IBGE; *Negro*, you know?) Note how he used the racial lexicon of the census to foreground the impact of Brazil's racial/color categories in the constitution of his newly emergent awareness. It became clear, however, that in his story, gaining consciousness had less to do with constructing a Black identity in and of itself than with his struggles against others' attempts to impose that identity on him in the first place.

What was striking about Deni's narrative as a whole was his ability to reflexively frame, through represented discourse, the many ways that words or utterances coming from other people have helped him construct different versions of his own self. For instance, toward the end of this excerpt, Deni used the word *enquadrei* in "me enquadrei nessa tipologia do IBGE" (I fit into one of the boxes of the IBGE) to link the idea of choosing a race/color to the idea of conforming to the language of the IBGE. *Enquadrei* (fit in with) is common slang in the military for "comply (or fit in) with the rules of the game." Deni's word choice indexes an ironic stance that encourages an anti-racist interpretation of the IBGE's racial categories: rather than using the official census term *preto*, Deni used *negro*, indexing Black consciousness. Next I asked him about his views before this point of discovery. He responded that he did not remember placing himself in any category, and he tried to elaborate on that idea: "Vamos dizer que . . . eu tivesse o senso comum . . . que na verdade era sem, na verdade ser sem saber que é, e tal." (Let me say it this way . . . I shared the common sensibility . . . honestly I was without, honestly to be and not to know you are, and such.) Deni could not articulate an understanding of himself as Black in the form of either a specific memorable story, person, or utterance or a distinct racial identity. He said he shared the common sensibility, meaning that although he never identified as Black, he had always sensed that he was. This became clearer when he used the phrase "ser sem saber que é" (to be and not to know you are). For Deni there was no option not to be Black, only the possibility of not knowing that he was. Deni's case exemplifies the experiences of Afro-Brazilians for whom self-describing as Black is intricately entwined with anti-racist consciousness. Gaining anti-racist consciousness helped them understand their racial position in Brazilian society.

This became even more evident in Catarina's personal stories, which were grounded in a succession of tension-filled encounters with the perspectives of others. Catarina was forty-six years old at the time of the interview; with a college degree in education, she worked as a literacy instructor for a non-profit organization dedicated to improving the reading and writing levels of sex workers. She described gaining racial consciousness as a moment of sudden insight mediated by another's words. As Catarina's story unfolded, several instances of represented discourse gave shape to her construction of anti-racist consciousness:

> Você acredita que eu não me via como negra, até entrar pra faculdade? Eu não me via como negra. Porque eu sou parda. E as pessoas me chamavam de moreninha. Eu não me via como negra. E aí eu participei de um seminário na faculdade, onde uma pessoa lá tava, a convidada, que fazia parte da mesa, e ela começou a falar de uma mulher, . . . , não sei se já aconteceu com você, numa missa numa igreja, e o pastor começar a dizer um monte de coisa, e você achar que ela tava falando com você? . . . Então essa pessoa, a palestrante, ela falava de uma mulher discriminada, de uma mulher que não tinha acesso, de uma mulher que não podia chorar, tinha que ser forte, de uma mulher que tinha que alisar o cabelo pra ser aceita, então nesse dia minha ficha caiu: Eu sou negra, negona.

> Can you believe that I didn't use to see myself as Black until I got into college? I didn't use to see myself as Black. Because I'm Brown. And people would describe me as a dark brown girl. I didn't use to see myself as Black. And then I participated in a seminar in college, where a person, the guest speaker, who was part of the panel, and she started talking about a woman . . .

because I don't know if this has ever happened to you, during a mass in church, and the preacher starts saying a lot of things, and you think she is talking to you? . . . So this person, the presenter, she talked about a woman who was discriminated against, about a woman who lacked access, about a woman who couldn't cry, who had to be strong, about a woman who had to straighten her hair to be accepted, so that day it clicked for me: I'm Black, a Black woman.

Catarina constructed the different facets of her experience of attaining consciousness through several instances of reported speech. Casting herself and others in her struggles with race, she reflexively situated and resituated herself with respect to being Black. She began with the rhetorical question, "Você acredita que eu não me via como negra?" (Can you believe that I didn't use to see myself as Black?). She then gave her own response to it, "Eu não me via como negra" (I didn't see myself as Black), thus providing an introduction to what she saw as her struggles with describing herself as Black. Next Catarina reported with a pinch of irony how, in the past, she justified her choice of a mixed-race identity: "Porque eu sou parda." (Because I'm brown). She then animated people's reference to her as "moreninha" (dark brown girl). She went on to describe a seminar she attended in college in which a female presenter told the story of a woman who was a victim of gender and racial discrimination. By reporting the presenter's narrative, Catarina highlighted the role of another's anti-racist and antisexist words in illuminating her own experiences as a victim of discrimination. Then Catarina used the metaphoric slang term "caiu a ficha" (it clicked) to describe the connection she made between the woman the presenter was talking about and her own experience. For Catarina, her own condition as a Black woman in a racist society became suddenly clear through the voice of another. Thus, Catarina's unfolding narrative defined anti-racist consciousness in terms of the different voices she created and brought together to make audible her many ways of relating to being Black, from ignorance or denial to understanding.

In other cases, however, Afro-Brazilians reported that they always understood themselves to be Black and were understood as such, but that it was only later, through a process of consciousness-raising, that they decided to embrace anti-racism. When I met Irene she was a twenty-nine-year-old college graduate and former Zumbi student who held a leadership position in an advocacy organization for Black youth. Her self-understanding as Black

emerged early in her life. Irene started off by telling me how difficult growing up Black had been for her, that she had a hard time accepting her Black
features, including her "pele muito retinta" (pitch black skin):

> Até meus vinte e três anos, eu odiava negro, tinha muita raiva dos meus
> traços, de ter a pele muito retinta, de ter os traços que eu tenho. Eu escondia,
> ficava dentro de casa pra não tomar sol. . . . Achava horrível. Eu só era no
> cabelo ou espichado ou alisado. . . . Então ele João sempre falava do racismo,
> que é o racismo que fecha as portas do nosso progresso, enquanto população
> negra. . . . E aí eu passei a entender melhor, a ideologia que o Zumbi tava
> defendendo. Não foi fácil, foi gradativa mesmo, porque a gente é educado com
> conceitos muito consolidados, né? Da própria família dizer "Não, você é feia,
> se você estudar, você não vai pra lugar nenhum." . . . Inicialmente eu tive
> resistência . . .

> Until I was twenty-three years old, I hated Blacks, I hated the way I looked,
> having pitch Black skin, looking the way I looked. I used to hide myself.
> I didn't go out, to avoid the sunlight. . . . I felt horrible, I always kept my hair
> either straightened or relaxed. . . . Then he, João [her teacher at Zumbi],
> always spoke about racism, that racism closes the doors of our progress, for
> our Black population. . . . And then I started to understand better the
> ideology that Zumbi was putting forward. It was not easy, it was gradual,
> because we are brought up with very consolidated concepts, you know in our
> own family, people saying "No, you're ugly, if you study, you won't go
> anywhere." . . . I was initially resistant . . .

After describing how difficult it had been for her to accept her physical
features, she discussed how learning about race and racism changed the
way in which she related to being Black. Here anti-racist consciousness
was captured as a dialogue between diverse understandings of race and
racism, strategically articulated as represented discourse to narrate Irene's
own struggles during the process of reorienting her own consciousness.
She quoted one of her teachers, voicing the ideology promoted by Zumbi
that recognized the cultural barriers to advancement for Brazil's Black
population and advocated for affirmative action. In the continuation of
her narrative, Irene shared the process of changing her relationship with
Blackness and orientation to racism. Note how she reported competing
positions as represented speech in her narrative to construe how anti-racist

consciousness was experienced, and further, that it was experienced from a position relative to others. She recounted what people—even her own family—had inculcated into her mind about Blackness. Through direct reported speech, she mocked someone in her family who harshly criticized her.

Irene's use of double voicing contrasted verbal equivalents of the principles and values associated with race and Blackness in Brazil with race consciousness. At this point, Irene construed anti-racist consciousness as an interpretive frame organizing and mediating her experience and self-understanding. Irene always understood herself to be Black, but it was only later, through a process of anti-racist consciousness-raising, that she embraced her Blackness. I suggest that learning to frame or stage ideas and principles about race and racism as voices was part of Irene's process of conscious self-formation (see Keane 2011).

In the next example, Pétala, a college graduate in her mid-twenties, talked about entering college. After attending a series of training workshops at Palmares, she found a teaching position at a church-based free school for at-risk youth. Preceding the excerpt below, Pétala reported that during her college preparatory period people often told her that it would be difficult for a Black person like her to succeed in college. She talked about how these messages made her self-conscious about her Blackness when she first entered college. In the process, she quoted her grandmother's warnings about the obstacles that Blacks face when it comes to career advancement:

Eu já entrei na faculdade um pouco—no sentido da questão de ser negra, de ser negro mesmo. Minha avó, ela é uma pessoa que ela dizia, quando a gente assistia televisão ela dizia, "Esse negócio de negro, Pétala, é tão difícil, é tão difícil entrar na faculdade, é tão difícil ser alguém." Então minha avó já tá imbuída de muita coisa disso.

I already entered college a little—I mean, biased toward being Black, for being Black really. My grandma, she was the kind of person who would say, when we sat down to watch television she would say, "Being Black, Pétala, is so difficult, it is so difficult to get into college, it's difficult to actually be someone." So my grandma has all that stuff inculcated in her.

Pétala engaged with a plurality of voices in saying "Esse negócio de negro, Pétala, é tão difícil, é tão difícil entrar na faculdade, é tão difícil ser alguém"

(Being Black, Pétala, is so difficult, it is so difficult to get into college, it's difficult to actually be someone.) She introduced the voice of her grand-mother as the source of what she learned about being Black, but simulta-neously, this utterance was also taken up by other voices, whose boundaries Pétala made clear in subtle but highly efficient ways. First she told me about how the issue of being Black affected her when she entered college. Then she linked those feelings to her grandmother's teachings about the chal-lenges of being Black. By constructing a quotation from her grandmother, she showed how those feelings and thoughts about Black people were com-municated to her and eventually influenced her self-confidence when she first started college. The quotation also embodies Pétala's own internal dia-logues about her Blackness. But these were not the only two voices present in this one utterance; Pétala also juxtaposed her anti-racist voice through a subtle, double-voiced move onto her grandmother's words and her own past voice. This third voice emanated a tension-filled critique of the other voices. The critique became more explicit when Pétala attempted to delineate, in terms of animator versus principal or author (Goffman 1981), the bound-aries between the various voices juxtaposed in the quoted utterance. Here she reflected back on her grandmother's words and, by recognizing that her grandmother could not be faulted for being the principal and/or author of her words, Pétala indicated the presence of others' voices in her grandmother's.

The central purpose of Pétala's complex combination of voices was to explore, in multiple and highly reflexive ways, the connections between others' ideas and words about Blackness and what being Black had meant to her. It also illustrated the role of voice, and tension among various voices, in Afro-Brazilians' process of self-formation—and even self-discovery—as they reflexively attempted to find their position among existing points of view on what it meant to be Black. The strong critique associated with Black activists' use of speech about speech (reported speech)—or, in Bakhtinian terms, voice about voice—in their narratives enabled them to highlight how their Blackness had been conveyed to them and how they continued to think about it and process it, even as they attempted to move away from these neg-ative tokens of their culture into more "conscious" positions. By staging (through voicing) coexisting but distinct discourses of race, Afro-Brazilians highlighted the processes and struggles involved in gaining anti-racist con-sciousness. Positioning themselves in relation to the various and competing languages of Brazil's racial heteroglossia became a tool by which they constructed and asserted their conscious selves. In addition, and related to my main point in this chapter, anti-racist consciousness and Black identity were not, for Pétala, identical. Remember that she recalled learning from others that she was Black, and in this excerpt, she told me that she had thought of herself as Black before entering college and was not ashamed of her race. Her anti-racist consciousness came later. In fact, most of the Afro-Brazilians whom I interviewed did not equate the experience of gaining anti-racist consciousness with self-identifying as Black.

Equally significant were the cases in which active support for Black social movements cut across racial and color lines, where light-skinned Afro-Brazilians said they decided to embrace the Black movement as they developed a allegiance to anti-racism. For them, self-identifying as Black was not part of their experience before or after gaining anti-racist consciousness. Ricardo, a seventeen-year-old, light-skinned high school student and Zumbi participant, commented on the racial categories in the Brazilian census. He told me that, if *negro* were an option, he would mark that, not *preto* or *pardo*, as his racial identity (since the use of *negro* in self-identification signals Black consciousness). As he explained,

Assim, eu não me utilizo de preto, porque as pessoas relacionam a *preto* a cor, e quando me veem assim, não enxergam a cor preta na minha pele. Sempre me veem como amarelo, pardo, sujo, mas não como preto. . . . Eu sou uma pessoa negra, mas as pessoas pensam que ser negro é questão de pigmentação da pele, só é negro quem tem a pele escura. Não, ser—como Steve Biko disse, "Negro não é questão de pigmentação da pele, mas sim reflexo de uma atitude mental."

Let me put it this way, I don't consider myself Black, because people relate [the word] *preto* to the color of one's skin, and when they see me, like [pointing to his own arm], they don't see my skin color as black. They always see me as yellow, brown, dirt colored, but not as black. . . . I'm Black, but people think that only those who have dark skin are Black. No, to be—as Steve Biko said, "To be Black is not a matter of pigmentation but a result of a mental attitude."

In this excerpt, Ricardo's choice not to mark *preto* on the census reflected what he saw as his position in the Brazilian racial classification scheme. As he noted, light-skinned Afro-Brazilians like him do not view themselves as *pretos* and are not perceived as such. Instead, they argue for the use of *negro* as they reorient their consciousness toward anti-racism. Note that Ricardo quoted Steve Biko to elaborate on his individual self-understanding as Black. This particular statement by Biko was widely cited in the Brazilian Black movement's expanding discourse of race, which Ricardo embraced and used to build his own argument regarding his preference to use the identifier *negro* but not *preto*. The articulation and evaluation of both societal racial frames that view him as non-Black—and the Black movement's discourse of race consciousness, as epitomized in Biko's words, and Ricardo's reflexive positioning with respect to those words—fulfill a common purpose for Ricardo and the other research participants: to construct and define their anti-racist consciousness.

A closely related case is my own. At this point, the reader might be wondering how I figure into the discussion. I do recognize that my own position may influence aspects of my research. I am Afro-Brazilian, born and raised in the city of Feira de Santana, Bahia, 105 kilometers from Salvador. At seventeen, I moved to Salvador, where I lived until I came to the United States in 2001 at the age of 39. My experiences of racial identification are in many ways like those of the people I research and write about, and my research and teaching interests are provoked by experiencing similar sorts of issues and questions. In January 2015, while I was back in Salvador, I went to replace my Brazilian identification card. I took a number and waited to be called for assistance. When my turn came, I handed over the requested documents, such as my birth certificate and my marriage certificate, and waited for the employee to enter my information on the computer. When he finished doing so, he printed a copy and asked me to confirm that the information at the top of the form (such as my parents' names, my date of birth, etc.) was entered correctly. After checking that part of the form, I scanned the other parts and was shocked to see he had described me as White without even asking me about it. Farther down, in a field labeled "Anomalies," I read "Effeminate." I took a picture of the form with my cell phone, then asked the employee to change my racial identity to *negro* and delete "Effeminate." He agreed to the latter request but said he would have to enter *pardo*, since I was not Black.

What happened should not have been a surprise, since I have lived with such experiences my entire life, but having those identities recorded in this particular circumstance and moment in my life was eye-opening. As a Brazilian of African descent with *pele mais clara* (literally, "skin that is a little lighter"—meaning I would not frequently be classified as Black in Brazil) and *cabelo bom* (literally, "good hair"—i.e., not too kinky), I grew up *moreno* (brown) in the context of Brazil's mixed-race ideology. I also learned to describe myself as neither Black nor White, but racially mixed or, better yet, Brazilian. After all, in the state of Bahia where I lived most of my life (and returned for my dissertation fieldwork), the large majority of the population is visibly of African descent, like me. I always knew that my brother-in-law and my nephew appeared "blacker" (with dark brown skin and kinky hair) and were seen and treated as Blacks by my family and society at large. I recall my sister (my nephew's mother) saying as she spotted him at a long distance, walking toward us on a white sandy beach, "Look, there is my Black dot on the horizon." I also knew that most of the people in the far south of Brazil looked mostly White, almost foreign to me. Growing up *moreno*, with some people darker than me, others lighter, and most of us fitting into a "mixed" category, I did not give much thought to my racial identity. Reflecting back today, I would say that as a *moreno* I rarely needed to think beyond Brazil's "national rhetoric of brasilidade, or Brazilian-ness, based on the uniqueness of a so-called Brazilian cosmic race, comprised of Africans, Europeans, and native peoples" (Davis 1999, 2). Today, even though I do not identify as *preto* (dark-skinned Black) I do embrace a *negro* identification as a form of affiliation with the Black movement and anti-racist activism.

Writing within the context of social and political changes in Brazil, researchers of Brazilian Black politics have placed the concepts of identity and identity transformation front and center in their inquiries (see, e.g., Caldwell 2007; French 2009; and Sansone 2003). This line of research has produced a significant amount of knowledge about the relationship between the construction of race and policy change in contemporary Brazil, but questions remain regarding Afro-Brazilians' understandings of race consciousness and its place in contemporary anti-racist activism. In this chapter, I have explored Afro-Brazilians' struggles occasioned by Black mobilization and anti-racist reforms, particularly with regard to the multiple and competing discursive notions of racial difference in Brazil today. I have shown the dialogic nature of Afro-Brazilians' relationships with Blackness, and it is this relationship that is most revealing of anti-racist consciousness among Brazilians of African descent. For some Afro-Brazilians, identifying as Black is indeed part of their process of gaining anti-racist consciousness. They self-identify as Black only after having reoriented their consciousness toward anti-racism and established a personal connection to the anti-racist cause of Black social movements. For others, however, understanding themselves to be Black is separate from gaining anti-racist consciousness. They self-identified as Black early in their lives, and embraced anti-racism later through a process of consciousness-raising. Finally, among light-skinned Afro-Brazilians, for whom self-identifying or being identified as *preto* was never part of their experience, the affirmative term *negro* has opened up new avenues for engagement in anti-racism. Their use of negro reimagines both racial identity and anti-racist consciousness, allowing them to reposition themselves in relation to race and racism.

Thus, the relationship between Afro-Brazilians' having anti-racist consciousness and self-identifying as Black is important to investigate. The main goal of this chapter is to explore the nature of anti-racist consciousness in Afro-Brazilians' contemporary struggles for racial justice. Offering a window into how Afro-Brazilians understand and experience race, racism, and affirmative action, Vânia Penha-Lopes (2017) demonstrates how affirmative action shapes Afro-Brazilians' racial identification. In *Politics of Blackness*, political scientist Gladys Mitchell-Walthour (2018) argues that awareness of "*negro* linked fate"—perceptions of racial discrimination and the political underrepresentation of Afro-Brazilians—explains Afro-Brazilians' pro-affirmative-action political behavior. Mitchell-Walthour's most relevant finding for my own work was that individuals who self-identified as *negro* (the affirmative term for Black) tended to have higher levels of awareness of *negro* linked fate, which led to *negro* group attachment. That is, the increase in *negro* self-identification among Afro-Brazilians is a result of increasing acknowledgment of the role race and racism play in the exclusion of and discrimination against Black Brazilians.

As shown in this chapter, an important dimension of anti-racist consciousness concerns the act of speaking, since language serves as a basis for the construction of the conscious self. Applying Bakhtin's dialogic approach, my analysis of Afro-Brazilians' self-narratives points to the conclusion that anti-racist consciousness is fundamentally dialogic or interactive—in other words, it exists in the interplay of one's own and others' voices. As Webb Keane notes, "To the extent that the self is drawing on voices or the materials for potential voices in the surround, it may be *discovering* something about itself and its social context through its encounter with the figures those voices embody" (2011, 175, emphasis in the original). My analysis reveals that anti-racist consciousness manifests in Afro-Brazilian speakers' ability to create double-voiced utterances (to use Bakhtin's term) that reflexively engage with the ideological weight of the many voices in Brazil's discourses of race. The people I interviewed used voice to dialogically organize the different ways in which racial meanings appear and mediate categories of people within Brazil's racial dynamics. Anti-racist consciousness for Afro-Brazilians is not primarily about the construction of a Black identity in and of itself; instead, it may be characterized by the capacity to delineate the boundaries—or edges—that separate Brazil's competing racial ideologies so as to intervene in how Brazilians think about race.

5

Who Can Be Black for Affirmative Action Programs in Brazil?

Responding to the unabated mobilization from the Brazilian Black movement organizations, the Brazilian state has implemented sweeping affirmative action laws and policies in education and civil service over the past two decades, including the Racial Equality Statute (Government of Brazil 2010), racial quotas in higher education (Government of Brazil 2012) and public service (Government of Brazil 2014),[1] and the Racial Identity Verification Committees (Government of Brazil, Ministério do Planejamento, Desenvolvimento e Gestão 2018). From the beginning there have been bitter fights over race-conscious policies and affirmative action policies nationwide. As I am writing this chapter, Brazil is squarely in the middle of another legal battle over racial quotas, this time in electoral politics. The decision over the proportional distribution of public electoral campaign funds between candidates who are *brancos* (Whites) versus *negros* (Blacks) reached the Brazilian Supreme Court. Fearing abuse of the affirmative action program, Black activists have been organizing to make sure that there is a system in place to guard against non-Blacks misrepresenting themselves as Blacks in order to gain the campaign funding allocated for Black Brazilians. With this new policy supporting Brazilians who tend to suffer from discrimination, especially in relation to political representation, the question of who is Black in Brazil for the purpose of affirmative action programs has again grabbed the public's attention.

Interested in the issue of who qualifies as Black under affirmative action in Brazil, I arrived in Brasília, the country's capital, in the summer of 2018 to meet Roseli Faria and Eduardo Gomor dos Santos.[2] Both held office in the Ministério do Planejamento, Orçamento, e Gestão, (MPOG; Ministry of Planning, Budget, and Management) and had been part of a task force during 2016–2018 in order to promote diversity and inclusion in public service and public policy. Faria, an economist, and Gomor dos Santos, a public administrator, were both working on federal social policy in the Brazilian capital. More recently, they had spearheaded the verification committees for the racial quotas system in government hiring to curtail applicants from falsely claiming to be Black in order to circumvent the quotas. These committees became known as Comissões de Heteroidentificação (CHs; Heteroidentification Commissions). *Heteroidentificação* (heteroidentification, or identification by others) is the process by which an individual's self-identification as belonging to a racial group is verified by a committee that decides whether the individual is indeed eligible or qualified for the racial quotas (F. D. Santos 2018). Whether praised as the most efficient means to control "racial fraud" or condemned for the manner in which they did so, the verification committees rapidly became divisive and polemical.

Faria and Gomor dos Santos offered their support to my research project and welcomed me in Brasília in June 2018. In this chapter, I discuss my findings relative to the experiences of policy makers and antiracism activists around the work of the verification committees. Then I tell the stories of two Afro-Brazilians, Marli and Júlio, who applied for the *negro* racial quotas and had their identifications verified by a CH. Marli's application was accepted, but Julio's was not. Marli's and Julio's attempts to assert their entitlement to racial quotas perform the discursive double duty of situating their Blackness within two ideological visions: the vision of the Black consciousness advocates who challenge Afro-Brazilians to embrace Black identification versus the vision of the proponents of redistributive and reparatory measures, for whom individuals must be phenotypically Black enough to be the most likely targets of racism. These conflicting visions about when Afro-Brazilians should think of themselves as Black or Brown complicate Blackness in a society attempting to address a racialized power structure.

On arriving in Brasília, I went to Esplanada dos Ministérios, located on the Monumental Axis that cuts east to west across the Pilot Plan. The area is a vast lawn surrounded by seventeen buildings of identical construction, which house the ministries of the executive branch of government. The axis ends at the National Congress. When I located Faria and Gomor dos Santos in their office in one of federal buildings, they introduced me to their colleagues and, since it was close to their lunch break, invited me to join them. The whole team had been working closely on the CH and, as a result, I ended up interviewing all of them during my two-day visit to Brasília. Over lunch we talked about the trove of challenges to the various race-based affirmative action laws, policies, and processes recently enacted in Brazil, and in particular the institution of the verification committees. We talked about the efforts to recruit qualified candidates and the challenges the committees face in attempting to differentiate dubious versus legitimate identifications in the context of quotas. "Não é fácil" (It is not easy), they repeated over and over. "Tem que haver uma forma a de a gente ser justo como os brasilieros que enfrentam exclusão contra o negro no dia a dia deles" (There has to be a way to do justice to Black Brazilians facing anti-Black racial exclusion in their daily lives), Faria added. We also parsed the importance of the debate over who is Black for affirmative action purposes and the need to weed out the unqualified candidates for the system to succeed. It became clear to me that the greatest challenge they faced as policy makers was to determine, in an ethical and fair way, who is a legitimate recipient of racial quotas and who is trying to game the system.

Referring to the recent turn toward affirmative action, they found themselves repeating, "We changed the face of public higher education in Brazil." Efforts to improve opportunities for the historically excluded Brazilian Black population have clearly reduced the number of students admitted from private schools while increasing the number of students, most of them visibly Black or Indigenous, admitted from public schools. Affirmative action has definitely improved the intellectual, psychosocial, socioeconomic, and political lives of Black Brazilians.

How Is Blackness Determined for Affirmative Action Programs?

The task force that Faria and Gomor dos Santos were leading was part of an affirmative action movement aimed at correcting or mitigating the impact of historical racial discrimination against Black Brazilians and securing their access to fundamental rights such as education and employment. All this, as Georgina Nunes (2018, 11) notes, has forced Brazilians to revisit such concepts as race, racism, miscegenation, and racial identity. The identification of both qualified and eligible affirmative action recipients has become crucial not only for the process but for the legitimacy and effectiveness of racial equity more broadly. Currently, the central challenge in affirmative action racial quotas is the problem of identifying who is or is not Black—and thus who does or does not deserve affirmative action—which in turn involves verifying candidates' racial identity.

Affirmative action programs have had a profound impact on how Afro-Brazilians relate to Blackness. They have also had huge ramifications in terms of the Black movement's strategies over the past forty years—that is, mobilizing Afro-Brazilians to embrace a Black identity as a political act, as seen in the preceding chapters. Between 2000 and 2010, the number of people self-identifying on the census as *preto* (Black) grew at a higher rate than the numbers of those identifying as *pardo* (Brown, mixed race) or White. Faria agreed that self-identification was very important in the Black and Indigenous collective struggles for rights but, she thought, given the history of non-Black people's taking advantage of redistribution systems for personal benefit, it became crucial to create ways to stop fraud. She recognized that verification of candidates' Black identities raises questions about the disparate impact of public policy on individuals in the intermediate *pardo* category—especially among those seeking access to competitive spaces in education and public service.

More specifically, the quota policies brought an unprecedented concept: that *pardo* could describe both Black and Brown people (Dias 2018, 149).[3] The MPOG's Norm 4 reaffirms that phenotype at the time of the verification interview is the only principle or standard by which a candidate's racial identity may be decided. The law actually goes so far as to prohibit any tracing of ancestry or the use of previous forms of identification. It establishes *pardo* as the middle color between *negro* (Black) and *branco* (White). There can be *pardos-negros* (Brown or mixed-race people who are dark enough to be viewed as Black) and *pardos-brancos* (Brown or mixed-race people who pass as White). The racial quotas for *negros* are intended for people who are *preto* or *pardo-negro*. Since early on in the implementation of affirmative action in Brazil, proponents of verification processes have warned against abuse of the system by *pardos-brancos* and *brancos*. Yet, some Black movement activists have been strong defenders of self-identification and have expressed reservations about phenotypical verification of Afro-Brazilians' chosen identities. The issue remains contentious, as Gomor dos Santos noted. In line with my overarching interest in Afro-Brazilians' reorientation toward Blackness, in this chapter I am most deeply concerned with the perspectives and experiences of Afro-Brazilians in the intermediate *pardo-negro* category who have applied for racial quotas as they describe their struggles to develop a clear sense of identity when other people have difficulty labeling their identity, particularly given the fluid racial categorization.

After lunch, Faria and I returned to her office for an interview. She is a dark-skinned Black woman with a degree in economics from the prestigious Universidade de São Paulo. When she realized upon being hired that she was the first Black person to occupy her budget and planning position in federal government, she believed that it was imperative to embrace racial equity issues: "Eu senti que eu estava representando minha raça naquele ambiente branco" (I felt I was representing my race in that predominantly White space), she explained. One of the critics' main objections to affirmative action in Brazil is that they believe it is impossible to draw racial lines in Brazil, and as a consequence, it is impossible to define who is Black among Afro-Brazilians. Very intrigued by this counterargument to Brazilian affirmative action, Faria decided to dwell on the issue. She thought, "Como assim, se a gente sabe discriminar, a gente vai conseguir identificar quem é o beneficiário legítimo?" (How is it that, if we know how to discriminate, we will be able to identify who are legitimate recipients?) In 2015 Faria and her colleagues embraced the affirmative action project and wrote the first pro-affirmative-action job description for competitive service in Brasília that included the CHs as part of the selection process. They have been involved in this process ever since.

When Faria asked me if I would be interested in a tour of her department, I enthusiastically accepted her invitation. Each large office space was subdivided into individual cubicles separated by half walls. As we walked through the aisles greeting and chatting with employees, she repeatedly pointed out how everyone except for her was White: "Os números em termos de gênero são claramente um problema, como você pode ver, mas quando as disparidades raciais são levadas em consideração aqui e ao nosso redor, as desigualdades saltam aos olhos." (The numbers in terms of gender are clearly a problem, as you can see, but when race disparities are taken into consideration here and around us, inequalities are even starker.) Similar to the situation on university campuses nationwide, the underrepresentation of Black people in well-paying, public-sector jobs is deeply troubling (Estanislau, Gomor dos Santos, and Naime 2015). This persists even after the implementation of affirmative action. For Faria, "there is clearly a need to intervene [*tem que intervir*] in the public sector." Besides changing the faces of higher education and the public sector in employment, another goal has been the epistemic transformations of these spaces of power historically restricted to White Brazilians (Nunes 2018, 19). As we walked back to her office, Faria also repeatedly emphasized that beyond diversity and inclusion in public service, her other motivation for working to increase racial diversification in the workforce was a genuine concern about the general lack of preparedness and awareness for preventing and detecting application fraud in the *concursos* (public service hiring exams). In a serious and determined tone, she stated that these were the main reasons why she took up the challenge of making sure the recipients of service job quotas were legitimate. With these concerns in mind, Faria, Gomor dos Santos, and others worked to come up with the CHs, and this subsequently resulted in its nationwide implementation.

Black into Brown, Brown into Black: Identifying Who Can Be Black for Brazilian Affirmative Action

When I asked Faria what about the process of heteroidentification concerned her the most, she spoke at considerable length about the nuances of answering the question, Who is Black in Brazil? Consensus is that the answer reflects Brazil's long experience with widespread miscegenation and a whitening ideology. Yet we also need to consider the influences of Black mobilization, antiracist policies, and social scientific research over the past thirty years or so. The answer to the question is based on physical appearance—above all on skin pigmentation. Light-skinned Afro-Brazilians are normally not publicly perceived as Black, "and they suffer infinitely less discrimination than those who are dark-skinned" (Pinho 2005 39, my translation). White blood can make a person "non-Black" and consequently privileged (Dzidzienyo 1973, 130), and the consensus position, even among Black Brazilians, is that light-skinned Afro-Brazilians are disassociated from Black identity.

As the Brazilian Black movement gained political clout over the past forty years, Black activists engaged in an increasingly successful campaign to motivate Afro-Brazilians with a range of skin tones to embrace a Black identity and self-identify as Black. I describe this as a "Brown into Black" movement. The idea that a person with any known African Black ancestry is Black emerged among Brazilian Black activists and is increasingly used among Afro-Brazilians generally. As Ivanir dos Santos has noted,

> Porque era um fator de desmerecimento você dizer a cor e o movimento trabalhou para valorizar como fator de orgulho, porque a cor deixou de ser apenas ônus. Porque antes era ônus. Ela passou também a ser um fator de direito. Então, juntado o orgulho, a consciência e esse fator de direito é natural que aqueles que se achavam marrom bombom, jambo, agora de forma orgulhosa se consideram como negros.

> It was shameful to self-identify as Black, so the [Black] movement worked to value Blackness as a matter of pride; being Black is no longer just a burden; it also becomes a matter of rights; by bringing together conscience, pride, and rights, it is natural that those who were candy brown now proudly consider themselves Black. (Quoted in *Jornal nacional* 2017, my translation)

With the advent of affirmative action, especially racial quotas, in higher education and subsequently public-sector employment, the political definition of Blackness becomes problematic. In Faria's words,

> A gente sabe que a grande polêmica sobre as comissões é isso. . . . Não tenho dificuldade e não vi pessoas com dificuldade de distinguir o negro do não negro. A gente sabe que tem negro retinto, negro com meu tom de pele, mais claros, não há dificuldade.

> We know that the big controversy [in the media] about verification committees is this [the identification as Black]. . . . I have no difficulty and I have not seen people [on the committees] having difficulty distinguishing Blacks from non-Blacks. We know that there are very dark-skinned Blacks, and Blacks with lighter skin tones like me; there is no difficulty.

Faria reminded me that verification of Black identity is as long standing as the racial quota system itself. She stressed that the process of verification has never been intended to define race but to identify, based solely on appearance (phenotype), those who are socially identified as Black and face discrimination in their everyday lives. Faria's position here echoes Sales Augusto dos Santos's argument, "We have no problem knowing who is black, pardo, white, yellow, or indigenous but categorically refuse to acknowledge racial discrimination and the universal or individualized programs necessary to counteract its ravages upon our society and collective conscience" (S. A. Santos 2006, 43). When I asked Faria whether there were any difficulties in the process of heteroidentification, she referred to "o continuo de cor que a gente tem no país" (the color continuum we have in the country), which creates confusion regarding racial quotas in citizens' minds. She also argued that although educating the public is difficult, doing so is extremely important since their goal is to mitigate inequalities of opportunity and give opportunity for those who have been left out:

> Quem não é representado em alguns ambientes ou na maioria dos ambientes de prestígio? E então eu acho que é mais fácil determinar pela ausência, certo? quem não está em altos cargos no serviço público? Quem não está na mídia? Fazendo papeis de destaque. Quem não está em 1 por cento mais rico, então a partir de quem não está é possível determinar quem deveria está.

> Who is not represented in some spaces or in the majority of prestigious spaces? And so I think this is easier to determine by absence, right? Who is not in high positions in public service? Who is not in the media? Playing prominent roles. Who is not among the 1 percent wealthiest, so taking into consideration who is not there it is possible to determine who should be.

In the webinar *Gênero e raça no orçamento público brasileiro* ("Gender and Race in the Brazilian national budget"), Faria (2020) talked about the effects of economic policies on Black communities in Brazil. She spoke of the ways in which racial inequality in terms of income and education has remained remarkably persistent throughout Brazilian history. While the Workers Party was in office (2002–2016), there was some improvement in these disparities due to policies such as Bolsa Família (cash transfer), a meaningful increase in the minimum wage, and race-based laws. All have had a huge impact on the lives of Black Brazilians. In spite of these measures, which focus on *políticas universais* (universal policies) to eradicate extreme poverty, the racial disparities remain staggering. Whereas 21 percent of Whites attend college, only 8 percent of Blacks do (Government of Brazil, Atlas do Desenvolvimento Humano no Brasil 2020, 2020). Also alarming are the disparities in income and literacy rates. The per capita income of White people is twice that of Black and Brown people, while illiteracy rates follow the opposite pattern (Magenta and Barrucho 2020). As most Brazilians know, Black and Brown people have historically faced problems of racial discrimination and unequal access to education and well-paying employment.

"Racial Fraud"

Soon after the quota system was implemented, several reports surfaced of "candidatos socialmente brancos" (socially White candidates) taking advantage of the system, a practice that became known as "afro-conveniência" (Afro-convenience; Vaz 2018, 35–36). As Faria and her team pointed out, even after the verification committees were created, there have been White candidates who have attempted to look *pardo-negro* or *preto* by wearing certain clothing, then coating their face with makeup, shaving their hair, and growing a beard. Others have even tried artificial tanning. Another common strategy is to claim Black ancestry, such as Black grandparents, even though candidates know that family history and genealogy are irrelevant in the process. Adapting an expression that denotes disclosing an LGBTQ+ person's sexual orientation or gender identity, critics have described claiming Black ancestors to advance one's career through affirmative action as "pulling Grandma out of the closet [*tirar vovó do armário*], or 'outing' Grandma" (Fontoura 2018, 129–130, 137, my translation). Law 12.990 (Government of Brazil 2014) uses the term *declaração falsa* (false declaration) to refer to fraudulent self-identifications (Dias 2018, 142–148; Freitas 2018, 185–186).

Another one of Faria's colleagues, Marcos Silva, also worked on the process of establishing the CHs and served on several committees. Silva, a White man who was at that time forty years old, was born and raised in Rio de Janeiro. He moved to Brasília to work for the federal government. During the interview, Silva stated that he became involved with racial quotas and the verification committees because of "fraude" (fraud). He realized that "sem nenhum sombra de dúvida, como se eu tivesse concorrendo a vaga para cotas para negros" (without any doubt, [White] people like me are competing for openings reserved for Blacks). That is when he made up his mind that the verification process was the right thing to do and joined the CH task force. He added, "Embora fosse controverso e fosse gerar muita polêmica, era necessário porque a entrada de candidatos assim claramente que estariam fraudando." (Even though it was controversial and would create a lot of polemics, it was necessary because people like that were clearly defrauding the system.)

Silva and his team did worry that externally verifying a person's self-identification as Black was a very delicate matter that could undermine affirmative action as a whole. They were relatively certain that affirmative action would be damaged, but the CH was worth the risk. As they served on committees, they realized that the vast majority of candidates were legitimate, and that only "pouquíssimas pessoas que claramente não deviam estar ali, por serem brancas" (a very few clearly shouldn't be there, because they were White). Reflecting back on how he felt in situations where White people clearly tried to appropriate Blackness for the purpose of benefiting from the quota system, Silva described his thoughts as follows: "Pelo amor de Deus você não tem o que fazer aqui. Ninguém nunca vai dizer que você é negro . . . cê sempre teve o privilégio de ser branco." (For the love of God, you shouldn't be here. No one will ever see you as a Black person . . . you have always enjoyed the privilege of being White.) This is how Silva defended the time and thought he devoted to the creation and implementation of the CHs as a way to exert internal controls on racial quotas.

I later interviewed Gomor dos Santos, a White man with a doctoral degree in social policy from the Universidade Nacional de Brasília (UnB). A researcher at the Center for Social Policy Studies at UnB, he was in his mid-forties. Hired by the federal government in 2010, his responsibilities include auditing federal agencies and administering the federal budget. Gomor dos Santos has been involved with what he called "agendas transversais," or a targeted approach to otherwise universal policies that promote equity in terms of gender, race, ethnicity, sexual orientation, homelessness, age, and other characteristics. They worked, in his words, "para assegurar que as demandas de igualdade sejam consideradas pelas políticas públicas nas áreas de saúde, educação, trabalho, et cetera, que historicamente adotam uma perspectivas universalistas" (to ensure that public demand for equal opportunities be factored into public policies in the areas of health, education, employment, et cetera, which historically follow universalist approaches). He had previously worked for the Secretaria Nacional de Políticas de Promoção da Igualdade Racial (SEPPIR; National Secretariat for Policies for the Promotion of Racial Equality), which is linked to the Ministry of Human Rights and was created in 2003 during the administration of President Luiz Inácio Lula da Silva. As Gomor dos Santos noted, the concern about fraud has been ongoing since the inception of racial quotas as a means of affirmative action. Additionally, fraud could make it harder for millions of eligible Black Brazilians to access higher education and public service jobs. For the task force, one of the keys to the appropriate functioning of the quota system is candidate integrity. Creating the verification committees was a means to that end.

Significantly, the understanding of social race, racial identity, and racism behind affirmative action is sociological, political, cultural, and historic (Rios 2018, 217), and as Enrico Rodrigues de Freitas (2018, 183) notes, self-identification has to do with how individuals subjectively see themselves as belonging to a racial group. In the context of public policy like racial quotas, however, it is reasonable that their self-identification be externally verified before establishing that they are eligible to benefit from the public policy. According to Georgina Nunes (2018, 17–18), Law 12.711 (Government of Brazil 2012) defines fraud in the quota system as occurring when a White or socially White person applies for a racial quota reserved for people who experience discrimination because they are externally identified as Black. Nunes adds that there are specific physical traits that White and socially White people lack but *pardos-negros* and *pretos* share, and which subject *pardos-negros* and *pretos* to racial discrimination and racial exclusion. Consequently, verification committees have a responsibility to guarantee that *pardos-negros* and *pretos* have access to higher education and public service through the quota system, as established by MPOG Norm 4 of 2018. The focus of this chapter is not individuals who are normally viewed as White (or socially White)—what Gleidson Renato Martins Dias (2018, 144) describes as "pessoas indubitavelmente brancas" (undoubtedly White persons)—but the intermediate and mixed category (Butler 1998; Piza and Rosemberg 1999), or "pessoas negras de pele preta ou pele parda (clara)" (Black people with darker or lighter skin; Dias 2018, 145).

Racial Discrimination in a Miscegenated Nation

Anti-Blackness in Brazil is so prevalent that it is often characterized as the cultural genocide of Black people (Cerqueira et al. 2020; Nascimento 1978). Major racial disparities are well documented.[4] In our interviews and subsequent conversations, Gomor dos Santos talked specifically about the broader context of inequality in higher education and public service: "O concurso público para mim é a reprodução da exclusão que é feita no vestibular." (The civil service competition is, for me, part of the same system of exclusion found in higher education admissions.). Notably, higher education and public service employment are dominated by White people, even in Bahia, where more than 80 percent of the population is Black or Brown. As Gomor sees it, both phenomena hinge on the fallacy of meritocracy, based on the notion of individual achievement.

Moreover, the vast majority of people who enter higher education or civil service perpetuate the ideology of meritocracy. As Gomor dos Santos explained, "O mais grave deles é que você traz para dentro do estado, pessoas . . . é a seleção adversa, você traz pessoas para dentro do estado que não tão interessadas em mudar o status que corre no estado, muito pelo contrário de manter." (The most troublesome of all is that, through the meritocratic process, you bring people into the national government who are not much interested in changing the status quo that runs through the state; quite the opposite, they are interested in maintaining it.) He further argued that they fail to recruit civic-minded people who are motivated by public service and willing to work toward the common good and general welfare: "O efeito simbólico de escurecer o estado é muito importante. Se a pessoa for atendida por um médico SUS, da saúde pública, um médico e uma médica negra. A criança negra vai ter outras . . . vai começar a ter outros referenciais para a vida dela." (The symbolic effect of darkening the state [national government] is very important. If the person is seen by a Black doctor in SUS [Sistema Único de Saudé], public health, the Black child will start to have other . . . will start to have other references for her life.) Thus, underrepresented students and workers are crucial for advancing diversity and inclusion. Consequently, increasing the diversity of public workers has been a particular priority for Faria and her team, and they have engaged in impactful diversity and inclusion projects. For them, diversifying the public workforce has been a key priority.

Since 2019, however, the challenges to affirmative action have gone way beyond fraudulent applications related to White or socially White people applying for racial quotas for Black Brazilians to include legislative action such as Bill 461/2020 (Government of Brazil 2020). On January 1, 2019, the extreme right-wing politician Jair Bolsonaro was sworn into office and announced on Twitter his intention to roll back significant policies setting aside land for Indigenous peoples and the descendants of runaway slaves. "More than 15 percent of national land has been demarcated as Indigenous and [for] quilombolas [descendents of slaves]," he wrote. "In reality, fewer than a million people live in those isolated areas of Brazil, and they are exploited and manipulated by nongovernmental organizations. Together, we're going to integrate those citizens and take care of all Brazilians" (quoted in Savarese 2019, my translation). Bill 461/2020 (Government of Brazil 2020) proposed changes to the racial quotas laws that reserve places for Black people in universities and civil service jobs. Most important, the bill proposed stopping the work of the verification committees. Legislators behind the proposed bill argued that the committees attacked human dignity because they humiliated candidates and fomented racism by dividing Brazilian society along color lines.

Gomor dos Santos was so incensed by Bill 461/2020, and particularly the provision banning verification committees, that he decided to draft a position paper opposing it. In his response, Gomor dos Santos emphasized the importance of the verification committees' work to monitor and control potential fraud. He also asserted that racial division has always existed in Brazil: "As pessoas negras são maioria em prisões e ocupações de baixa qualificação e estão sub-representadas em profissões de prestígio e espaços de poder como o Congresso Nacional." (Black people are the majority in prisons and low-skilled occupations, and are underrepresented in prestigious professions and spaces of power such as the National Congress; Gomor dos Santos 2020, my translation). For Gomor dos Santos, behind the attempt to stop the verification committees is the larger national project to undo the affirmative action laws and policies that have granted Black Brazilians minimal access to spaces of power that have historically been denied them. It was clear that, for Faria and her colleagues, expanding educational and employment opportunities and dismantling the barriers that Black and Brown people face in higher education and public service was a moral imperative. To achieve this end, it was critical for the Brazilian government to address the contributing factors, and fraud was one of them.

Pardos and Who Can Be Black for Affirmative Action in Brazil?

Faria, Silva, and Gomor dos Santos repeatedly stressed, "O primeiro ponto este: Quem é o sujeito de direito das políticas raciais . . . , das cotas raciais no Brasil? Sujeito de direito." (The first point is this: Who is the target of the directive on racial policies . . . , of racial quotas in Brazil? Purpose of the law.) Conflict over who is Black enough to qualify for affirmative action is widespread in Brazil, particularly as more Afro-Brazilians compete for places in higher education and prestigious civil service jobs. How the middle category *pardo* relates to Blackness has been the most challenging aspect in the development and implementation of the verification committees.

For example, Faria recalled the case of a young man whose skin color and facial features made him look Black, but his straight hair made him look Indigenous. His first affirmative action application was rejected because they believed he was trying to commit fraud passing as *preto*, but on appeal, a different committee approved it. Faria, a member of the second verification committee, explained their decision as follows: "Ele tinha características comuns aos negros, suficientes pra ele ser vitíma de racismo contra o negro." (He had characteristics common to Black people, enough for him to be a target of anti-Black racism.) This was reminiscent of what she had said before about considering the applicants whose absence from spaces of power, public service, mainstream media, and so forth, is easy to detect. I asked her about whether the inclusion of *pardos* in affirmative action quotas was consistent with the argument about absence from spaces of power. Responding about the reasons for including them, she first pointed out that the law states applicants for the quotas for *negros* may identify as Black or *pardo*. She admitted that the inclusion of *pardos* in the racial quota system created a degree of ambiguity in the law, a loophole that sparked applications by non-Blacks and led policy makers to identify remediation strategies, such as the verification committees. It is important to note that Norm 4, which regulates the committees, uses the term *negro* only, instead of *preto* and *pardo*, to avoid defining the complex and ambiguous status of *pardos* in the racial quotas. Job and admissions announcements still use the terms *preto* and *pardo*, however. This only complicates matters even more. As Faria explained, "A gente estaria traindo o espírito da lei, se a gente incluísse beneficiários que são vistos como brancos, né, pode ter uma pele mais bronzeada, mas são visto como brancos." (We would be betraying the spirit of the law if we included beneficiaries who are seen as White, you know, they may have more tanned skin, but they are viewed as White.) The bottom line is *pardos* who pass as White are not eligible for the same quotas for Black people.

During the course of our conversation, Faria went on to discuss her sense of racial recognition. She explained that she knew how to identify a Black person in Brazil. In fact, research has long shown that there has always been racial categorization based on characteristics such as skin color, hair texture, and lip shape. For example, Oracy Nogueira (1998) once described this as "racismo de marca," meaning that Brazilians discriminate based more on phenotype (*marca*), while racial background or ancestry (*origem*) are less relevant. Brazilian racial mixing inspired various intermediate categories to describe those who are between Black and White. As the ideal of racial whitening spread popularly and widely, skin pigmentation became the primary factor driving prejudice and discrimination among Brazilians. The extent to which a person looks more or less Black will determine how much discrimination he or she will face. The greater opportunity for social mobility of the middle category *pardo* (Brown, mixed race)—which Carl Degler has astutely described as an "escape hatch" for Blacks—has also "encourage[d] them to dissociate themselves from [Blacks]" (1971, 107–109). In reference to *pardos*, Lívia Maria Santana e Sant'Anna Vaz (2018) has noted that their darker skin tone does not cause them to be targets of anti-Black racism. Racial quotas are available for *pardos* who appear Black but not for those who look socially and culturally White. The verification committees base their identification of candidates solely on phenotype.

Norm 4 reflects a sociological understanding of what it means to be Black in Brazil, in line with the Movimento Negro Unificado's (Unified Black Movement's) description of Black people as "all those who have in skin color, in facial appearances, and in hair, signs characteristic of the race" (Covin 1990, 132). As Dias (2018) explains, black and brown are not races, not even in sociological terms, but are skin tones. In this sense, a person with dark brown skin color will always be *negro*, but a person with brown skin may be brown-white, brownish, or tanned—meaning they are brown in color but in terms of sociological race they are White. Thus, what drives the verification of *pardos-negros* is the familiar question in Brazilian affirmative action, Are they Black enough?

Heteroidentification Procedures

Clearly there is nothing simple, straightforward, or predictable about the work of the verification committees. While there are some differences in the operation of the committees, the basic procedure is the same, and candidates are informed about it when the hiring or admissions recruitment is announced. The main goal of the verification committee is to carry out *heteroidentificação* (external identification) to validate a candidate's self-identification. The committee is normally composed of at least three voting members, selected with consideration of diversity (gender and race), socio-cultural background (lived experience in the candidate's home city), and representation of the Black movement (see, e.g., Vaz 2018, 54–56). All selection committees must include at least one woman and one man. Given the importance of committee members and candidates having shared experiences and social perceptions, the committee must include people with the same contextual background as the candidate. Finally, for representation and expertise in critical race studies, committees must include at least one member of the Brazilian Black movement. The committee must meet the candidate in person to prevent the use of disguises to conceal a White or socially White appearance and racial position. Committees must observe skin color (the main factor), hair texture, and facial features rather than the candidate's reports of his or her experiences of discrimination or genealogy (see Dias 2018, 151).

At the Universidade Federal da Bahia (UFBA), there are four stages to the verification process. When candidates arrive they are introduced to the committee members, who describe their background, occupation, affiliation, and so on. In the second stage, candidates attend an orientation on topics such as the history of quotas in Brazil, the functioning of the evaluation process, and the reasons verification is needed. Then candidates move on to the third stage, the verification itself, where they receive a form to confirm the self-identification they reported when applying for the quota: "negro de pele parda ou preta" (*negro* with brown or black skin). After that, they answer questions posed by the committee that relate to racial identification. Faria, Gomor dos Santos, and Silva all stated that candidates' answers to these questions have absolutely no bearing on the committee's decision to approve or reject an applicant's racial self-identification. Finally, in the fourth stage, a photo of each candidate is taken to attach to their individual file. Candidates also have an opportunity to provide feedback on and an assessment of their verification experience and how it can be improved. Candidates are informed of the results within twenty-four hours.[5]

As described in Chapter 4, in their struggles with self-identification *pardos-negros* come to recognize a multiplicity of perspectives and voices on what it means to be Black. Through interactions between their own experiences and other people's perceptions of them, they construct their own identity narratives. This can be thought of as a struggle to claim a position among contrasting ways of seeing oneself, often weighted with contradictory ideologies. Continuing my exploration of the engagement of *pardos-negros* with Blackness, I conducted ethnographic interviews with *pardos-negros* who applied for a racial quota. I demonstrate that they, caught between Brown and Black identities, face uniquely difficult questions about race in the age of Brazilian affirmative action.

In 2018, I began to research the work of the CHs and candidates' experiences of the verification process. As an initial step in this research, I conducted twenty-six in-depth, semistructured interviews with policy makers, verification committee members, and both accepted and rejected quota candidates. The interviewees lived in three different regions of Brazil: Salvador (in the state of Bahia), and Brasília and Florianópolis (in the Distrito Federal), and were recruited through a combination of purposive and snowballing sampling strategies. The multisite approach allowed me to triangulate data from locales that have been key in the larger struggle for racial quotas: the UFBA and the Universidade Estadual da Bahia in Salvador, the Universidade Federal de Santa Catarina in Florianópolis, and the MPOG and the UnB in Brasília. A former UFBA student whom I met during my two-year postdoctoral position there in 2014–2015 served as a key informant and research assistant to help in recruiting individuals to interview. The interviews in Brasília and Salvador were done in person at a place chosen by the interviewee; those in Florianópolis were conducted via Skype. The questions addressed why the individuals decided to apply for the quota system, their experiences of having their identities verified, and their reactions to the results. Data were analyzed using an ethnographic approach to discourse that focused on language use within ethnographic and sociopolitical contexts (Roth-Gordon 2020). My concern was with identifying how Afro-Brazilians develop their orientation to Blackness in an environment where terms like *preto*, *pardo*, and *moreno* are imbricated in a language of exclusion that delimits the positions available to Blacks in a racialized power structure (Martins 1995, 36).

Marli and Júlio

As part of their applications for federal jobs, Marli and Júlio were both required to present themselves before a verification committee. It was Marli's first experience of applying for affirmative action, and her application was approved by the verification committee. She had previously held a federal job and had earned a BA and an MA, yet she had never previously used affirmative action opportunities to advance herself. Marli believed that throughout her life she had enjoyed a privileged position because of her relatively light skin tone. In a lot of ways she dissociated herself from Blackness. This time, however, she felt that she had the right to use the quota program: "Simples assim, eu tinha direito a isto." (As simple as that, I had the right to do it.) At the time, she realized that most people are fairly oblivious to the effort it takes for non-Whites to achieve their goals, and that they have to work harder than other people just because they are Black, "só pelo fato de ser negro" (only for the fact of being Black). At the time of our interview, Júlio was still trying to come to terms with the process of verification and the rejection of his application by the verification committee. He expressed his frustration with such statements as "O cara não precisa ser muito negro, né? Meio negro já é negro." (A guy doesn't need to be very Black, right? Half Black is Black enough.) Compounding his feelings of being caught between racial positions was the world of his identity as *pardo* in present-day Brazil. He felt he was trapped between the traditional whitening ideal and, more currently, its affirmative values.

Using an Althusserian perspective on ideology and ideological subjection for my analysis, I explore the stories of Marli and Júlio through the ways they talked about their application and verification experience. I do so with an eye to how their ideological relationships to Blackness intersect with different conceptions of Blackness and the assumptions that underlie them, all weighted with contradictory ideologies. Although Marli's application was accepted, she found the process anything but easy. At the time of her application, she knew that there would be "uma comissão de avaliação" (an evaluation committee) because she worked for SEPPIR. Marli did not question her identification as Black, but not knowing what kinds of questions the committee would ask made her uncomfortable: "É um sentimento meio esquisito de ser avaliado por isto. . . . É muito esquisito." (It is a sort of weird feeling to have your racial identity evaluated. . . . It is very weird.) She reiterated that she felt uneasy over the possibility of her Black identity being challenged. As a light-skinned Black woman she sometimes felt like a fraud, that "até passa na sua cabeça se você é negro o suficiente" (it crosses your mind whether you are Black enough). Compounded by the fact that she came from a working-class family but had never needed to apply for affirmative action before, this confused her further still: "Parece uma ambiguidade, você sabe que é merecedor daquilo, mas ao mesmo tempo lhe passa uma sombra na cabeça, como se você não fosse." (It almost feels ambiguous, you know you deserve it, but at the same time, it becomes fuzzy, as if you don't deserve it.) Although she knew she was Black, she was unsure whether it was fair for her to apply for a quota, in "uma espécie de síndrome do impostor" (a kind of imposter syndrome). When the committee asked her whether she considered herself Black, she said, "Sim. Sou" (Yes. I am.) She followed this with "Mas sei lá . . . também me passou pela cabeça, assim, como se. . . . (But I don't know, the thought also crossed my mind, like, as if. . . .) That is, Marli is did not think she was Black enough to use the quota system.

When she was a child, both Marli and her mother had difficulty identifying as Black. For a long time, her mother straightened Marli's hair and never braided it, all in an effort to help her appear White and thus better succeed. Wanting Marli to disassociate herself from Blackness, she said, "Você não é neguinha." (You're not a Black girl.) Marli grew up near a middle-class neighborhood, where she went to school, and she was the only dark-skinned student in her school. They called her "carvão mineral" (mineral coal). In that anti-Black environment she could not escape Blackness. Later she attended a prestigious public high school where she studied with Black students who were ascending the socioeconomic ladder and White students who were descending it, she explained. She hung out with the nerds, Black, White, and in between. She added, "Isto era muito legal, assim como um laboratório de autoestima." (This was very cool, like a laboratory of self-esteem."

In the process of verification, Marli thought a lot about the boundaries between Brown and Black, whether it was really possible for her to separate them when she was caught so deeply between them. She also felt weird about an evaluation to determine whether she was Black enough to deserve the right of a quota. She said that she kept thinking about the stereotypical images of a Black person based on which the CH would evaluate her, especially if the members were White. All the popular and pervasive stereotypes of Black women, and particularly the Black dancers of samba schools in Rio de Janeiro's carnival, haunted her. Marli also spoke about her experiences among people in middle-class circles who would "politely" refer to her as *morena* instead of Black: "É como se fosse uma ofensa, né, eu sinto um pouco isto; é como se você fosse embranquecendo." (It is like an offense, right, I sense that; it is as if you whiten in situations like that.) She wondered whether she would have passed the verification if she had straightened her hair, for example. All these ideas and representations, which constituted her as a subject of Brazilian racial ideology, swirled around in Marli's head and were discernible in her words as she talked.

In contrast, Júlio identified himself as *pardo*, and until he decided to apply for the federal job, he had not been well informed about affirmative action or the quota system in Brazil. All he knew about it was what he saw in mainstream media. Then he saw the posting for the federal job competition. He said, "O edital já tava publicado, e eu estudei o edital e nisso eu vi esse negócio de cota." (The open job announcement was out, and I studied the announcement and saw the thing about the quota.) He went to great lengths to distance himself from the culture of *concurseiros*—those who learn all about the exams, spend a lot of time preparing for them, and take several in hopes of eventually passing one—and thus was unfamiliar with the notion of quotas, which had been around since 2014. When Júlio decided to apply for a federal civil service position in 2015, and saw the part about applying for a *negro* quota, he had no doubt he would meet the criteria: "Nunca declarei outra coisa que não fosse pardo, moreno. Depende da pesquisa, né. Tem pesquisa, 'Ah, qual é sua raça?' Tem lá, moreno." (I have never identified as anything but *pardo* [the census term for mixed race] or *moreno* [the popular, unofficial term for Brown or mixed race]. Depends on the survey, right? There are surveys, "Oh, what is your race?" It is there, *moreno*.) He added,

> Nunca me marquei como branco, nem negro puro, eu não me marcava negro puro, porque eu achava que tivesse, vamos dizer assim . . . pô, eu . . . seu eu disser que sou branco, eu tô negando o lado da minha mãe . . . do meu pai, desculpa. Aí alguém poderia até questionar, "Pô, cê tem vergonha de ser negro?" Não. Se eu falasse que eu sou negro, eu estaria negando o lado da minha mãe.

> I never checked White or pure Black, I never checked pure Black, because I thought I had, let's put it this way . . . damn, I . . . if I say that I'm White, I'd be denying the side of my mother . . . sorry, of my father. Then people could ask, "Damn, are you ashamed of being Black?" No. If I said that I was Black, I would be denying the side of my mother.

After trying very hard to explain his position again, Júlio summed it up by saying that if the option on a form were *pardo*, he would pick *pardo*; if it were *moreno*, he would pick *moreno*; and if it were a choice of Black or White, he would pick Black. As was common among candidates who had their applications rejected, Júlio told me that he had enough documentation, such as photos of different generations of his family, to prove his Black origins: "Eu tenho foto de família, meu pai, minha vó, todos negros." (I have pictures of my family, my father, my paternal grandmother, all Black.)

Talking about his experience with the verification interview, Júlio said he was surprised by how quickly the whole process went. In hindsight, it bothered him that they did not ask him questions beyond whether he identified as Black or Brown. At the time of the interview and until he received the rejection, he believed that the speed of the process was vindication of his identification as *pardo*. In the interview he gave vent to his frustration by describing the whole process as a trick played on him at his expense: "A impressão que eu tive é que parecia uma pegadinha do malandro." (The impression I had was that they poked fun at me). Júlio was more than aware that he occupied an ambiguous racial position and that his racial identity is fluid and that he can be melded into different racial categories like portals. He did not accept that the committee had closed one of those portals on him.

Júlio decided to appeal the committee's decision: "Não sei dizer sinceramente o que aconteceu, que chegaram a conclusão, mas . . . é . . . não se buscou a verdade isso eu garanto a você." (I sincerely don't know what happened, how they arrived at that conclusion, but . . . uh . . . they didn't aim for the truth, and I can assure you of that.) In his appeal Júlio included several documents that attested to his race. Convinced that the committee's decision was unfair, he added, "Eles olham para você e dizem, pelo fenótipo, não é pela história . . . se você tem pai negro ou mãe branca ou mãe negra, entendeu?" (They look at you and decide, based on your phenotype, not on your history . . . if you have a Black father or a White mother or Black mother, you understand?) Júlio would have preferred that the committee ask him why he identified as Black, as he would have answered, "porque eu tenho um pai negro" (because I have a Black father). He added that throughout his life people had often referred to him as *branco*, and every time that happened, he would respond by denying he was White and identifying himself as *pardo*. Some of the ideas and representations about race Júlio brought forward had parallels with the ones that Marli engaged in. Both expressed that at times they felt like they were in a separate Black and Brown world and, at other times, they were in interacting and converging worlds.

A Note on Ideology

In his essay "Ideology and Ideological State Apparatuses: Notes Toward an Investigation," the French philosopher Louis Althusser analyzes at length a characteristic of everyday life that he called "ideological recognition." According to Althusser, every person is inherently distinguishable and "irreplaceable" as a subject of ideology within a particular social formation (religious, political, or racial). Althusser defines ideology as "the system of ideas and representations which dominate the mind of a man or social group" (Althusser 1971, 107). These ideas and representations mold people's relationships with their everyday conditions of existence. People "act according to [their] ideas" (113). Thus, these ideas and representations have concrete existence in the many ways people conduct their daily lives and are thus keys to the formation of social relations, including racial relations (112–113). Explaining the conditions under which "ideological recognitions" take place, Althusser states that "all ideology hails or interpellates individuals as subjects" (119). He defines interpellation as the operation through which ideology transforms concrete individuals into concrete subjects of some sort (118–120) This casts a bright light on the power of social and legal principles of racial categorization to transform concrete individuals into racial subjects based on their morphology and/or ancestry.

Central to my understanding of quota candidates' participation in the verification process is Althusser's discussion of "ideological constraints and pre-appointment" and the fact that "an individual is always-already a subject, even before he is born" simply because of the ideological configurations into which he comes to exist (1971, 119). It is thus extremely difficult if not impossible in Brazilian racial ideology to choose one's race outside the limits of morphology and context. As Ian Haney López (1998, 14) affirms, "choices [regarding racial identities] are exercised not by free agents or autonomous actors, but by people who are compromised and constrained by the social context." In Brazil, people's phenotypes and racial meanings have a close, stable relationship. In the context of the CHs, talk of racial ancestry is not deemed relevant in that racial categorization becomes closed to the discourse of ancestry. But the combination of phenotype and ancestry in the narratives of quota candidates—Marli's and Júlio's being two examples—reflects a certain ideological conflict in antiracism in Brazil today, which is emboldened by the promotion of self-declaration but is also complicated, in part, because of the authentication process.

Back to Marli and Júlio

With this background, we can try to make sense of the words of Marli and Júlio. Starting with the case of Marli, her position and place in Brazilian society matches those of other interviewees whose applications for a quota had been approved. Her position and place reflect to a large extent the intermediate tone of her skin. She was called "carvão mineral" by her classmates to denote that her skin was darker than theirs. This highlights the importance of color to Brazilians, and the widespread pejorative attitudes and insulting remarks toward dark-skinned Afro-Brazilians. In her classmates' ideological insinuations, Marli became a subject of color and race. More important for the present discussion, however, is that Marli described her racial identity as often being in tension with the ideology of racial mixture in Brazil—particularly the whitening ideal and the possibility for some Black Brazilian to escape Blackness. Marli is not a Black person per se, but one who is constantly hailed by Brazilian mixed-racial ideology and its obsessive concern with Blackness, racial mixture, and the whitening ideal. Several instances of this emerge in her narrative: one example was her and her mother's daily struggles to escape Blackness ("You're not a Black girl"). Another was Marli's self-doubt about whether she would be "Black enough" in the committee's eyes. In this admission, Marli was expressing an instance of being summoned as a racial subject constituted by the Brazilian racial ideology, and thus caught between the whitening ideal and possibilities that racial quotas for Blacks could afford her. When deciding to apply for a racial quota, Marli reasoned that multiple versions of her race coexisted. Furthermore, she decided not to dwell on a single way of being as if no other way existed.

In Júlio's case, which is representative of some of my other interviewees who identified as *pardo*, there are several relevant cultural factors. One way to view applications by lighter-skinned *pardos* like him is that they are wrongful or criminal deceptions (*jeitinho brasileiro*) aimed at personal gain. Alternatively, they can be viewed as a form of anti-Blackness that fails to recognize the structural problems affecting Black people in Brazil and afford them their rights. Cases like Júlio's offer yet another way to understand the problem of ideological subjectivization in Brazil affecting Afro-Brazilians whose physical appearance is "not White enough" to be White and "not Black enough" to be Black. As Pierre Macherey notes in his study of Althusser, ideology is "an effective agent of the process of social reproduction in which it is directly implicated" (2012, 9). So, as Althusser puts it, ideology "practically always gets its man" (as translated and quoted in Macherey 2012, 12). In his important exposition of Brazilian racial dynamics, Degler uses the metaphor of the "escape hatch" (1971, 178) to posit a means of upward social mobility for Brazilians whose intermediate (*pardo*) category allows them to occupy a social position between Whites and Blacks (178). What strikes me in Degler's exposition is how it underscores the nature of the ideology of race in Brazil that "gets its man," which is to note the impossibility of evading it. Though an astute observer of Brazilian race relations, Degler focuses only on escape in one direction, from Blackness toward Whiteness. Marli is an example of this struggle. Degler's focus obviously reflects the conditions he studied. Now, however, could the escape hatch go both ways, toward Blackness as well, if social mobility is also possible through affirmative action? A central premise of my analysis is that the possibility for improving one's life through racial mobility can happen not just through benefits that accrue from Whiteness but also through those that accrue from Blackness. As Brazil takes its sharpest turn yet toward positive action for the social advancement of Blacks, it is not surprising that Júlio shifted from seeing himself as Brown, or even socially White, to seeing himself as Black in order to enjoy some privilege of being Black.

Fundamentally, it does not matter whether Júlio was manipulating the system to take advantage of recent affirmative action legislation. He may not have recognized the structural problem affecting dark-skinned Blacks whose rights were being appropriated by people like him, and how his identity shift toward Blackness for the purpose of individual advancement perpetuated structural inequality. As Freitas points out, "Although they self-declare as Black or Brown on well-founded grounds, they do not seem to be the real beneficiaries for effective antiracial prejudice policy" (Freitas 2018, 178, my translation). After all, we cannot "negate the racial singularity and uniqueness of Black discrimination victims that make them eligible to benefit from programs promoting greater access to power and privilege" (S. A. Santos 2006, 43). Rather, I am keenly interested in the overarching ideological dimension characterizing race relations in Brazil that has historically played a role in the relationship of its people, like Marli and Júlio, with Blackness. What their cases speak to are Afro-Brazilians' persistent encounters with racialization, which have an added dimension in the context of affirmative action. The entrenched racial calculus and color arithmetic of anti-Blackness has historically relegated Blackness to others. In the age of affirmative action, Blackness has become a political force to be reckoned with.

6

The Complex Calculus of Race and Electoral Politics in Salvador

At the heart of Black mobilization efforts in Salvador is activists' struggle to mobilize the Afro-Brazilian vote. This chapter offers a window into how Afro-Brazilian voters feel about and reflect on race-based politics and how Black activist candidates for office emphasize race-specific messages with their constituencies. Their messages are steeped in double-voiced discourse—different ways of adjusting their political communication in response to competing ideological leanings—around ideas about racial justice. The number of Black Brazilians in electoral politics in Salvador, and Brazil more broadly, has seen a significant increase (*Estado de Minas* 2020), and the theme of Black life and its challenges has become more prominent in campaigns. There is no clear evidence that focusing on the challenges of Black life carries any weight with Afro-Brazilian voters, yet the "blackening" of electoral politics in Salvador does have important implications for understanding Afro-Brazilians' relationship with Blackness in the era of affirmative action in Brazil. The following examples of campaign slogans, presented in chronological order, frame the complex calculus of race and electoral politics in Salvador:

Olívia Santana, a negona da cidade. (Olívia Santana, a Black woman of the city)

—Olívia Santana, 2014

A Bahia é negra. Vote contra o racismo. (Bahia is Black. Vote against racism.)

—Luiz Alberto, 2014

Educação, igualdade e respeito. Um compromisso de vida. (Education, equality, and respect. A life commitment.)

—Sílvio Humberto, 2014, 2016, 2020

Nossa força, nossa voz. E a força e a voz do povo no poder. (Our strength, our voice. And the strength and the voice of the people in power.)

—Olívia Santana, 2018

Pra trabalhar, para construir . . . sem excluir. (To work, to build . . . without excluding.)

—Olívia Santana, 2020

These campaign slogans capture a change underway in the current political discourse that Black candidates use to court Afro-Brazilian voters in Salvador. Santana's and Alberto's early campaign slogans flirted with multicultural ideas, focusing on an appeal to Afro-Brazilian group identity and Blackness. Humberto, in contrast, opted to treat Blackness more subtly, engaging in a discourse of rights and appealing to all segments of the population. In her 2018 and 2020 races for state deputy and mayor of Bahia, respectively, Olívia Santana adjusted her campaign messages, branching out to address a broader theme of inclusion in an attempt to appeal to a wide range of voters regardless of color. The various slogans encapsulate the different, and sometimes divergent, campaign strategies directed toward social justice that Black activists have deployed in Salvadorean electoral politics. They illustrate the ways in which candidates have attempted to traverse the large expanse of racial justice discourse. From initially expressing minoritized people's interests as united by common identity (e.g., "Bahia is Black"), they have increasingly begun to privilege a citizenship rights approach to addressing issues of broader concern. In Brazilian discourse on social justice, João Feres Junior and Luiz Augusto Campos (2016, 273) have noted a pattern of oscillations toward or away from multiculturalism, or demands for group-specific rights by the oppressed and the excluded (Hale 2002) versus progress for all citizens.

This chapter outlines more distinct trend in Black candidates' political communication, whose origins can be traced to a particular form of multiculturalism articulated within some Black movement circles in Salvador. In their attempts to connect with a larger constituency of voters, Black activists running for office have increasingly foregrounded issues of structural disadvantage of interest to the Afro-Brazilian constituency while subtly referencing issues of importance to a broader political alliance. In line with the overarching dialogic approach in this book, I argue that this shift in electoral strategies reveals Black candidates' need to dialogize the discourse of Blackness and thus present choices where none may have been evident before. In other words, broad-based distributive justice has started to play a more significant role in campaigns compared to appeals to Black people's shared experiences of injustice. This shift of discourse has contributed to syncing Black candidates' political communications with the institutional redistributive and reparatory measures the Brazilian government has been undertaking to redress racial disparities. In order to blacken electoral politics in Salvador, Black Brazilians running for office have expanded the conversation about racial justice, and consequently the discourse about Blackness itself.

Brazil's Turn toward Multiculturalism

Brazilian constitutional reforms in the 1980s were steeped in the discourse around ethnoracial rights, the most important result of which was the recognition of Black communal land rights. Armed with the language of multiculturalism—the idea that different cultural groups coexist within Brazilian society—Black communities emerged as discrete cultural entities. As Tianna Paschel convincingly demonstrates in her book, *Becoming Black Political Subjects* (2016), the Brazilian Black movement as a whole played an important role in scripting the political arguments supporting the authentic and legitimate Black identity of the groups claiming collective rights. Brazil's political sphere became imbued with multiculturalism. As the word *multicultural* entered the vocabulary of electoral politics, Brazilian society witnessed a broader ideological shift. I begin this chapter by reviewing the scholarship on multiculturalism in Latin America that fundamentally supports the idea of leveling the playing field for minorities across the hemisphere while simultaneously critiquing its logic of ethnoracial inclusion. Ultimately, the ways in which Blackness and Black rights were conceived in multicultural terms during the 1980s reflect a neoliberal approach.

Since the term *multiculturalism*, together with its by-products, recurs throughout this chapter, it is worthwhile to examine the concept of multiculturalism, its limitations, and its possibilities as a way of understanding the rationale behind Afro-Brazilian collective action, including struggles for political representation. First, I use *multiculturalism* to broadly describe the reforms that started in the 1980s and 1990s and were designed to address the challenges associated with diversity in society. Multiculturalism can be defined as a response to demands for rights by marginalized groups on the basis of ethnic and racial differences (Hale 2002, 490). In this vein Craig Calhoun (2003a, b), Charles Mills (2007), and Jessé Souza (1997) use multiculturalism to describe the shift from a national ideology that promoted a combination of assimilation and a homogeneous Mestizo citizenry to a recognition of the existence of cultural minorities and an emphasis on pluralism. Simultaneously, they describe multiculturalism as a discourse of opposition and participation based on identity formation through which minoritized groups entered the national discussion about cultural differences and rights. Both global and national, public and private, institutions played important roles on both sides of this movement. The umbrella of multicultural rights would come to include language, education, law, and participation in governance. In sum, the heart of the multicultural movement in Latin America was to replace the myth of a national identity based on a homogeneous mixed-race citizenry with a recognition of cultural difference (Afro-centrism, Black nationalism, Africa as the homeland).

While casting light on the processes of the state's endorsement of minority rights and subaltern people's collective responses to them, research on Latin America's multicultural turn has produced an important critical analysis of the contradictions permeating multicultural reforms implemented in a neoliberal context (e.g., Hale 2002; Larson 2018; Paschel 2016;

Postero 2007).[1] Under neoliberal governments, a salient aim of multiculturalism has been to transfer responsibility for social welfare (i.e., a physical and material safety net for people in need) and for redistributive measures to combat inequality from the state to nongovernmental organizations (NGOs). NGOs thereby became the primary social institutions protecting and promoting the welfare of a nation's citizenry. Further, the paradox facing minoritized groups across the Americas is that whereas equality is emblazoned across the flags of multiculturalism, the approach has produced limited and short-lived benefits. As a rule, inequities were not reduced, and in some situations were exacerbated, while racial inequality rose rapidly in the era of multiculturalism.

Presently scholars are also engaged in an important argument over the transformative potential of state-sponsored and society-endorsed multicultural mobilization. Charles Hale's noting that "multiculturalism is the discourse of *mestizaje* for the new millennium" (Hale 2002, 491) encapsulates most scholars' views of multiculturalism—that is, lingering exclusion is disguised behind the discourse of diversity and inclusion. Like *mestizaje*, multiculturalism can be viewed as a mechanism for social control, enacting restraints on anyone who dares to oppose the status quo. In a study of the contradictions of anti-racist politics and the limits of multiculturalism in Guatemala, Hale documents how Ladinos, members of Guatemala's dominant culture, harbor "deep anxiety" about Indigenous empowerment, and particularly fears of losing the benefits from ingrained racial privilege. In order to establish limits on collective mobilizations that have potential to upset the balance of power, Ladinos are repressing minoritized groups who are pushing for radical transformation and changing the history of their societies. Although Ladinos in Hale's study claim to believe in racial justice, they fear that equality struggles would go too far.[2] Hale uses the term *indio permitido* to refer to the condition in which Indigenous cultural politics is welcomed but limits are place on Indigenous rights activism. It is difficult for Indigenous people to confront and address the unspoken subordination of their culture to the dominant culture (Hale and Millamán 2015, 300–301). As Shannon Speed (2005, 31) also notes, the ceding of certain rights occurs in the context of controlled political subjectivities. In many cases poverty and income disparity have grown in locations where identity-based rights movements have been backed by transnational neoliberal institutions such as the World Bank or the Inter-American Development Bank. Simply put, neoliberalism is a political project to curb the power of labor (Harvey 2016). In Latin America, multicultural policies have been enmeshed in neoliberal reforms that have exacerbated inequality.

On the other hand, many scholars agree that the positive effects of state-endorsed multicultural mobilization have, in some respects, been greater than imagined, with larger processes of political restructuring giving rise not only to new forms of governance but also new forms of opposition. Consider, for example, the Brazilian Black movement, which resurged in the 1970s and has increasingly become a force to be reckoned with. Afro-Brazilians' growing awareness of and concern about inequality has shaped attitudes regarding racial exclusion. Marginalized groups' enhanced awareness of the inequalities holding them back have driven the reconstitution of political subjectivities to ensure that neoliberal multiculturalism has not gone unchallenged for long (Paschel 2016). In Salvador, Blacks have gained a foothold in their efforts to blacken electoral politics—that is, increase Black representation that is committed to racial justice—though they still face unequal representation compared to White Salvadoreans.

Even as some Black activists argued passionately for Afro-Brazilians to embrace the politics of recognition, others acknowledged that identity-based mobilization would do little to promote systemic change. Though activists hold divergent views, many see the politics of redistribution as more important for addressing widespread race-based structural violence affecting Black Brazilians (see Postero 2007, 14). Seeking to strengthen the cultural politics of identity-based struggles, Sílvio Humberto explained that he viewed Blacks building a path out of inequality as the only solution; redistribution policies would only be enacted if Blacks worked together to attain their political goals at the local, regional, and national levels, dealing with the state and civil society on their own terms. His political communication emphasized a progressive, rights-based politics that invested its efforts in challenging inequalities and promoting resource redistribution (see Speed 2005, 32). Many Black Brazilians running for office view political representation, or the blackening of electoral politics, as a potential catalyst for increased racial equality. Inspired by the work of Gloria Anzaldúa (1987) and Chela Sandoval (1991), Hale uses the notion of "*mestizaje* from below" to mean that lessons for successful mobilization can often come from unexpected places: "Cultural rights movements have little choice but to occupy the spaces opened by neoliberal multiculturalism, and that they often have much to gain by doing so; but when they do, that we should assume they will be articulated with the dominant bloc, unless this decision forms part of a well-developed strategy oriented toward resistance from within, and ultimately, toward a well-conceived political alternative" (Hale 2002, 522).

Even under neoliberalism, Indigenous communities have been able to build power from below. Speed also notes that "human rights and multi-culturalism are multiple discourses and have different meanings and effects depending on how, and by whom, they are deployed" (2005, 29). Brazil is an outstanding case study of the intersecting of discourses of multicultur-alism and anti-racism. As Feres Junior and Campos note, Brazilian affirma-tive action is quite distinct from multiculturalism as strictly defined—that is, the recognition of cultural difference—as it also embodies an alternative approach to social justice. For Black activists in Salvador, achieving the goal of getting more Black people elected to office entails juggling different, equally important aspects of racial justice.

Race in Politics in Salvador

Since Brazil's return to civilian government in the 1980s, Afro-Brazilian activists have been able to press their collective claims for access to resources and rights for Brazil's Black population (Bairros 2008; Hooker 2008). Yet Afro-Brazilians have been severely underrepresented in the electoral arena, even in the state of Bahia, where around 80 percent of the population is of African descent. Because Brazil's dominant ideology of racial mixture con-tends that Brazil is not divided along racial lines, Black candidates have, by and large, avoided race-conscious messages in their political campaigns. As Brazil enacted an agenda that responds to the struggles and desperation of Black Brazilians through extensive affirmative action laws and policies, Black Brazilians running for elected office began using race as an electoral strategy. The persistence of Brazil's racial ideology has, however, forced them to confront the question of how to effectively utilize racial or group con-sciousness to enlist the political support of Afro-Brazilians (Guimarães 2001; G. Mitchell 2009; M. Mitchell 1999).

Since 2014, I have engaged in a project to examine the racial orienta-tions of Black candidates' political campaigns. The original project had two objectives: (1) to describe Black candidates' various campaigns, how these campaigns unfolded, and the messages each used to win political support; and (2) to investigate how voters received and interpreted those campaign communications and assessed which candidates to vote for. This project was timely given current trends in the study of race in electoral politics in Brazil and elsewhere (Crowley 2008; Reiter and Mitchell 2010; Valentino, Hutchings, and White 2002). Interest in the complex nexus of race and politics in the United States is resurging, and much debate and research revolves around the extent to which campaign messages should focus on issues of race or ethnicity rather than on universal issues independent of race. Similar concerns arise in electoral politics in Salvador. Traditionally, Brazilian national identity has had at its core the identification with *brasilidade*, an essential "Brazilianness." By challenging this dominant ideology, community-based Black organizations have had considerable influence on the public discourse about race in Brazil. As addressed previously, particularly in chapters 2 and 3, the anti-racist pedagogy promoted by Black NGOs brings to the surface two juxtaposed, often contradictory themes—racial integration and racial disparity—that shape Afro-Brazilians' understandings and interpretations of Blackness, Black consciousness, and anti-racist activism. These themes are linked to the dual discourses involving the traditional narratives of racial mixture versus race-conscious legislation and policies.

In electoral politics, however, Black candidates have faced an uphill battle in wooing Afro-Brazilian voters, even in Salvador, known as the Black capital of Brazil. As of the 2017 Brazilian census, Salvador is home to 2.425 million people, of whom 81.1 percent identify as either Brown (44.7 percent) or Black (36.5 percent; State of Bahia, Secretaria do Planejamento 2020). Between 2017 and 2018 in the state of Bahia, 308,000 more citizens identified themselves as Black, while those identifying as Brown or White dropped by 155,000 and 124,000, respectively. In 2018, self-declared Blacks accounted for 22.9 percent of the 14.7 million inhabitants of Bahia, or one in every five residents of the state, while Whites were at 18.1 percent (Muniz and Amorim 2019). Yet "pigmentocracy" (social stratification based on race, where one's socioeconomic position is determined by one's skin color and physical features) and devaluation of Blackness remain central to Brazilian racial ideology. Salvador is also known for the worst racial income inequality in the country: the average income of its Black population is one-third (67 percent) that of White residents. Despite the large proportion of Afro-descendants in Salvador and some gains in Black representation, holders of public remain overwhelmingly White. As of 2018, thirteen out of forty-three city council members are Black (30 percent). Notably, seven out of ten candidates for the sixty-four legislative positions in Bahia were Black, but only four out of ten of those candidates won election (*Estado de minas* 2020).

Black Brazilians running for office have traditionally not used racial and group consciousness as a political resource to connect with the large Afro-descended segment of the population. Their approach to campaigning has always been to avoid race-specific messages and instead to frame their political agendas as intended to help Brazilians of all backgrounds. In the past twenty years, however, race has increasingly played a significant role in campaign messages. Consider the competing slogans in the 2014 election. Luiz Alberto's slogan was "A Bahia é negra. Vote contra o Racismo" (Bahia is Black. Vote against Racism). Olívia Santana's slogan, on the other hand, employed style shifting with "Olívia Santana, negona da cidade" (Olívia Santana, a Black woman of the city); she described herself as *negona*, an in-group word Brazilian Blacks use to refer to themselves. In her shift in style, Olívia astutely used a form of the vernacular spoken among her potential constituents, and in doing so, she created a projected linguistic relationship with them. Given the deeply entrenched racism and ideology of miscegenation in Brazil, it is worthwhile to investigate how much weight racial messages actually lend to Black candidates' campaigns and how the evolving racial climate is affecting politics from campaign strategies to voter patterns.

The Research Project

When Barack Obama ran for the U.S. presidency in 2008 and 2012, he had enormous backing from the African American community. In contrast, Afro-Brazilians are a much less unified voting bloc. In part this is because, for them, anti-racist consciousness does not require or even privilege a Black identity. Rather, it crosses racial identities and becomes an ideological critique of dominant ideas about race and racism in Brazil. Researchers are asking how much Brazil's affirmative action turn has increased Afro-Brazilian support for race-conscious initiatives (see, e.g., Penha-Lopes 2017). A review of studies on Black candidates' racial messaging in their political campaigning reveals that the effect of their racial calibrations on Afro-Brazilian voters' political choices is not well understood (see, e.g., Johnson 1998, 2006; Mitchell 2009; Oliveira 1995, 2007; S. A. Santos 2000; Soares and Silva

1987; and Valente 1986). Political speech targeting a specific racial group has not been a traditional strategy in Brazilian campaigns. The focus of scholarship so far has been on candidates, not voters, exploring whether racial issues are important to Afro-Brazilian politicians and how they use racial cues. Research is lacking on the impact of racial appeals on Afro-Brazilian voters.

My task, then, was to examine the elements of the race production and interpretation process as experienced by and meaningful to both Black candidates and Afro-Brazilian voters. During the 2014 elections, when Salvador elected a governor, one senator, federal and state deputies, and the national president, I conducted six months of fieldwork covering the entire election cycle. Because of the interactional and rapidly evolving nature of electoral politics, it was important to collect two synchronous sets of data: campaign messages and voter responses to those messages. It was important to monitor for new and changed messages, as well as how voters' individual decision-making processes actually unfolded. Therefore, both campaign data and voter data were collected during the entire election season, through ongoing observations, repeated interviews, and informal conversations. For both data sets, the study considered racial identification by self and other. To determine whether a candidate was Black (*preto*), both candidates' self-identifications and voters' comments on the candidates' racial identities were considered. With regard to voters, only self-identification as Afro-Brazilian was considered. In campaign messages, verbal and nonverbal cultural indicators of race orientation (racial politics versus universal politics) were identified.

Between July and October 2014 (from the nomination process to election day), and ever since, I have monitored campaign activities. A corpus of political messages was compiled from the following sources: (1) individual, on-the-record interviews with candidates, staffers, speechwriters, and political strategists; (2) written publications, such as articles, editorials, and think pieces in newspapers, newsletters, flyers, and on social media posts; and (3) public events, such as radio and television broadcasts, conventions, rallies, and ground-level campaigning. Verbal and nonverbal elements that revealed different themes in the political communications were recorded and organized systematically. The project involved all players in Brazil's multiparty system. During this period, I compiled lists of (1) Black candidates and their local campaign organization (staffers, consultants, allied interest groups, civic associations, and individual volunteers); (2) locally known indicators of racial and deracialized campaign themes and strategies; and (3) the most prevalent campaign themes and strategies. To assist with identifying and describing indicators of racial themes and strategies (e.g., Blackness, race consciousness, anti-racism), I purposively recruited interviewees from targeted constituencies, Black activists, and political journalists. A similar categorization exercise was done for indicators of deracialized themes (e.g., Brazilianness, meritocracy, and universalism). Through participant observation of what voters did (e.g., wearing campaign merchandise) and said about candidates, I traced their everyday responses to Black candidates' campaign messages.

Between July and December (from the general election through election day and to the postelection period), I conducted repeated interviews with a random sample of voters to document their decision-making process as the political campaigns evolved. Individuals were interviewed at least three times throughout the campaign season regarding (1) their knowledge of the various candidates and their campaign messages, (2) their perspective on each type of message and on the candidates, and (3) their consideration of campaign messages in deciding their vote. The study population was defined as voters who self-identified as Afro-Brazilian and lived in neighborhoods with the highest concentrations of Black residents in Salvador (Carvalho and Barreto 2007, 240). I aimed for reasonable variation among interviewees along several important demographic dimensions (gender, economic class, and education). Three subsections from each neighborhood were randomly selected. Within each subsection, voters were identified in all households, and five voters per subsection were randomly selected. The goal was to include at least fifteen voters per neighborhood, with a total of at least forty-five voters.

Semistructured and open-ended interview questions were created based on information in the campaign data set. I asked voters to identify and rank the candidates according to whom they were most likely to vote for. To collect specific information on voters' decision-making, I asked them (1) which political messages they recalled, (2) what factors influenced their voting decisions, and (3) how they used information in their decision-making. Audio- and video-recorded interviews were transcribed and qualitatively analyzed for manifestations of race orientation in each campaign's practices and for voters' interpretive perspectives.

My analysis herein builds on several approaches within linguistic anthropology in order to examine both direct and nuanced expressions of racial notions. As John Gumperz (1982) has noted when writing about ethnic style in political rhetoric, racial meaning is generated as language use simultaneously reflects on and indexes situated identities as a function of broader social, economic, and political forces. Scholarship in linguistic anthropology has yielded considerable knowledge about how race both shapes and is shaped by larger social dynamics as well as by daily communicative practices. For example, Bonnie Urciuoli (2011, E118) points out that race is hierarchically locative, discursively produced, and politically and economically structured. Race is something a person enacts in social interactions or communicative events, and language plays a crucial role in enacting race. As various scholars have shown, even discourse that is not explicitly about race can send out critical racial meanings (see, e.g., Hill 2008). Bakhtin's concept of dialogism and its related concepts—particularly double-voiced discourse, or speech with a double agenda—can shed some light on this intriguing quality of discourse about race. In Bakhtinian terms, the use of double voicing allows the speaker to engage in a discursive double duty: expressing a particular opinion while acknowledging other ideological standpoints and concerns (Bakhtin 1981).

In order to study the complex calculus of race and electoral politics in Brazil, I made comparisons between campaign input and voters' uptake, assessment, and political choices. This was the basis for identifying common interpretive perspectives and voting decisions. The goal was to elucidate shared strategies for interpreting and evaluating candidates and their campaign messages specifically. Following the framework of linguistic anthropology, I viewed Black candidates and voters as social actors and viewed race as a simultaneously real and imaginary entity whose existence is constantly being reshaped and negotiated in social interactions through myriad acts of speaking. The findings add to our knowledge of the shifting ways racial meanings figure in and mediate Afro-Brazilians' orientation to Blackness in the era of affirmative action.

The Afro-Brazilian Vote

Unlike any other event since, the 2014 election was revealing in terms of the decisions that voters made, which are still reverberating in Black activists' 2020 campaigns. The 2014 contest presented perhaps the starkest choice between two competing visions for Black electoral mobilization, and it continues to shape political messaging. In 2014, out of the sixty-three state legislators who won their elections, only two (3.17 percent) were Black. At the federal level: out of thirty-nine elected congressmen from Bahia, six (15.3 percent) were Black. None of the three elected senators was Black. Whereas Luiz Alberto, Olívia Santana, and other veteran Black movement activists whose campaigns were strongly aligned with a Black identity lost their races, both Bebeto Galvão and Sílvio Humberto, who took more universalist approaches, won. These results indicate the complexity of race in electoral politics in Salvador.

The results of the 2014 elections were certainly not good news for Black candidates as a group, as they did worse than in previous elections. They went from four to two elected state legislators, and their low level of representation persists to this day. These numbers imply that Afro-Brazilians did not support Black candidates, so beyond the numeric results it is crucial to investigate voter attitudes and behavior. How did Afro-Brazilian voters interpret Black candidates and the race orientation of their campaign messages, and what did they consider relevant in assessing candidates?

Between August and November 2014, I met and talked with voters in the three Black neighborhoods I chose to study because they had been consistent targets of race-based community organizing. During the interviews I asked about everyday problems they faced in their communities, whose job was it to solve those problems, and citizen engagement. Some of the common themes were lack of safety, poor education, long distances to public transportation, and lack of sewers. But they also talked about the accumulations of garbage and dog excrement on pathways throughout the neighborhoods:

> DAMILA Não é só a questão que ela é suja, cocô de cachorro por toda parte, que as casas não têm reboco, é uma questão que o transporte é muito longe. (It is not just the issue that it is dirty, dog poop everywhere, that the houses have no stucco, the issue is that public transportation is far away.)
>
> PEDRO O povo sofre, paga seus impostos e não tem saúde e segurança. (People suffer, pay their taxes, and lack health care and safety.)
>
> DANIEL Matando um ao outro, essas coisa, por causa de droga. (Killing each other, stuff like this, because of drugs.)

Regarding what should be done to change the situation, Ana's response was typical:

ANA Estudando nossos governante, quem ele é, a proposta dele, o que é que ele fez. (Studying our government officials, who they are, their proposal, what they accomplished.)

Some respondents spontaneously brought up government or politicians before I even asked who should address the problems:

DANIEL O prefeito deveria olhar mais pela nossa Bahia. (The mayor should look after our Bahia.)

Many expressed their commitment to the electoral process as a way to change things and their awareness of the importance of voting:

PEDRO A solução, o povo votar e tirar o político também de acordo com o trabalho dele, por exemplo, o político não faz nada e tem que sair . . . botar o político e ficar de olho. (The solution, the people should vote and remove the politician according to his work, for example, the politician who does nothing has to leave . . . elect the politician and keep an eye on him.)

ANA Vou pesquisar que quem é esse cara, o que é que ele já fez. (I research who this guy [the candidate] is, what he has done.)

Clearly the criteria are a combination of ability, talent, and personal qualities like leadership and civic-mindedness. For these voters, the race or skin color of political candidates was a secondary consideration. There was considerable diversity in Black political opinion beyond the appeal of racial issues.

As they talked about the issues that affected their communities, most respondents displayed considerable awareness of the existence of racial inequality and the importance of taking an active role to improve the situation. For instance, when directly asked about Black representation in elected office, most expressed concern about race relations and inequities, as in this example:

MARCELINO São minoria realmente. É aí que a cota ajuda ao negro a conseguir a mesma coisa que em si só o branco antigamente tinha. (They [Blacks in local offices] are the minority, really. This is where the quota helps Blacks to achieve the same thing that only White people did in the past.)

In general, respondents believed that Blacks in Brazil experience a lot of discrimination, and some anti-racist measures garner majority support among low-income Afro-Brazilians. They agreed that public policies, such as creating university scholarships for racial minorities, should be promoted to provide broader access to higher education for those in need:

MARCELINO O negro era empregado doméstico . . . hoje em dia já tá sendo bem mais fácil. Tá fazendo faculdade. (Black people used to be domestic servants . . . nowadays it's becoming a lot easier. They're going to college.)

In addition to being aware of race-related issues, most voters had considerable awareness about the work of local and national Black resistance activities. Even when they disagreed with racial politics—or what they described as people thinking about individuals, races, and social groups in Black or White terms—their comments about Black activism were permeated with the feeling that racial disparities are a serious problem that needs to be addressed. Yet they were unsure how to act systematically about such disparities and inequities:

PEDRO Então por que ter o jornal do preto? (Why there should be such a thing as a Black newspaper?)

When I asked for clarification, he related this story:

PEDRO Eu tava trabalhando na faculdade Católica. A menina tava assim lendo um jornal. Ela fazia filosofia história, um bocado de coisa. E ela tava lendo um jornal do, o jornal do negro. "Se tivesse assim o jornal do branco, aposto como você não ia gostar. Então porque ter o jornal do preto?" (I was working at the Catholic university. There was this girl reading a newspaper. She was majoring in philosophy, history, or something like that. And she was reading a newspaper, the black newspaper. [I approached her and asked,] "If there were such a thing as the white newspaper, I bet you would not like it. So why do we need a black newspaper?)

Although he did not favor a newspaper specifically for the Black community, he agreed with the need for inclusion of Blacks across society:

PEDRO Tem que botar o negro na sociedade em termo geral. (Black should be everywhere.)

When asked about Black representation in electoral politics, most interviewees had substantial familiarity with Black candidates' electoral campaigns and were able to name at least one Black candidate. Marcelino was one of the few who reported having no awareness:

MARCELINO Eu não vou mentir pra você. Eu não ando muito ligado em política. Não ando muito antenado no que se passa em termos de candidature. (I will not lie to you. I don't really care about politics. I'm not very up to date in terms of who's running.)

Pedro talked critically about his neighbors, followers of the Candomblé religion who were supporters of Olívia Santana and advocated voting along racial lines. In 2014, as well as previous elections, Santana's campaign rhetoric revolved around her identity as a Black woman. According to Pedro, she came across as a political and social radical who wanted to portray herself as a new type of candidate for whom race should be the central issue:

PEDRO Ela chamava a si mesma de "negona da Bahia" e queria que os negros como ela votassem nela porque ela era negra como eles. (She referred to herself as "a black woman of Bahia" and wanted Black people like her to vote for her because she was Black like them.)

He also reflected on Olívia's losses in previous elections:

PEDRO É isso irmão. Votou pela raça. Votou pela cor. Mas não votou pela qualidade do candidato. (That's it, brother. They voted her race. They voted for her skin color. They didn't vote for the quality of the candidate.)

Eliangela mentioned Luiz Alberto, whom she voted for in previous state and national congressional elections as "um candidato negro" (a Black candidate). I prompted to explain, and she said the following:

ELIANGELA Luiz Alberto tem projetos de educação. E eu acho que educação é a solução para nosso país. É um negro. Ele é até do Steve Biko. Foi um dos fundadores do Steve Biko.... Tem um discurso racial bom.... Não vou dizer pra você que eu ignoro. Eu acho também pros negros ainda tem muito poucas. Aliás as pesquisas tá dizendo aí né. Que os negros ainda não chegaram perto que os brancos chegam. (Luiz Alberto sponsors and promotes education projects. And I think education is the solution for our country. He is a Black man. He is even from [the] Steve Biko [Institute].[3] He was one of the founders of Steve Biko.... his position and the way he frames racial politics is effective.... I will not tell you that I ignore it [racial discourse]. I also think that there are still very few Black people [who understand the significance of racial discourse]. In fact, research is saying that, right? That Black people have not yet come close to White people.

For Eliangela, Alberto seemed to care for everyone, not just for Blacks; he was not one of those politicians who practiced identity politics, people who wanted to look out only for their own.

Damila spoke about her admiration for Sílvio Humberto's active involvement in the Bahian Black movement. She also described herself as a product of his organizing efforts and spoke of the importance of the racial vote:

DAMILA Ele foi responsável por muitas conquistas pra gente.... Sou fruto, entendeu? Porque como eu sou nova.... Eu fico aqui recebendo só os frutos dessa luta.... O problema no negro também não é só econômico.... Ele vai chegar lá e ainda vai ter que pegar o elevador e o cara vai olhar pra ele e dizer, "Por que você não está no elevador de serviço?" ... Então acho que o problema do voto. De votar na questão racial. Por isso que eu gosto de Sílvio. (He was responsible for a lot of achievements for us.... I'm a product, understand? Because, as I'm young.... I'm only collecting the fruits of this struggle.... The problem for Black people is not only economic. He will get there, and when he takes the elevator [the other rider] will look at him and say, "Why aren't you in the service elevator?" ... So I think that is the problem of voting. To vote on the racial issue. That's why I like Sílvio.

As respondents spoke at length about Black candidates, I began to ponder the low Black representation in local and national politics. I told them there was a widespread pattern among Afro-Brazilian voters of not voting in bloc for Black candidates, unlike what happens in the United States. In their reactions and discussions about race, they sounded fundamentally liberal—even those with strong ties to the Black movement—but the sentiment was not monolithic. In other words, there were various responses.

PEDRO Tem que votar na qualidade do candidato. A gente não pode julgar pela raça cor ou o que for nada. Eu voto assim, na condição do trabalho dele. Pode ser branco negro. Pode ser o que for. (You have to vote for the candidate. We can't judge solely by race, color or anything. I vote like that, based on his work his accomplishments. He may be Black, White. He can be anything.)

MARCELINO O que eles tão fazendo de melhoria para as pessoas. Mas se dependesse de mim. O meu voto poderia ser de um deles. ([You have to see] what they are doing to improve people's lives. But if it were up to me, my vote could be for one of them [Black people].)

DAMILA Meu voto é também racial. Mas não é só o racial. (My vote is also based on race. With that said, it's not solely racial.)

The prevailing attitude in the Brazilian electoral arena of being unwilling or disinclined to consider race in political decision-making was clearly evident in the interviewees' voting preferences. When asked about their personal political choices, enduring resistance to racial voting was evident. Previous quantitative data from political scientists suggest that when faced with too many options to pick from, Afro-Brazilian voters took a "racial identity shortcut," relying on racial identities more and political identities less (Aguilar et al. 2015). Simply put, voters chose candidates who were like them racially. The broader point is that racial identity's impact on behavior increased as voting became more complex and burdensome for citizens (Aguilar et al. 2015, 181). My ethnographic data shed light on an intriguing paradox. Even voters like Damila with close ties to the Black movement and Black activist candidates were lukewarm about the concept of voting along racial lines. This attitude reflects the persistence of Brazil's popular and wide-ranging ideology of race: Afro-Brazilian voters acknowledged racial inequality but committed to liberal ideals as the solution based on beliefs that assimilation and integration are good for society. Similarly, interviewees were inspired by the meritocratic ideal, committed to choosing candidates on the basis of their abilities rather than promotion of equal rights.

Daniel and Jandira (who did not know each other) were two voters of this type. Both were high school graduates in their late twenties, and both self-identified as Black. Daniel was stocking shelves at a local supermarket, and Jandira was looking for a job as an office assistant. I asked their opinions about the absence of Black Brazilians in politics, and Daniel was the first to answer:

> DANIEL É com certeza. Pra mim é porque [os brancos] são os que mais tiveram oportunidade na vida. É muito difícil o senhor ver um negro na faculdade, de 30 pessoas você vai ver um ou dois negros, então é muito difícil ver até na política, um escritório, um advogado, entendeu? (I see the point. To me, the reason is that they [White people] were the ones who had more opportunities in life. We rarely see a Black person in college, out of thirty people, you see one or two Blacks, the same in politics, office jobs, lawyers, you know?)

I asked them if they took this into consideration when deciding whom to vote for, and received the following responses:

> DANIEL Não, eu não; esse negócio de cores de pessoas assim, raças, eu não ligo não. Pra mim é, pra mim é tudo a mesma coisa, todo mundo é ser humano. (No, I don't; this thing of races I don't care about. To me, to me they are all the same, they're all human beings.)
>
> JANDIRA Eu acho que é falta de oportunidade para os negros, ou eles não têm estudos suficientes . . . então é sempre essa desigualdade, porque quando a gente ver uma pessoa, um conhecido nosso e sabe da capacidade dela e tal . . . e vê que essa pessoa negra é um candidato e tal, eles mesmos, nós negros mesmos, dizemos, "Ah que nada, isso aí não vai pra lugar nenhum, que esse negro aí, coitado, não vai pra lugar nenhum." (I think it is about lack of opportunities for Blacks. Either they don't have adequate formal education . . . it is always a matter of inequality, because when we see a person, someone we know is prepared, and all that, and we see this Black person is a candidate, and all that, and Black people themselves, we Black people, say, "No way, that one isn't going to go anywhere, that poor Black isn't going anywhere [so why would I throw my vote away?]")
>
> ANTONIO Quais são as coisas que contam pra você na hora de você escolher, gênero, religião, raça? (What counts when you make your choice: gender, religion, race?)
>
> JANDIRA Essas questões pra mim são irrelevantes, de cor, de sexo, pra mim são irrelevantes, eu procuro mesmo é ver a postura dele, o que é que ele já fez

em prol da sociedade. Eu já vi muito homens falar, "ah, eu não voto em mulher!" Eu não tenho essa questão, acho que o que vale é a inteligência e a intenção da pessoa . . . não é a raça que vai fazer diferença, é o conhecimento, a experiência que já tem e a vontade de fazer alguma coisa. (These things are irrelevant, color, sex, to me, are irrelevant, what I pay attention to is his attitude, what he has done for society . . . what counts is how smart the person is, her intentions . . . race won't influence my vote, but knowledge and experience, and the willingness to do something for the Black population will.)

In sum, respondents were caught between a logic of integration into the arena of institutional politics and a logic of contestation. Daniel and Jandira were hardly alone in their views on race in politics. Afro-Brazilians recognized the racial gap, and many suggested that racism was the real reason for disparities in education, income, and the like in Brazil. They were also aware of the benefits that racial equality could provide to them as individuals and to their communities. However, most believed that committing to a race identity vote would be racist. The majority of my Afro-Brazilians respondents boldly argued that race-based voting was not the most effective strategy to achieve racial justice. Similarly, Gladys Mitchell-Walthour (2018, 214) has examined the effects of awareness of discrimination and exclusion on Afro-Brazilians' stance toward race-conscious redistributive policies, finding that perception of discrimination increased support for the politicization of group identity. Their rejection of voting along racial and color lines reflects Afro-Brazilians' struggles with the competing discourses of race and racism in Brazil today. On the one hand, they are influenced by remnants of the ideology of a racial democracy based on liberal values, such as individual freedom and equality of opportunity; on the other hand, they are aware of efforts to inform and educate people about the existence of widespread institutional racism, which have mobilized public opinion toward redressing racial discrimination through institutional recognition. Caught between the two positions, voters in my study came down on the side of liberal solutions to racial inequality.

Campaigning for the Afro-Brazilian Vote

"This coming election for mayor of Salvador is pivotal," notes journalist Zulu Araújo in an article for *Revista raça* about the 2020 mayoral election in

Salvador. Araújo envisions a spirited racial discourse occurring in the local political campaign, comparable to the heightened ideological battle between left and right in Bolsonaro's election: "In addition to the tough ideological struggle that lies ahead, between the Right and the Left, driven by local and national Bolsonarists . . . , there will also be a strong racial discourse" (Araújo 2020, my translation). He emphasizes the fact that Salvador, the Blackest city outside the African continent, had never elected a Black mayor in its long history. Araújo expresses concern that Brazilian society's historical conservatism is breeding negative attitudes among voters to Black candidates' racial appeals: "Centuries-old conservatism emanates a sharp and to some extent already planned discourse that what matters are ideas and proposals and not skin color" (Araújo 2020, my translation). Alluding to Brazil's nationalist narrative that racial blending has made race irrelevant, Araújo argues for a reevaluation of race and a recognition of the country's ethnoracial differences. In a very interesting twist, he argues that the existence of White privilege is evident in the elections of White candidates who lacked merit: "It is as if the candidacies of contenders such as Bruno Reis (Democrats), Léo Prates (Democrats), and Guilherme Bellintani (unaffiliated) that are placed on the succession board for 2020, across the political spectrum, inherently enjoyed racial privilege and, for that reason, do not need to present programs and proposals" (Araújo 2020, my translation).

Araújo's point is that people should recognize that race always matters, and they should stop using the conservative argument that it does not when Black candidates deploy race to court Afro-Brazilian voters. He cites examples from past campaigns in which Black candidates like Olívia Santana and Sílvio Humberto were accused of reverse racism and of inciting racial conflict whenever they used race to appeal to Afro-Brazilian voters. Yet Black candidates in Salvador indisputably remain deeply aware of racial exclusion and equally determined to address Black underrepresentation in elected office. Thus, it is not a matter of *if* but of *how* they should address racial exclusion in their campaigns. In what follows I examine how some Black candidates used race in their political communications.

The stigmatization and exclusion of Black Brazilians have been targets of Afro-Brazilian activism in various sectors of society. Still, few Blacks run for and win political office, but Black activists are increasingly aiming to change that dynamic. Araújo quotes Vovô do Ilê, founder of the famous Carnaval group Ilê Ayê, talking about the political debate over Blacks in electoral politics that has taken place within the Afro-Brazilian communities: "In 2006, at the Black Beauty Night promoted by Ilê Aiyê, at the end of the event, I said: I want this! A Black face as mayor of Salvador. . . . On July 2, we took to the street with all our strength, demanding what I asked for in 2006, a Black face in the city hall of Salvador" (Araújo 2020, my translation).

For almost three decades, Black activists have been attempting to bring identity-based voting into the political discussion. In a way, multiculturalism became one of the leading emblems of electoral politics among Black activists seeking elective office. In 2014 Luiz Alberto's claim that "Bahia is Black" and entreating "Vote against Racism," and Olívia Santana's using ingroup terminology (*negona*) to tout herself as "a Black woman of the city" were clearly dominated by a cultural politics of difference. Both lost their elections that year. In contrast, Black activist candidates since then have sought to speak only indirectly on the political relevance of identity-driven differences. To accomplish this, they have embraced more citizenship-based, egalitarian claims by adding a new layer of ideological imbrication to their voice (double voicing). Aiming for redistributive measures to create equality, they downplay appeals to distinct cultural identities. In contrast with the earlier political messages of Alberto and Santana, the hallmark of Sílvio Humberto's campaign was equality in education: "Education, equality, and respect. A life commitment." Humberto avoided an explicit appeal to a specific racial identity, instead rallying voters behind a narrative of education and moral progress for all. Even in his choice of the word "respect," one hears the deep intertwining of the language of equality with the language of egalitarian citizenship.

Multiculturalism is not an outdated notion in Brazil, as multicultural approaches to social activism are still widespread throughout the country. But Black candidates are becoming less concerned with grounding their campaigns in a politics of difference than with promoting difference-neutral equal rights. Clearly this signals a shift toward recasting the politics of Blackness in dialogic terms that appeal to a much wider Afro-Brazilian constituency.

Prior to his first political campaign, Humberto was involved in three Black NGOs in Salvador. Since 1992 he has been at or near the center of the Black movement in Salvador. During informal conversations, I once asked him his thoughts about what Black consciousness entailed. He answered, "Adquirir consciência racial é aprender uma nova maneira de ouvir, sentir, ver, ler, reagir e questionar o mundo racista em que vivemos."

(To gain race consciousness is to learn a new way of hearing, feeling, seeing, reading, reacting to, and questioning the racist world we live in.) This led to a question about the Black movement's goals, to which he asserted,

> No passado, grande parte da luta política foi travada para tornar a questão racial visível. Conseguimos traduzir nossas agendas em políticas públicas. Temos várias leis e políticas de ação afirmativa em vigor. Agora, o escopo do movimento negro deve ser estendido para abranger não apenas a política cultural, ou a luta por subjetividade e identidade, mas também a luta por espaços de poder dentro do governo e da política. Só podemos conseguir isso vencendo as eleições para um cargo público.

> In the past, much of the political struggle was waged to make the racial issue visible. We succeeded in translating our agendas into public policy. We have several affirmative action laws and policies in place. Now the scope of the Black movement must be extended to encompass not just cultural politics, or the struggle over subjectivity and identity, but also the fight for spaces of power within government and politics. We can only accomplish this by winning elections to public office.

Humberto recognized a world of urgent discourse beyond cultural politics that could be used to change the dominant cultural conceptions of race, gender, and other individual differences. His first foray into politics came in 2012 when he ran for and won a seat on Salvador's city council. I began to follow his campaign in 2012, before I began my fieldwork, due to a deep interest in exploring race in electoral politics. Humberto's 2012 campaign was a success: well organized and appealing, full of political and policy promises. His speeches were always confident and centered, delivering fiery defenses of social justice. It also became clear early on that he did not engage with the politics of identity and culture; instead, his overarching message was premised on a clear vision of citizenship-based equality. Promoting education for all, Humberto's message targeted the institution that all Brazilians most value and trust.

In the 2014 elections, Humberto, then in office, endorsed Bebeto Galvão's campaign for federal deputy. Galvão had a background in labor union organizing, which he consistently highlighted, and he portrayed his campaign as a defense of workers' rights. Throughout his campaign, Galvão never made any substantial sort of multicultural appeal, even when speaking to mostly

Black crowds. When Humberto appeared at one of Galvão's rallies to endorse him, the endorsement message focused on Galvão's background in the labor union movement. Humberto presented Galvão as a Black "ally" rather than a Black movement insider, portraying him as an external resource who would benefit multiple constituencies. In his endorsement, Humberto did, of course, speak of racism and the importance of anti-racism, stating that Galvão was committed to anti-racism, but he couched his support in reference to Galvão's commitment to the construction of a nation that is equal, democratic, and without discrimination. It appeared that Humberto was avoiding framing rights struggles as dependent on the recognition of distinct group identities. In order to support Galvão, Humberto had to withdraw his support from Luiz Alberto, a longtime Black activist who was seeking reelection to the same seat Galvão was vying for. As has been noted, Alberto's campaigns had always had strong multicultural appeal. During his speech Humberto mentioned that he still supported Alberto's candidacy but chose to endorse Galvão based on his belief that Brazilian Blacks needed to forge a new path to social justice more broadly and to representation in government more specifically. Galvão acknowledged the support of Black activists like Humberto and expressed concern for the welfare of the Black population. Without talking directly on the topic of race, he adjusted the way he spoke to take into account others' views and concerns. In their separate speeches during the rally, both Humberto and Galvão offered telling snippets of their thoughts and rhetoric around race in electoral politics. Their messages conveyed concern about racial inequality without foregrounding the politics of culture or Black identity.

Olívia Santana made several bids for election in 2016 (for mayor, which she lost), in 2018 (for state deputy, which she won), and 2020 (for mayor, which she lost, while serving her term as a state deputy). In her 2018 campaign for state deputy, after consecutive failed election attempts, she inserted double voicing in her messages, expanding her focus on Black voters toward a broader coalition of Black, Indigenous, and White voters. In a 2018 campaign video posted on Facebook, Santana first appeared surrounded by Black women, but then tailored her message to all women: "Mulheres negras, mulheres não negras, mulheres brancas, mulheres indígenas . . . as mulheres sofrem situações muito próprias da condição de mulher." (Black women, non-Black women, White women, Indigenous women . . . women suffer as a result of situations very specific to the condition of womanhood.) Toward the end of the Facebook video, two White women asked voters to support Santana due to her experience and long history of work for the people of Salvador (O. Santana 2018). Santana seemed to be attempting to balance an embrace of Black life and its challenges with a recognition of the need to dialogize the discourse of Blackness. During her 2020 campaign Santana's message shift toward attracting a broader coalition of voters became clearer, with an additional focus on disparities between affluent residents and the marginalized, low-income majority who lacked access to city resources. Her campaign jingle was designed to appeal to the working class (Bochicchio 2020). Campaign jingles were sung by well-known local singers and sometimes became hits, or even "classics," and were replayed in several election cycles. Olivia's 2020 jingle included the lines

> Salvador é uma só
> Pra trabalhar, para construir
> Pra trabalhar sem excluir
> Olívia vem aê.

> Salvador is only one
> To work, to build
> To work without excluding anyone
> Olívia will win.

The reference to "construir" (build) conveys the idea that the city is good only for those who live in wealthy neighborhoods. Here she alluded to the previous administration, which invested disproportionally in the revitalization of wealthy areas at the expense of development in historically marginalized areas, or *comunidades* (literally, communities, but an in-group term for favelas).

Brazilian Black activists running for political office seem to be engaging in a broad and expansive strategic realignment in how they address race in their political communication. This shift is happening, I suggest, because they have sensed that Afro-Brazilian voters are reluctant to engage in identity politics—that is, Black identity alone is not their most important consideration in choosing a candidate does not seem to be relevant to candidate choice. In response, candidates are decentering issues of identity recognition and re-centering rights-based approaches to realizing broader racial equality. As in other areas of the Black struggle in Brazil, we are witnessing a change from a time when discourses of Black identity were central to anti-racist mobilization to one where more nuanced conversations about anti-racism and Blackness are foregrounded.

The larger question here is, What does this realignment imply about Afro-Brazilians' relationship with Blackness? Afro-Brazilians' awareness of racial injustice and the liberal common sense with which it is entangled cannot be dismissed as distortions resulting from a century of the ideology of racial mixture and racial harmony. Nor should we write and talk about Afro-Brazilians and their political perspectives through a single simple frame. Between Brown and Black, Afro-Brazilians display considerable diversity in their political opinion. They are often inclined to downplay the racial vote. And on questions of racial identity in electoral politics, many Afro-Brazilians, both Brown and Black, tend to disaggregate the terms and the order of racial politics by avoiding "branding or messaging" as Black, Brown, or White and focusing instead on issues of inequality and rights more broadly.[4] In other words, the discourse of universal rights is being broadened to reach Afro-Brazilians, who are the most vulnerable constituents.

And Black activists running for office in Salvador are rediscovering that in the range from Brown to Black there might be no such thing as a mono-logic discourse of Blackness that attracts all Afro-Brazilian voters. As they contemplate the changes underway, Black candidates are realizing that, if they truly want to represent Afro-Brazilians, they must listen to the multi-vocality Afro-Brazilian voters use to speak about the things they care about. The shift to a broader discourse of rights that reaches more constituents in Salvador is a sign that candidates are listening, and this fact has had political and electoral implications.

Conclusion

Afro-Brazilians' Black and Brown Anti-racism

This conclusion by no means finally settles the dialogue about Afro-Brazilians' relationship with Blackness, which every day presents new specificities and complexities to be explored. I am also reminded that anti-racism is constantly evolving, as are race and racism. As I started to write this chapter, a friend sent me a photo from the wrapping of a chocolate bar that he had received as a Christmas gift. The label on wrapper in the photograph that my friend sent to me looked exactly like the label in the image I include here, which I obtained directly from the chocolate company (see figure C.1). The label reads "Do Lado de Dentro Só Tem Amor" (Inside There Is Only Love). This brand of chocolate is made in Bahia. The image in the center of the wrapper shows a same-sex couple embracing: a fair-skinned man is hugging his dark-skinned partner from behind, they are looking at each other, and both are wearing Santa Claus hats. In the background we can see a Christmas tree, and Christmas lights hang in the window that frames the couple. This was my favorite image of the Christmas season—one that perfectly depicted not only our current time (gay love) but also, and more significantly, our long-standing ideology of racial harmony

FIG. C.1 "Do Lado de Dentro Só Tem Amor" (Inside There Is Only Love). (Courtesy of Natucoa.)

updated to current times, with a gay couple and "Inside There Is Only Love." Inside the package is the chocolate that everyone loves; inside the widow, a same-sex, biracial couple in love. One of my motivations in writing this book was to contribute to a deeper understanding of some of the issues and tensions surrounding Brazil's discourse of racial integration, a key theme in this imagery.

The age-old adage "A picture is worth a thousand words" is only partly true with regard to the image on this Natucoa candy bar wrapper. Widespread cohabitation of Black, Brown, and White people is indeed a reality in Brazil, but the fact remains that structural violence against Black Brazilians casts dark shadows on the country's dubious claim of not being a racist society. Brazilian racial democracy remains an unrealized ideal at best. As

Christen Smith writes about the city of Salvador, and Brazil more broadly, Black Brazilians "confront visible and invisible human walls in their everyday attempts to access resources and dignity in the city, and these walls are often subtle, elusive, and guileful" (Smith 2016, 79; see also Bairros 2008, 5n1). All of this has fomented discussion on the benefits, and especially the costs, of policies to counter racial discrimination and racial exclusion in Brazil. At the heart of these discussions reside different questions: How do Afro-Brazilians begin to self-identify as Black to articulate opposition, resistance, and rights claims in the context of contemporary legal and political changes in the country? How do Afro-Brazilians' Black identities work strategically as driving forces in the rights struggles in Brazil, a country that has long denigrated Blackness while celebrating racial mixture? How are essentialisms embedded within these movements magnified and refracted through various governmental and commercial institutions? And how does racial politics help to interpret in new ways the entrenched notions of race and Blackness? While there are field-specific differences in how scholars approach these questions, their research provides much-needed historical background and exposes the political and social structures underpinning identity-related claims. In particular they show how, over the last three decades, Brazilian Black movements have changed racial politics in Brazil, challenging the myth of "racial democracy."

I have covered a lot of ground to illustrate analytically various facets of the Brazilian Black movements that have shifted the ways in which Afro-Brazilians connect to Blackness. I have observed several nongovernmental organizations whose mission is socializing Afro-Brazilians into anti-racism. A key part of that effort is challenging them to embrace and organize around being Black. I have also worked with policy makers and anti-racism activists more directly involved with the implementation of redistributive and reparatory measures, such as racial quotas in higher education and public service. Because racism in Brazil harms dark-skinned people the most, these policy makers and activists are determined to do justice to Afro-Brazilians whose phenotype (especially dark skin) makes them targets for anti-Black racism. Their main goal is to make sure Afro-Brazilians benefiting from the racial quotas are legitimate recipients. I have also addressed the complex calculus of race and electoral politics in Salvador, particularly the ways in which Black activists running for office tailor their political communication to take into account that, for Afro-Brazilians, Blackness is not "one size fits all." Bridging Black mobilization and the everyday lives of Afro-Brazilians,

Black candidates' political campaigns further highlight both the limits of race in electoral politics and the dialogic possibilities of anti-racist activism among Afro-Brazilians.

The latest elections, in the year 2020, brought some good news. They diversified the country's leadership as a record number of Black Brazilians running for elected office claimed victory. From Curitiba's first Black councilwoman, Carol Dartora (elected with 8,874 votes, the candidate with the third highest number of votes in the capital of the state of Paraná) to Eliana de Jesus, age fifty-two, the first Black woman to serve as mayor of Cachoeira in the state of Bahia, the cradle of Black resistance in Brazil. The 2020 elections nationwide were marked by a legendary debate that laid down questions of race, justice, and history in Brazilian electoral politics. There were clearly important signs of change. But just as important as those signs of change is a larger reality. It did not take long for overt anti-Black racism to show itself in more insidious ways in Brazilian electoral politics. As I was in the later stages of writing this book, I noticed a rising tidal wave of racist attacks on Black public officials nationwide (with Black politicians and their families receiving death threats and violently worded texts) from those wanting to impose their exclusionary political projects at time when Black people hope to change democratic participation in Brazil. And evidence was everywhere. This conclusion's moment coincides with the news of threats to Eliana de Jesus, which started during her campaign and continue to this day.

Well known for her labor union activism and defense of distributive justice activism, particularly in terms of land reform, Eliana de Jesus was elected mayor of Cachoeira in 2020 with 55.94 percent of the votes against Fernando Pereira (aka Tato). Tato is a forty-nine-year-old light-skinned Afro-Brazilian who identifies as *pardo* (Brown, or mixed race); in Bahia his light skin would make him a *pardo-branco*, or socially White. He is from a political family in Cachoeira whose members have been heavily involved in the electoral arena for over twenty years. If he had won reelection as mayor of Cachoeira, Tato would expand his political reach in the region. Tato had not anticipated, however, that his ascent to power would be challenged by Eliana de Jesus, who noted that the violence against her originated during the campaign and intensified after the results, with some messages asking for her resignation in order to bring an end to the threats (Alma Preta 2021). Her private residence has been targeted by harassment online and by phone; social media were flooded with protests, with people calling for justice and highlighting connections between the threats and racism and misogyny. This forced Eliana de Jesus to move out of her home in Cachoeira for fear of attacks against her and her family. The case sparked outrage among Black movement leaders, who demanded measures against the perpetrators; in a letter signed by several national and local Black organizations, they expressed their concerns about the threating remarks the new mayor was receiving daily, and specifically denounced the racist and sexist nature of those remarks. They also connected the problem in Cachoeira to the political killing of Black women more generally, including the assassination of Marielle Franco in 2018, and feared that it could become part of Brazilian daily life (Silva and Larkins 2019). Another example was that of Talíria Petrone, a thirty-five-year-old Black woman whose close association with Franco and her 2020 election to the National Congress to represent the state of Rio de Janeiro gave rise to threats to her safety. When asked in an interview if she though that the threats she had been subjected to, and what happened to Franco, could prevent other women (and especially Black women), from entering politics, Petrone answered, "I do not have any doubt. The level of political violence that the bodies of women, especially Black women, experience when they occupy politics is very high" (quoted in Batista 2020, my translation). Thus, the threats to Eliana de Jesus, Marielle Franco, Talíria Petrone, and others are interlocked, whether the majority of Brazilians are willing to admit it or not. Targeting Black public officials exposes the shortcomings of Brazil's widely held racial exceptionalism. The violence against Black politicians in Brazil is part of an organized reaction of conservative forces working to defend privileges while suppressing mobilizations for social justice in the form of anti-racism, feminism, and the like. Incidents of anti-Black violence are clearly attempts to destroy the power of projects for progressive change and to stop marginalized communities, especially Black women, from entering spaces of power.

Understanding how Afro-Brazilians situate Blackness within these peculiar dynamics is crucial for understanding Afro-Brazilian anti-racism itself. In his studies of the new social movements, Richard Day (2004, 2005) distinguishes what he refers to as the politics of the act from the politics of demand. In the politics of demand (recognition and integration) framework, which Day argues has dominated new social movement theory, struggles for recognition of rights from a hegemonic state that regulates those rights are directly linked to the notion of a collective identity. For instance, applying the politics of demands framework to Brazil's Black land rights movement is contingent on separating the groups who are demanding land rights from one another based on shared identities. The goal of these struggles is to have the state apparatus respond to demands of particular segments of the population by granting them rights and, ultimately, letting them participate in the current hegemonic order provided that they fulfill identity requirements. As I have discussed in this book, and as Day also points out, Mikhail Bakhtin's notion of the dialogized self has unsettled this notion of identity as unitary and all-knowing. A dialogized self presupposes a "plurality of consciousnesses" of equal value, a plurality of "independent and unmerged voices," each inhabiting their world of experiences, (Bakhtin, 1984, 4–5). By contrast, Day's second framework, the politics of the act, acknowledges the impossibility of perceiving a tightly bounded identity. The politics of the act framework recognizes the diversity inherent to the self (and to consciousness). Yet, as Day notes, "The impossibility of a purely universal identity does not relieve us from the necessity of attempting to be in solidarity with others—note that I say solidarity, not identity. Solidarity occurs *across* identifications, which means that without a multiplicity of subject positions there can only be identity of struggles, at which point the concept of solidarity becomes meaningless" (2005, 90).

In the politics of the act framework, activists and theorists alike seek to create alternative forms of autonomous identity and solidarity to contest the structures of domination. The politics of the act framework thus allows us to understand Afro-Brazilian racial consciousness as not necessarily contingent on a Black identity in and of itself. More fundamentally, Afro-Brazilians share knowledge about racism and the ability to critically reflect on where they are situated within it, ultimately allowing them to engage in anti-racist action. Affiliation with the Black cause is not determined by people's individual position within Brazil's racial identification and categorization system but by their engaging in what Day calls "affinity-based action."

Where my book differs from other scholarship of Brazil's framework of race is that it focuses on Afro-Brazilians' engagement with language to create a new anti-racist discourse that challenges long-standing racial ideologies. The specificities and complexities of Afro-Brazilians' relationship with Blackness can be observed with clarity at the level of language, which serves as both a vehicle for anti-racist socialization and a primary means of foregrounding and interpreting the meanings of Blackness in Brazil today. Bakhtin's work on voice and dialogism helps us to understand how Black activists represent and contest, project and embrace, different articulations of Blackness that are intricately woven in their own words and the words of others. Linguistic anthropologists' definition of "voice" as the linguistic embodiment of points of view, subject positions, and consciousness enables a deep analysis of Afro-Brazilians' use of language (in, for example, instances of speech habits, lexical choices, and speech reporting). Careful consideration of Bakhtin's notion of polyphony reveals how Afro-Brazilians use language to navigate multiple voices that are weighted with competing ideologies about race and racism—and, ultimately, how their commitment to being anti-racist manifests in their language choices.

The concept of "voice" is another powerful tool to seek clarity or offer a fresh perspective on Afro-Brazilians' relationship to Blackness. Language around race and racism has become a site of struggle in which voices—which may be juxtaposed even within a single word spoken by a single speaker—compete with one another to project a point of view on Blackness. In multiple individual and collective attempts, Afro-Brazilians stage "voices" that range from perpetuating the dominant system of racial identification and categorization to challenging those established frameworks. In their individual and collective processes of challenging Brazil's racialized power structure, Afro-Brazilians negotiate Blackness as an anti-racist voice within miscegenated national narratives of assimilation. As they develop active consciousness about race and racism and realize they can play a role in ending it, Afro-Brazilians challenge their internalized racism and join other Afro-Brazilians in confronting racial inequities in Brazil.

This book continues where other scholars have left off, paying substantive attention to the emergence of anti-racist knowledge in Afro-Brazilian grassroots politics. Afro-Brazilians have engaged in interactive processes of socialization, learning to understand, identify, and address racism through interactions with more knowledgeable community activists and with each other. Moving the analytical focus of Black activists' linguistic strategies beyond an identification of the various voices (of family, friends, teachers, the media, and society at large) woven into their speech to an exploration of how they socialize one another into actively scrutinizing the ideological and practical significance of the fusion of voices in their own and others' speech adds a new dimension to the study of dialogism. Via growing awareness of the ways in which racism structures Brazilian society, Afro-Brazilians have increasingly engaged in grassroots politics against the racial discrimination and racial exclusion of Black Brazilians.

After delving into how Afro-Brazilians acquire critical race consciousness and how their views on race shape and are shaped by it, I set out to explore the dialogic nature of their self-identification as *negro*. Reworking current approaches to Afro-Brazilian racial consciousness in contemporary community organizing is a fruitful avenue for exploring the interplay of voice, dialogism, and participant roles in anti-racist activists' work to articulate Afro-Brazilians' understandings of themselves and Brazilian society without reducing racial consciousness to an identification as Black. Additionally, Afro-Brazilians do not demonstrate their own version of anti-racist consciousness through the construction of a Black identity as such but instead forge that consciousness through linguistic strategies that foreground each individual's ability to critically evaluate Brazil's dominant racial ideologies. Afro-Brazilian anti-racist consciousness is characterized by the capacity to articulate Brazil's competing racial ideologies and set them in opposition to one another in order to nurture a new, *anti-racist*, way of thinking about race relations. Through creative uses of voice, Afro-Brazilians are able not only to articulate the multiple contemporary discourses about race and racism but also—armed with the language of anti-racism—to separate anti-racist consciousness from Black identification. Decoupling anti-racist consciousness from self-identification as Black has allowed them to critically engage with Brazil's dominant racial ideologies to promote a new anti-racist way of thinking about race and racism and to project their own individual relationships with Blackness.

Further, dialogical analysis of Afro-Brazilians' anti-racist language practices in the context of their ethnographic situation enables identification of the words and actions by which they reclaim their histories, influence policy, and compete in the electoral arena. Their adoption of voice, polyphony, and dialogism in communicative practices is part of a larger political project concerning racism in Brazilian society. As Sílvio Humberto, one of the leading Black activists in Brazil today, points out, "When you do not know how racism works, it affects you without your being aware of it. When you are conscious of it, it wants to be dialogued with 24/7" (personal communication, February 28, 2010). Humberto's evocative words—particularly about racism being perceived as an embodied position with which Blacks can dialogue—gives insight into Brazilian Black activists' current attempts to maintain a certain distance from racism. In their anti-racist discourses they make racism a "voice" (in Bakhtin's sense) to which they can respond in ongoing negotiations with and interrogations of Brazil's dominant racial ideologies. Caught between Brown and Black, Afro-Brazilians face unique questions regarding their role in changing the way Black Brazilians are treated on the one hand versus their rights under affirmative action on the other.

The chapters in this book are sequenced to move step-by-step through different facets of Afro-Brazilian anti-racist activism. I begin in Salvador with three Black activist organizations that educated Afro-Brazilians on Black consciousness and citizenship, including a teacher preparation course on African and Afro-Brazilian history and culture. My early research, presented in chapters 2 and 3, examines how Black activists creatively challenge the entrenched belief that race and color do not matter in Brazil. Inspired by Bakhtin's work on voice and dialogism, I closely attend to how Afro-Brazilians' discourse strategies function as claims to and displays of anti-racist consciousness. Participants in Black organizations frame anti-racist consciousness as intersubjective and dialogic—embodied in the interplay of words between self and others—and therefore as distinct from "identity politics" as we know it. Of primary importance is an analysis of how anti-racism is taught and learned in Afro-Brazilians' quest for social justice. They devote considerable time to sharing new ideas, challenging their peers to think about the construction of racial identities in new ways and identifying ways to apply the newly learned content and consciousness-raising strategies back in their communities. In my fieldwork, it was very common to see instructors and more experienced learners socializing other students in skills and knowledge that would inform their activism. Their activity made clear the changes in their positions relative to Brazil's competing racial ideologies as they juxtaposed historical ideas about racial mixture, particularly Brazil's racial exceptionalism, with the discourse of new anti-racist struggles. This dialogic approach to race consciousness reveals an untold story of anti-racism among Afro-Brazilians.

At this point I began to reflect on how policies influenced Afro-Brazilians' struggles for racial justice on different levels. New policies create ideological contradictions on the community and individual levels. In chapter 3, I bring together memory studies and critical race theory to illustrate Black activists' efforts to dispute misconceptions about Black people and Blackness that are present in the dominant narrative of Brazilian society. These activists are accomplishing something of broad social significance: an agentive revision of the history and collective memory of race relations and Blackness in Brazil.

Chapter 4 deepens the understanding of anti-racist consciousness among Afro-Brazilians by departing from an identity-based analysis of racial politics. In examining interviewees' stories of how they became involved in struggles against racism, it is striking that, in some cases, self-identification as Black emerges as intricately tied to their evolving awareness of their racial position in Brazilian society, but in other cases, self-identification as Black occurred in childhood, long before they gained racial consciousness and embraced anti-racism. Most significant are the cases of Afro-Brazilians who identify as Brown and whose engagement with anti-racism largely transcends their identification in terms of skin color. "I don't consider myself Black," Ricardo said; "when they see me ... they don't see my skin color as black. They always see me as yellow, brown, dirt colored, but not as black. ... I'm Black, but people think that only those who have dark skin are Black. No, to be—as Steve Biko said, "To be Black is not a matter of pigmentation but a result of a mental attitude." Ricardo's choice not to self-identify as *preto* reflects how he perceives his position in the Brazilian racial classification scheme. For Afro-Brazilians, embracing Black struggles does not require or even privilege a Black identity. Rather, it crosses racial identities to become an ideological critique of the dominant ideas about race and racism in Brazil.

Chapter 5 centers on the dynamics of redistributive and reparatory measures to offset racial stratification that have powered Afro-Brazilians' quest for racial equity in the past decade. Unequal social and economic status in Brazil is mainly a function of how others perceive an individual's physical features—especially skin color. The people viewed as *negro* or *preto* are those whose skin color, hair texture, and facial features indicate "pure" African ancestry. Darker-skinned Brazilians with visibly African features are most adversely affected by anti-Black racism. The race verification committees were established to counter fraudulent attempts by light-skinned Brazilians of African descent to further their careers through the quota system. Both government officials and Black movement activists have been influential in the implementation of these committees to inspect affirmative action applicants, and a diverse panel is empowered to decide which candidates are "Black enough" to merit reparation through the quota system. Redistributive and reparatory measures intertwine with and interweave through the Brazilian discourse of race and identity and have caused a fundamental change in what it means to be Black in Brazil.

Chapter 6 explores how Afro-Brazilians living in areas of Salvador that were consistently targeted for anti-racist outreach respond to the use of race as an electoral strategy. Black candidates' approach to campaigning has always been to avoid race-specific messages and to frame political agendas as aimed at helping *all* Brazilians. Given the deeply entrenched racism and ideology of miscegenation in Brazil, how successful are racial messages—like "A Bahia é negra. Vote contra o Racismo" (Bahia is Black. Vote against racism)—in bolstering Black candidates' campaigns? How is the new racial climate affecting politics from campaign strategies to voter patterns? The answers lie in the verbal and nonverbal messages Black candidates use to articulate the issues that affect their constituents and market themselves to voters. On the other side, voters deploy interpretive perspectives to make sense of and decide how receptive they are to candidates' messages in deciding how to cast their vote. Afro-Brazilians do not vote along racial lines. Black candidates in Salvador who define their campaigns based on race encounter obstacles in the intersection between a liberal form of citizenship and racial politics. A prominent factor in the complexity of political campaigning seems to be that voters struggle to reconcile what they understand to be conflicting viewpoints—namely, Brazil's dominant ideology of race mixing, the obligations of liberal citizenship (to treat all people as equal citizens), and government policies on affirmative action. Faced with competing forms of democratic participation—one based on "minority" rights and the other on a nondiscriminatory liberal stance—Afro-Brazilians lean toward the liberal form in their voting behavior. Interacting variables contribute to Black candidates' complex calculus of race and politics in Brazil. The evolution of Black candidates' campaigns and the messages they use to win political support provide more nuanced understandings of the ways in which campaign messages construct identity and how voters react to that identity. In terms of the political relevance of race in electoral politics in Salvador, Black activists running for office must constantly adjust the ways they speak about race to accommodate the evolving ways in which Afro-Brazilians relate to Blackness in contemporary Brazil.

Afro-Brazilians' anti-racist consciousness has long fascinated scholars of race relations in Brazil. Discourse practices shine new light on how Afro-Brazilians situate Blackness in relation to Brazil's reality of racial mixture and racial integration, on their everyday lived experiences of anti-Black racism, and on their anti-racist consciousness. These practices convey sociocultural meanings at both micro- and macroanalytical levels. These meanings, in turn, open a window to the processes of identity negotiation and the ways in which organized struggles have reshaped the lives of many

Brazilians of African descent. In closing, I return to the conflicting ways in which Afro-Brazilians' lives have been affected by the complex succession of Black mobilization to affirm Black identity among a broad range of Afro-Brazilians and affirmative action programs that rely on phenotype to narrow down who counts as sufficiently disadvantaged to be eligible for racial quotas.

Afro-Brazilians' demand for racial justice is palpable in contemporary Brazil. Black consciousness advocates are challenging Afro-Brazilians to define themselves and politically organize around being Black while redistributive and reparatory measures are taking aim against the racial discrimination and racial exclusion of Black Brazilians. Without doubt, anti-racist activism has already produced enormous changes. In the process, Afro-Brazilians are presented with a range of identity choices, from how they classify themselves to how they vote. The very question of what it means to be anti-racist is bound up in the idea of a single consciousness and, consequently, in the distinction of Blackness from a miscegenated identity. Afro-Brazilians tell stories of dialogic negotiations around their racial positions, how they act and are acted upon. As they realize that they do not fit neatly into any one category, they are critically exploring their own Blackness in the world between Brown and Black. There is growing resistance to categorical expressions of Blackness and increasing political will to build anti-racist coalitions. The conflicts that motivated this book are real and to some extent unavoidable. For a broader analysis of anti-racist activism among Afro-Brazilians, we need more research that explores ethnographically Black identity and politics in Brazil, ethnographies that directly engage with and place the voices of those involved in collective efforts within the multitude of social contexts. As this book demonstrates, in Afro-Brazilian anti-racist activism, Brownness and Blackness are increasingly in dialogue, with one informing the other to construct a collective vision of racial justice.

Acknowledgments

After twelve years of study and research, I am grateful to so many people, and I am sure these words of acknowledgement will not do justice to their time and dedication. I first thank activists from the Brazilian Black movements who have worked tirelessly for social justice in a country with entrenched structural racism and a relentless denial of this racism. As Brazil and the world continue a downward spiral of racial violence, your work is truly needed, and I continue to be impressed by your efforts.

There is an endless list of people from whom I learned much about race, racism, and anti-racist activism among Afro-Brazilians in Salvador (Bahia, Brazil). I would like to acknowledge some of those with whom I worked most closely at different stages of fieldwork. I benefited from discussions with Denise Cabral, Michel Chagas, Fernando Conceição, Lázaro Cunha, Bartolomeu Dias, Roseli Faria, Sílvio Humberto, Tarry Cristina Santos Pereira, Eduardo Gomor dos Santos, Rosy Mary Santos, Jucy Silva, and Marcos Silva. I am indebted to them not only for the informed, critical, and insightful conversations but for the many doors they opened for me.

At the Coordenadoria de Informações e Produção de Indicadores Urbano-Ambientais (Office of Information and Production of Urban-Environmental Indicators) in Salvador, I am thankful to Elba Guimarães Vega and her team for their help with neighborhood mapping for my 2014 project on electoral participation. My work in Salvador was facilitated by Clécio Macedo, Maria Helena Meyer, Patrícia Teles dos Santos, Willys Santos, Marli dos Santos, and Josane Silva. They helped me arrange interviews and contact organizations through which I could learn different perspectives on anti-racist activism among Afro-Brazilians. I am grateful to them. I am particularly grateful for the critical comments and suggestions on parts of this text that were provided by Michel Chagas, Roseli Faria, Jennifer Roth-Gordon, Eduardo Gomor dos Santos, and Marcos Silva. I would like to thank my former students and academic colleagues, Eduardo Oliveira, Marieli Pereira, and Adelmo dos Santos Filho for the invaluable discussions on the ideas contained in this book.

I am grateful to faculty members in the School of Anthropology at the University of Arizona (UArizona). I am deeply indebted to the generous and thoughtful mentorship of Ana Alonso, Ellen Basso, Jane Hill, Norma Mendoza-Denton, Susan Philips, and Qing Zhang. They assisted me in exploring the field of anthropology, and their wealth of insights and information shaped the trajectory of my research and career. I also benefited from innumerable discussions with the late Bert Barickman in the Department of History at UArizona. Bert offered me a broader understanding of Brazilian history. The passing of Bert Barickman and Jane Hill left a deep intellectual, professional, and personal hole in my life. In addition, I shared many valuable and enjoyable discussions with many fellow graduate students at UArizona, including Paola Canova, Joon-Beom Chu, Ben McMahan, Jessica Nelson, Ashley Stinnett, Maisa Taha, and Wendy Vogt.

During my time as a graduate student at UArizona, I had the opportunity to work as a teaching assistant for numerous semesters for the Department of Spanish and Portuguese. I am especially thankful to Ana Carvalho and Malcolm Compitelo, whose guidance and material support helped me survive in graduate school. Ana's friendship and profound insights within the areas of language, culture, and Portuguese foreign language pedagogy are deeply appreciated. I also thank the entire staff at the Department of Spanish and Portuguese, and especially Isela Gonzales-Cook, Nichole Guard, Mary Portillo, and Mercy Valente for the many ways they made my work there as productive and pleasant as possible. At UArizona I am grateful as well to Laura Tabili in the Department of History for sharing her knowledge and experience with successful book proposals.

I owe thanks to James Riordan and Athiná Arcadinos Leite at Associação Cultural Brasil-Estados Unidos in Salvador. Their support in my early professional life helped set the foundations for my academic career. Among friends and colleagues whom I owe gratitude to are Erika Robb Larkins, Alba Riva Brito de Almeida, and Michelle de Sá e Silva. At the

University of Arizona, I was fortunate to join ever-supportive colleagues at the Center for Latin American Studies (CLAS). They create a collegial atmosphere that I am proud to be a part of. I am extremely thankful for the camaraderie of Clea Conlin, Jennifer Cyr, Colin Deeds, Javier Duran, Mia Guimarães, Katie O'Brien, Liz Oglesby, Erin Tyo, Margaret Wilder, Susan Brewer-Osorio, students, and student-workers. I want to express special gratitude to my student Ezra Zvaigzde Gonda for creating the artwork on the front cover of the book. I would like to express my strong appreciation of Marcela Vasquez-Leon for her leadership in turning the center toward a successful future and enhancing the research, teaching, and service opportunities it provides to faculty, staff, and students. I am indebted to her for so many professional opportunities and for our personal friendship.

I have been fortunate to receive financial support during different stages of my academic career from several sources, including the CLAS at UArizona, the Coordenação de Aperfeiçoamento de Pessoal de Nível Superior (CAPES) in Brazil, the Fulbright Foundation, the School of Anthropology at UArizona, the University of Arizona itself, and the Wenner-Gren Foundation. During my CAPES postdoctoral fellowship at the Universidade Federal da Bahia, I benefited from the supportive mentorship of Sávio Siqueira. This fellowship helped me complete my two-year home residence as required by the Fulbright Foundation.

I would also like to thank Jasper Chang, Kim Guinta, and the publishing team at Rutgers University Press for their enthusiasm for this book and for supporting me through the publication process. I cannot thank the anonymous reviewers enough for their substantial feedback, which greatly improved the book. I thank Kirsteen Anderson for her detailed and brilliant editing work. I thank G. Reginald Daniel, whom I had the opportunity to meet days before I submitted the final manuscript for production, for an insightful exchange about the complex issues surrounding multiraciality and anti-racism. Thanks are also due to my former student, Ezra Ann Gonda, for the amazing artwork on the front cover of the book.

I am immensely thankful to Jennifer Roth-Gordon, my former adviser turned mentor and friend, for her guidance, support, and inspiration. Jen's passionate commitment to a robust anthropology of race has pushed me to be a better anthropologist and scholar. In writing a book like this, while I have relied on my own experiences, Jen's incisive comments and challenging questions helped me get unique perspectives on what was happening in anti-racisracist activism among Afro-Brazilians.

I am deeply grateful to Edward Gervasoni for his unending support and enthusiasm for my academic career throughout the entire period this book was in the making. Ed was always available to read my graduate school papers, grant proposals, dissertation chapters, job application materials, journal manuscripts, and parts of this book no matter the time, day, or location. I could not have done it without you!

My friends and family, both near and far, have encouraged me with emotional support, and my gratitude is deep and permanent. Carlos Alberto Neves and Patrícia Neves da Rocha have shared the gift of their time to edit my writing in Portuguese. I am indebted to Carlos Alberto for his hospitality, opening his home to me in Brasília many times, including the time I was there to conduct research for this book. I thank my friends Reynaldo Castro, Selene Dias, Vera Gonçalves, Clécio Macedo, Líbia Régia Oliveira Alves, Nete Silva, and Olga Tartaruga, who provided excellent company, often over beer and caipirinhas, during the time I spent in the field. I would like to express my thanks to my friend Jen Cole, who read earlier versions of the book proposal with great care. I would like to give a special acknowledgment to my mother, Yêda Maria Bacelar da Silva, who invested precious resources, effort, and energy so that I could be the first in my family to attend college, learn English, and travel to the United States. I know this book would have meant the world to her, and I regret that she did not live to see it published. This book is for you, Mãe!

Much of this book was written during one of the most difficult times of my personal life. I thank Ana Carvalho, Jennifer Roth-Gordon, and Marcela Vasquez-Leon, who offered me the strength, peace, and healing that enabled me to reach the finish line. Some debts are incalculable. At the end of it all, there is your love, which I thank you for.

This book is also for all the strong black women in my life who shaped who I am.

—June 5, 2021

Notes

Chapter 1   Black into Brown, Brown into Black

1   For a critique of the characterization of U.S. race relations as strictly based on hypodescent, also known as the one-drop rule, see the work of Kerry Ann Rockquemore (2002) on biracial Americans and Lauren Davenport (2016) on biracial Americans and political opinions.

2   Mary Lorena Kenny (2018, 48) updates the definition of *quilombolas* to include current legal language.

3   Some institutional and individual names have been replaced by pseudonyms to ensure anonymity.

4   There is growing scholarship on anti-Blackness in Brazil; see, for example, Alves 2018 and Vargas 2018.

5   For the scholarly debate about the analytical usefulness of identity, see Brubaker 2003; Calhoun 2003a, 2003b; and Weinstein 2015, 22–24.

Chapter 2   The Language of Afro-Brazilian Anti-racist Socialization

1   An earlier version of this chapter appeared as Antonio José Bacelar da Silva, "Dialogism as Antiracist Education: Engaging with Competing Racial Ideologies in Brazil," *Anthropology and Education Quarterly* 45 (4), 2014, 319–336, https://doi.org/10.1111/aeq.12073. © 2014 by the American Anthropological Association. All rights reserved.

2   See the interview with Kabengele Munanga (2010), a well-known Black activist, in which he provides an explanation similar to Ana's.

Chapter 3   Performing Ancestors, Claiming Blackness

1   Both Instituto Lutas de Zumbi and the name César Silva are pseudonyms, as are the names of the Zumbi teacher and students.

2 Focusing on a later period (after the 1970s), Patrícia Santana Pinho (2018) writes about Brazil becoming a destination for African American tourists seeking the cultural roots of the Black Atlantic diaspora.

Chapter 4 Becoming an Anti-racist, or "As Black as We Can Be"

1 An earlier version of this chapter appeared as Antonio José Bacelar da Silva, "Voicing Race and Antiracism," *Journal of Anthropological Research* 71 (1), 2015, 49–68, http://dx.doi.org/10.3998/jar.0521004.0071.103. Copyright © The University of New Mexico.
2 See Pardue 2008 and R. Santos 2010, both of which examine Afro-Brazilians' alternative forms of anti-racism in which Black identity does not play a crucial role in terms of sustaining a racial justice mission.

Chapter 5 Who Can Be Black for Affirmative Action Programs in Brazil?

1 Sales Augusto dos Santos (2021b) has mapped the implementation of the committees in federal public universities across the country. He concludes that there was a significant increase in the number of universities that adopted the verification process. The Black movement organizations, Black scholars, and Black students themselves have been successful in pressuring the universities to guard against fraud.
2 With their permission, I use the real names of Roseli Faria, Eduardo Gomor dos Santos, and Marcos Silva in this chapter.
3 I use words like *Brown* because they are the closest in English, and I am trying to be as faithful as possible to what I heard or read.
4 On the underrepresentation of *pardos* and *negros* in higher education, see Vaz, 32. On disparity in public service, see N. L. Costa, 2018, 91. Both Fontoura 2018, 111–118, and Jardim 2018, 195–196, write about the 1988 constitution to address inequality.
5 For a more detailed account of the procedures, see V. Nascimento 2019.

Chapter 6 The Complex Calculus of Race and Electoral Politics in Salvador

1 On the notion of "contradictory brew," see Hale and Mullings 2021, 41
2 Regarding preventing a broader radicalization, see Larson 2018, 23.
3 Founded in 1992, the Instituto Cultural Steve Biko (Steve Biko Cultural Institute) created the first college preparatory course aimed at Blacks in Salvador. Inspired by anti-racist struggles around the world, the institute promotes the insertion of Black youth into the academic space as a strategy for their social ascension and the fight against racial discrimination (Instituto Cultural Steve Biko 2020).
4 On marketing language in politics, see Silverstein 2011.

References

Aguilar, Rosario, Saul Cunow, Scott Desposato, and Leonardo Sangali Barone. 2015. "Ballot Structure, Candidate Race, and Vote Choice in Brazil." *Latin American Research Review* 50 (3): 175–202. https://doi.org/10.1353/lar.2015.0044.

Alberto, Paulina L. 2011. *Terms of Inclusion: Black Intellectuals in Twentieth-Century Brazil.* Chapel Hill: University of North Carolina Press.

Alma Preta. 2021. "Primeira prefeita mulher e negra de Cachoeira (BA), Eliana Gonzaga denuncia ameaças." Yahoo News, April 21, 2021. https://br.noticias.yahoo .com/primeira-prefeita-mulher-e-negra-de-cachoeira-ba-eliana-gonzaga-denuncia -ameacas-164559001.html.

Althusser, Louis. 1971. *Lenin and Philosophy, and Other Essays.* Translated by Ben Brewster. New York: Monthly Review Press.

Alves, Jaime Amparo. 2018. *The anti-black city: police terror and black urban life in Brazil.* Minneapolis: University of Minnesota Press.

Andrade, Miguel. 2020. "Barbaric Murder by Brazilian Security Guards Sparks Protests, Repression." *Wall Street Journal*, November 29, 2020. https://www.wsws .org/en/articles/2020/11/30/bras-n30.html.

Andrade, Oswald de. [1928]1973. "Manifesto Antropófago." In *Vanguarda Européia e Modernismo Brasileiro: Apresentação crítica dos principais manifestos, prefácios e conferências vanguardistas, de 1857 até hoje* edited by Gilberto Mendonça Teles. Petrópolis, RJ: Editora Vozes Ltda.

Anzaldúa, Gloria. 1987. *Borderlands / La Frontera: The New Mestiza.* San Francisco: Aunt Lute Books.

Appelbaum, Nancy P., Anne S. Macpherson, and Karin Alejandra Rosemblatt. 2003. *Race and Nation in Modern Latin America.* Chapel Hill: University of North Carolina Press.

Araújo, Zulu. 2020. "Uma face negra para a Prefeitura de Salvador." *Revista raça*, January 17, 2020. https://revistaraca.com.br/uma-face-negra-para-a-prefeitura-de -salvador/?fbclid=IwAR16AUdh9bwsThAQkFV8lYKUr9WoUW2Sf6T-TqTd1 VNzbLhElR6GRQl4pEs.

Bairros, Luiza. 2008. "A Community of Destiny: New Configurations of Racial Politics in Brazil." *Souls* 10 (1): 50–53.

Bakhtin, Mikhail M. 1981. *The Dialogic Imagination: Four Essays*. Edited by Michael Holquist. Translated by Caryl Emerson and Michael Holquist. Austin: University of Texas Press.

———. 1984. *Problems of Dostoevsky's Poetics*. Edited and translated by Caryl Emerson. Minneapolis: University of Minnesota Press.

———. 1986. *Speech Genres and Other Late Essays*. Edited by Michael Holquist and Caryl Emerson. Translated by Vern W. McGee. Austin: University of Texas Press.

Batista, Fabiana. 2020. "Deputada Talíria Petrone: Tarefas e ameaças me deixam exausta e amedrontada." *UOL*, October 15, 2020. https://www.uol.com.br /universa/noticias/redacao/2020/10/15/taliria-petrone-deputada-do-rio-diz-estar -exausta-e-com-medo-das-ameacas.htm?cmpid=copiaecola.

Bernstein, Mary. 2005. "Identity Politics." *Annual Review of Sociology* 31 (1): 47–74. http://dx.doi.org/10.1146/annurev.soc.29.010202.100054.

Bochicchio, Regina. 2020. "Em Salvador, a disputa paralela pelo 'axé-jingle' nas eleições 2020." *Estadão*, October 17, 2020. https://noticias.uol.com.br/eleicoes /estadao-conteudo/2020/10/17/em-salvador-a-disputa-paralela-pelo-axe-jingle-nas -eleicoes-2020.htm.

Bourdieu, Pierre. 1977. *Outline of a Theory of Practice*. Translated by Richard Nice. Cambridge, MA: Harvard University Press.

Brubaker, Rogers. 2003. "Neither Individualism nor 'Groupism': A Reply to Craig Calhoun." *Ethnicities* 3 (4): 553–557. https://doi.org/10.1177 /1468796803003004006.

Brubaker, Rogers, and Frederick Cooper. 2000. "Beyond 'Identity.'" *Theory and Society* 29 (1): 1–47. http://links.jstor.org/sici?sici=0304-2421%28200002%2929%3 A1%3C1%3AB%22%3E2.0.CO%3B2-W.

Burdick, John. 1998. *Blessed Anastácia: Women, Race, and Popular Christianity in Brazil*. New York: Routledge.

Butler, Kim D. 1998. *Freedoms Given, Freedoms Won: Afro-Brazilians in Post-abolition São Paulo and Salvador*. New Brunswick, NJ: Rutgers University Press.

Cabrera, Nolan L. 2020. "'Never Forget' the History of Racial Oppression: Whiteness, White Immunity, and Educational Debt in Higher Education." *Change* 52 (2): 37–40. https://doi.org/10.1080/00091383.2020.1732774.

Caldwell, Kia Lilly. 2007. *Negras in Brazil: Re-envisioning Black Women, Citizenship, and the Politics of Identity*. New Brunswick, NJ: Rutgers University Press.

Calhoun, Craig. 1994. "Social Theory and the Politics of Identity." In *Social Theory and the Politics of Identity*, edited by Craig Calhoun, 9–36. Cambridge, MA: Blackwell.

———. 2003a. "'Belonging' in the Cosmopolitan Imaginary." *Ethnicities* 3 (4): 531–553. https://doi.org/10.1177/1468796803003004005.

———. 2003b. "The Variability of Belonging: A Reply to Rogers Brubaker." *Ethnicities* 3 (4): 558–568. https://doi.org/10.1177/1468796803003004007.

Camargos, Marcia. 2002. *Semana de 22: Entre vaias e aplausos*. São Paulo: Boitempo.

Carneiro, Sueli. 2011. *Racismo, sexismo e desigualdade no Brazil*. São Paulo: Selo Negro.

Carvalho, Inaiá Maria Moreira de, and Vanda Sá Barreto. 2007. "Segregação residencial, condição social e raça em Salvador." *Cadernos metrópole*, no. 18: 251–273.

Celarent, Barbara. 2010. "*The Masters and the Slaves* by Gilberto Freyre." *American Journal of Sociology* 116 (1): 334–339. http://www.jstor.org/stable/10.1086/655749.

Cerqueira, Daniel, Samira Bueno, Renato Sergio de Lima, Cristina Neme, Helder Ferreira, Paloma Palmieri Alves, David Marques, Milena Reis, Otavio Cypriano, Isabela Sobral, Dennis Pacheco, Gabriel Lins, and Karolina Armstrong. 2019. *Atlas da violência 2019*. Brasília: Instituto de Pesquisa Econômica Aplicada / Fórum Brasileiro de Segurança Pública.

Cicalo, André. 2012. *Urban Encounters: Affirmative Action and Black Identities in Brazil*. New York: Palgrave Macmillan.

Costa, Alexandre Emboaba da. 2014. *Reimagining Black Difference and Politics in Brazil: From Racial Democracy to Multiculturalism*. New York: Palgrave.

Costa, Najara Lima. 2018. "A implementação da Lei de Cotas Raciais nos Concursos Públicos Federais: Análises dos orocessos de execução da ação afirmativa." In *Heteroidentificação e cotas raciais: Dúvidas, metodologias e procedimentos*, edited by Gleidson Renato Martins Dias and Paulo Roberto Faber Tavares Jr., 80–107. Canoas, Brazil: IFRS Campus Canoas.

Covin, David. 1990. "Afrocentricity in O Movimento Negro Unificado." *Journal of Black Studies* 21 (2): 126–144.

Crowley, Michael. 2008. "Skin Deep." *New Republic*, February 13, 2008, 9–10. https://newrepublic.com/article/65713/skin-deep.

Cunha, Olivia Maria Gomes da. 1998. "Black Movements and the Politics of Identity in Brazil." In *Cultures of Politics / Politics of Cultures: Re-visioning Latin American Social Movements*, edited by Sonia E. Alvarez, Evelina Dagnino, and Arturo Escobar, 220–251. Boulder, CO: Westview.

Daniel, G. Reginald. 2001. *More Than Black: Multiracial Identity and New Racial Order*. Philadelphia: Temple University Press.

———. 2006. *Race and Multiraciality in Brazil and the United States: Converging Paths?* University Park: Pennsylvania State University Press.

DaMatta, Roberto. 1990. "Digressão: A fábula das três raças, ou o problema do racismo à brasileira." In *Relativizando: Uma introdução à antropologia social*, 58–87. Petrópolis: Editora Vozes.

Darnton, Robert. 2010. "Talking about Brazil with Lilia Schwarcz." *New York Review of Books*, August 10, 2010. https://www.nybooks.com/daily/2010/08/1//talking-about-brazil/?lp_txn_id=1008150.

Davenport, Lauren D. 2016. "Beyond Black and White: Biracial Attitudes in Contemporary U.S. Politics." *American Political Science Review* 110 (1): 52–67. https://doi.org/10.1017/S0003055415000556.

Davis, Darién J. 1999. *Avoiding the Dark: Race and the Forging of National Culture in Modern Brazil*. Aldershot, UK: Ashgate.

Day, Richard J. F. 2004. "From Hegemony to Affinity." *Cultural Studies* 18 (5): 716–748. https://doi.org/10.1080/0950238042000260360.

———. 2005. *Gramsci Is Dead: Anarchist Currents in the Newest Social Movements*. London: Pluto Press.

Degler, Carl N. 1971. *Neither Black nor White: Slavery and Race Relations in Brazil and the United States*. New York: Macmillan.

Dias, Gleidson Renato Martins. 2018. "Considerações à Portaria Normativa no 4 de 6 de abril de 2018 do Ministério do Planejamento, Desenvolvimento e Gestão." In *Heteroidentificação e cotas raciais: Dúvidas, metodologias e procedimentos*, edited by

Gleidson Renato Martins Dias and Paulo Roberto Faber Tavares Jr., 142–176. Canoas, Brazil: IFRS Campus Canoas.

Drumond, Angel. 2020. "Bolsonaro critica protestos contra o racismo em discurso na Cúpula do." *O Tempo*, November 21, 2020. https://www.otempo.com.br/politica /bolsonaro-critica-protestos-contra-o-racismo-em-discurso-na-cupula-do-g20-1 .2415756.

Du Bois, John W. 2009. "Interior Dialogues: The Co-voicing of Ritual in Solitude." In *Ritual Communication*, edited by Gunter Senft and Ellen B. Basso, 317–340. New York: Berg.

Dzidzienyo, Anani. 1985. "The African Connection and the Afro-Brazilian Condition." In *Race, Class, and Power in Brazil*, edited by Pierre-Michel Fontaine, 135–153. Los Angeles: Center for Afro-American Studies, University of California.

Dzidzienyo, Anani, and Suzanne Oboler. 2005. "The Changing World of Brazilian Race Relations." In *Neither Enemies nor Friends: Latinos, Blacks, Afro-Latinos*, 137–155. New York: Palgrave Macmillan.

Estado de Minas. 2020. "Salvador tem cinco pré-candidatos negros." *Estado de Minas*, September 2, 2020. https://www.em.com.br/app/noticia/politica/2020/09/02 /interna_politica,1181802/salvador-tem-cinco-pre-candidatos-negros.shtml.

Estanislau, Bárbara, Eduardo Gomor, and Jéssica Naime. 2015. "A inserção dos negros no serivço público federal e as perspectivas de transformação a partir da lei de cotas." In *Servidores públicos federais: Novos olhares e perspectivas*, edited by Pedro Palotti and Alessandro Freire, 108–133. Brasília: Fundação Escola Nacional de Administração Pública.

Fanon, Frantz. 2008 [1967]. "The lived experience of the Black man." In *Black skin, white masks*, 89–119. New York: Grove Press.

Farfán-Santos, Elizabeth. 2016. *Black Bodies, Black Rights: The Politics of Quilombo-lismo in Contemporary Brazil*. Austin: University of Texas Press.

Faria, Roseli. 2020. *Gênero e raça no orçamento público brasileiro*. Webinar, September 20, 2020. https://www.youtube.com/watch?v=kmi60iQoG9o.

Faustino, Oswaldo. 2016. "Oswaldo Faustino escreve sobre Chiquinha Gonzaga, que por toda sua vida quebrou inúmeros tabus." Revista Raça (website), October 14, 2016.

Feres Júnior, João, and Luiz Augusto Campos. 2016. "Ação afirmativa no Brasil: Multiculturalismo ou justiça social?" *Lua nova: Revista de cultura e política*, no. 99: 257–293. http://www.scielo.br/scielo.php?script=sci_arttext&pid=S0102-64452016 000300257&nrm=iso.

Fontoura, Maria Conceição Lopes. 2018. "Tirando a vovó e o vovô do armário." In *Heteroidentificação e cotas raciais: Dúvidas, metodologias e procedimentos*, edited by Gleidson Renato Martins Dias and Paulo Roberto Faber Tavares Jr., 108–141. Canoas, Brazil: IFRS Campus Canoas.

Freire, Paulo. 2004. *Pedagogia da autonomia: Saberes necessários para a prática educativa*. São Paulo, SP: Paz e Terra.

Freitas, Enrico Rodrigues de. 2018. "Heteroidentificação e quotas raciais: O papel do Ministério Público." In *Heteroidentificação e cotas raciais: Dúvidas, metodologias e procedimentos*, edited by Gleidson Renato Martins Dias and Paulo Roberto Faber Tavares Jr., 177–193. Canoas, Brazil: IFRS Campus Canoas.

French, Jan H. 2009. *Legalizing Identities: Becoming Black or Indian in Brazil's Northeast*. Chapel Hill: University of North Carolina Press.

Freyre, Gilberto. (1933) 1987. *Casa-grande & senzala: Formação da família brasileira sob o regime de economia patriarchal.* Rio de Janeiro: Schmidt.

Garcia, Januário. 2006. *25 anos 1980–2005: Movimento negro no Brasil.* Brasília: Fundação Cultural Palmares.

Goffman, Erving. 1981. *Forms of Talk.* Philadelphia: University of Pennsylvania Press.

Gomor dos Santos, Eduardo. 2020. "Ofensivas Neoliberais contra as políticas afirmativas raciais." Unpublished manuscript.

Government of Brazil. 2003. Lei 10.639/03 de 9 de janeiro de 2003. "Ensino sobre História e Cultura Afro-Brasileira." Brasília: Government of Brazil.

Government of Brazil. 2010. Lei 12.288 de 20 de julho de 2010. "Estatuto da igualdade racial." Brasília: Government of Brazil.

Government of Brazil. 2012. Lei 12.711 de 29 de agosto de 2012. "Cotas raciais em universidades federais e nas instituições federais de ensino técnico de nível médio." Brasília: Government of Brazil.

Government of Brazil. 2014. Lei 12.990 de 09 de julho de 2014. "Reserva aos negros vagas em concursos públicos." Brasília: Government of Brazil.

Government of Brazil. 2017. Projeto de lei 482/2017: Estabelece Dia da Consciência Negra como feriado nacional.

Government of Brazil. 2020. Projeto de Lei 461/2020. "Para vedar a realização de procedimentos de heteroidentificação racial." Brasília: Government of Brazil.

Government of Brazil, Atlas do Desenvolvimento Humano no. 2020. 2020. "Retratamos o desenvolvimento humano sustentável e as desigualdades no Brasil, combinando dados de qualidade com formas amigáveis de visualização." http://www .atlasbrasil.org.br.

Government of Brazil, Ministério do Planejamento, Desenvolvimento e Gestão. 2018. Portaria normativa n.4. In *Diário oficial da união,* Edição 68, Seção 1, Página 34, Brasília: Government of Brazil.

Gramsci, Antonio. 1972. *Selections from the Prison Notebooks of Antonio Gramsci.* Translated and edited by Quintin Hoare and Geoffrey Nowell-Smith. New York: International.

Guimarães, Antonio Sérgio Alfredo. 2001. "A questão racial na política brasileira (os últimos quinze anos)." *Tempo Social* 13(2):121–142.

Gumperz, John J. 1982. "Ethnic Styles in Political Rhetoric." In *Discourse Strategies,* 187–203. Cambridge: Cambridge University Press.

Gumperz, John J., and Dell Hymes. 1972. *Directions in Sociolinguistics: The Ethnography of Communication.* New York: Holt.

Hale, Charles R. 2002. "Does Multiculturalism Menace? Governance, Cultural Rights and the Politics of Identity in Guatemala." *Journal of Latin American Studies* 34 (3): 485–524.

Hale, Charles R., and Rosamel Millamán. 2015. "Cultural Agency and Political Struggle in the Era of Indio Permitido." In *Cultural Agency in the Americas,* edited by Doris Sommer, 281–304. Durham, NC: Duke University Press.

Hale, Charles R., and Leith Mullings. 2021. "A Time to Recalibrate: Understanding and Resisting the Americas-wide Project of Racial Retrenchment." In *Black and Indigenous Resistance in the Americas: From Multiculturalism to Racist Backlash,* edited by Juliet Hooker, 21–66. Lanham, Maryland: Lexington Books.

Hanchard, Michael George. 1994. *Orpheus and Power: The Movimento Negro of Rio de Janeiro and São Paulo, Brazil, 1945–1988.* Princeton, NJ: Princeton University Press.

Haney López, Ian F. 1998. "Chance, context, and choice in the social construction of race." In *The Latino/a Condition: A Critical Reader*, edited by Richard Delgado and Jean Stefancic, 9–16. New York: New York University Press.

Harvey, David. 2016. "Neoliberalism Is a Political Project: An Interview with David Harvey," by Bjarke Skærlund Risager. *Jacobin*, July 2016. https://www.jacobinmag.com/2016/07/david-harvey-neoliberalism-capitalism-labor-crisis-resistance/.

Haviland, John B. 2005. "'Whorish Old Man' and "One (Animal) Gentleman": The Intertextual Construction of Enemies and Selves." *Journal of Linguistic Anthropology* 15 (1): 81–94. http://www.anthrosource.net.ezproxy1.library.arizona.edu/doi/abs/10.1525/jlin.2005.15.1.81.

Hill, Jane H. 1995. "The Voices of Don Gabriel: Responsibility and Self in a Modern Mexicano Narrative." In *The Dialogic Emergence of Culture*, edited by Dennis Tedlock, 97–147. Chicago: University of Illinois Press.

———. 2008. *The Everyday Language of White Racism*. Malden, MA: Wiley-Blackwell.

Holquist, Michael. 1990. *Dialogism: Bakhtin and His World*. London: Routledge.

Hooker, Juliet. 2008. "Afro-descendant Struggles for Collective Rights in Latin America: Between Race and Culture." *Souls* 10 (3): 279–291. http://www.informaworld.com.ezproxy2.library.arizona.edu/10.1080/10999940802347764.

Instituto Cultural Steve Biko. 2020. "Quem Somos." https://www.stevebiko.org.br/sobre-nos.

Jardim, Sílvio Guido Fioravanti. 2018. "Cotas Raciais nos Concursos Públicos: Edital e Jurisprudência." In *Heteroidentificaçõa e Cotas Raciais: Dúvidas, Metodologias e Procedimentos (Heteroidentification and Racial Quotas: Doubts, Methodologies, and Procedures)*, edited by Gleidson Renato Martins Dias and Paulo Roberto Faber Tavares Jr., 195–215. Canoas, RS: IFRS campus Canoas.

Johnson, Ollie A. 1998. "Racial Representation and Brazilian Politics: Black Members of the National Congress, 1983–1999." *Journal of Interamerican Studies and World Affairs* 40 (4): 97–118.

———. 2006. "Locating Blacks in Brazilian Politics: Afro-Brazilian Activism, New Political Parties, and Pro-Black Public Policies." *International Journal of Africana Studies* 12 (2): 170–193.

Jornal Nacional. 2017. "Número de crianças no Brasil cai e sobe o de idosos, afirma IBGE." *Jornal Nacional*, November 24, 2017. http://g1.globo.com/jornal-nacional/noticia/2017/11/numero-de-criancas-no-brasil-cai-e-sobe-o-de-idosos-afirma-ibge.html.

Kaufmann, Roberta Fragoso. 2008. "Cotas geram ódio racial: Entrevista com Roberta Fragoso Kaufmann," by Hugo Marques. *Istoé*, May 28, 2008, 6–10.

Keane, Webb. 2011. "Indexing Voice: A Morality Tale." *Journal of Linguistic Anthropology* 21 (2): 166–178. https://doi.org/10.1111/j.1548-1395.2011.01104.x.

Kenny, Mary Lorena. 2018. *Deeply Rooted in the Present: Heritage, Memory, and Identity in Brazilian Quilombos*. Toronto: University of Toronto Press.

Kroskrity, Paul V. 2000. "Identity." *Journal of Linguistic Anthropology* 9 (1–2): 111–114.

Larson, Eric D. 2018. "Tradition and Transition: Neoliberal Multiculturalism and the Containment of Indigenous Insurgency in Southern Mexico in the 1990s." *Latin American and Caribbean Ethnic Studies* 13 (1): 22–46. https://doi.org/10.1080/17442222.2018.1416895.

Leitão, Míriam. 2002. "A imprensa e o racismo." In *Mídia e racismo*, edited by Sílvia Ramos, 42–50. Rio de Janeiro: Pazzas.

Lemon, Alaina. 2009. "Sympathy for the Weary State? Cold War Chronotopes and Moscow Others." *Comparative Studies in Society and History* 51 (4): 832–864. https://doi.org/10.1017/S0010417509990156.

Lowenthal, David. 1998. *The Heritage Crusade and the Spoils of History*. 1st pbk. ed. New York: Cambridge University Press.

Macherey, Pierre. 2012. "Figures of Interpellation in Althusser and Fanon." *Racial Philosophy* 173 (May/June): 9–20.

Magenta, Matheus, and Luis Barrucho. 2020. "Protestos por George Floyd: Em seis áreas, a desigualdade racial no Brasil e nos EUA." BBC News Brasil, June 4, 2020. https://www.bbc.com/portuguese/brasil-52916100.

Martins, Leda Maria. 1995. *A Cena em Sombras*. São Paulo: Editora Perspectiva.

Mendoza-Denton, Norma. 2002. "Language and Identity." In *The Handbook of Language Variation and Change*, edited by J. K. Chambers, Peter Trudgill, and Natalie Schilling-Estes, 476–499. Malden, MA: Blackwell.

Mills, Charles W. 2007. "Multiculturalism as/and/or Anti-racism?" In *Multiculturalism and Political Theory*, edited by Anthony Simon Laden and David Owen, 89–114. New York: Cambridge University Press.

Mitchell, Gladys. 2009. "Campaign Strategies of Afro-Brazilian Politicians: A Preliminary Analysis." *Latin American Politics and Society* 51 (3): 111–142. https://doi.org/10.1111/j.1548-2456.2009.00058.x.

Mitchell, Michael. 1999. "Racial Consciousness, Afro-Brazilian Electoral Strategies, and Regime Change in Brazil." In *Race and Ethnicity in Comparative Perspective*, edited by Georgia A. Persons, 64–83. New Brunswick, NJ: Transaction.

Mitchell-Walthour, Gladys L. 2018. *The Politics of Blackness: Racial Identity and Political Behavior in Contemporary Brazil*. New York: Cambridge University Press.

Morris, Aldon D. 1992. *Frontiers in Social Movement Theory*. New Haven, CT: Yale University Press.

Moura, Clóvis. 1994. *Dialética radical do Brasil negro*. São Paulo: Editora Anita.

Munanga, Kabengele. 2010. "Nova legislação e política de cotas desencadeariam ascensão econômica e inclusão dos negros, diz professor." Pambazuka News, March 1, 2010. https://www.pambazuka.org/pt/security-icts/nova-legislação-e-pol%C3%ADtica-de-cotas-desencadeariam-ascensão-econômica-e-inclusão-dos.

Muniz, Lauro César, writer, Marcílio Moraes, writer, Jayme Monjardim, director, Luis Armando Queiroz, director, and Marcelo Travesso, director. [1999] 2008. *Chiquinha Gonzaga,* DVD. Rio de Janeiro: Som Livre.

Muniz, Tailane, and Gabriel Amorim. 2019. "Questão de identidade: Autodeclarados pretos ultrapassam brancos na Bahia." *Correio*, May 23, 2019. https://www.correio 24horas.com.br/noticia/nid/questao-de-identidade-autodeclarados-pretos -ultrapassam-brancos-na-bahia/.

Muñoz Acebes, César. 2016. "'Good Cops Are Afraid': The Toll of Unchecked Police Violence in Rio de Janeiro." Human Rights Watch, July 7, 2016. https://www.hrw .org/report/2016/07/07/good-cops-are-afraid/toll-unchecked-police-violence-rio -de-janeiro#.

Nascimento, Abdias do. 1978. *O genocídio do negro brasileiro: processo de um racismo mascarado*. Coleção Estudos Brasileiros. Rio de Janeiro: Paz e Terra.

———. 1983. "Padê de Exu libertador." In *Axés do sangue e da esperança (orikis)*, edited by Robson Achiamé Fernandes, 31–37. Rio de Janeiro: Edições Achiamé Ltda.

———. 1989. *Brazil, Mixture or Massacre? Essays in the Genocide of a Black People*. 2nd rev. ed. Dover, MA: Majority Press.

Nascimento, Vinícius. 2019. "Entenda como funciona a verificação dos candidatos às cotas raciais na UFBA." *Correio*, January 31, 2019. https://www.correio24horas .com.br/noticia/nid/entenda-como-funciona-a-verificacao-dos-candidatos-as-cotas -raciais-na-ufba/.

Nogueira, Oracy. 1998. *Preconceito de marca: As relações raciais em Itapetininga*. São Paulo: EDUSP.

Nunes, Georgina Helena Lima. 2018. "Autodeclarações e comissões: Responsabilidade procedimental dos/as gestores/as de ações afirmativas." In *Heteroidentificação e cotas raciais: Dúvidas, metodologias e procedimentos*, edited by Gleidson Renato Martins Dias and Paulo Roberto Faber Tavares Jr., 11–30. Canoas, Brazil: IFRS Campus.

Oliveira, Cloves Luiz Pereira. 1995. *A luta por um lugar: Gênero, raça e classe; Eleições municipais de Salvador-Bahia, 1992*. Salvador, Brazil: Programa A Cor da Bahia.

———. 2007. "A inevitável visibilidade de cor: estudo comparativo das campanhas de Benedita da Silva e Celso Pitta às prefeituras do Rio de Janeiro e São Paulo, nas eleições de 1992 e 1996." Ph.D., Instituto Universitário de Pesquisa do Rio de Janeiro.

Paixão, Marcelo, Irene Rossetto, Fabiana Montevanele, and Luiz Carvano. 2011. *Relatório Anual das Desigualdes Racias no Brazil, 2009–2010*. Rio de Janeiro: Garamond.

Paixão, Marcelo, and Rossetto, Irene. 2019. "The Labyrinth of Ethnic–Racial Inequality." In *Comparative Racial Politics in Latin America*, edited by Kwame Dixon and Ollie A. Johnson, 288–317. New York: Routledge.

Pardue, Derek. 2008. *Ideologies of Marginality in Brazilian Hip Hop*. New York: Palgrave Macmillan.

Paschel, Tianna S. 2016. *Becoming Black Political Subjects: Movements and Ethno-racial Rights in Colombia and Brazil*. Princeton, NJ: Princeton University Press.

Penha-Lopes, Vânia. 2017. *Confronting Affirmative Action in Brazil: University Quota Students and the Quest for Racial Justice*. Lanham, MD: Lexington Books.

Perry, Keisha-Khan Y. 2005. "Social Memory and Black Resistance: Black Women and Neighborhood Struggles in Salvador, Bahia, Brazil." *Latin Americanist* 49 (1): 7–38. https://doi.org/10.1111/j.1557-203X.2005.tb00063.x.

———. 2013. *Black Women against the Land Grab: The Fight for Racial Justice in Brazil*. Minneapolis: University of Minnesota Press.

Pinho, Patricia de Santana. 2005. "Descentrando os Estados Unidos nos estudos sobre negritude no Brasil." *Revista Brasileira de Ciências Sociais* 20 (59): 37–50.

———. 2018. *Mapping Diaspora: African American Roots Tourism in Brazil*. Chapel Hill: University of North Carolina Press.

Piza, Edith, and Fúlvia Rosemberg. 1999. "Cor nos censos brasileiros." *Revista USP* 40: 122–137.

Porfírio, Francisco. 2020. "Consciência negra." Brasil Escola. https://brasilescola.uol .com.br/sociologia/consciencia-negra.htm.

Postero, Nancy Grey. 2007. *Now We Are Citizens: Indigenous Politics in Postmulticultural Bolivia*. Stanford, CA: Stanford University Press.

Racusen, Seth. 2004. "The Ideology of the Brazilian Nation and the Brazilian Legal Theory of Racial Discrimination." *Social Identities: Journal for the Study of Race, Nation and Culture* 10 (6): 775–809.

Reiter, Bernd, and Gladys L. Mitchell. 2010. *Brazil's New Racial Politics.* Boulder, CO: Lynne Rienner.

Rios, Roger Raupp. 2018. "Pretos e pardos nas ações afirmativas: Desafios e respostas da autodeclaração e da eeteroidentificação." In *Heteroidentificação e cotas raciais: Dúvidas, metodologias e procedimentos*, edited by Gleidson Renato Martins Dias and Paulo Roberto Faber Tavares Jr., 215–249. Canoas, Brazil: IFRS Campus Canoas.

Risério, Antonio. 2017. "Movimentos negros repetem lógica do racismo." *Folha de São Paulo*, December 16, 2017. https://m.folha.uol.com.br/ilustrissima/2017/12/1943569-movimentos-negros-repetem-logica-do-racismo-cientifico-diz-antropologo.shtml.

Rockquemore, Kerry Ann. 2002. "Negotiating the Color Line: The Gendered Process of Racial Identity Construction among Black/White Biracial Women." *Gender and Society* 16 (4): 485–503. https://doi.org/10.1177/0891243202016004005.

Roth-Gordon, Jennifer. 2017. *Race and the Brazilian Body: Blackness, Whiteness, and Everyday Language in Rio de Janeiro.* Berkeley: University of California Press.

———. 2020. "Situating Discourse in Ethnographic and Sociopolitical Context." In *The Cambridge Handbook of Discourse Studies*, edited by Anna De Fina and Alexandra Georgakopoulou, 32–51. New York: Cambridge University Press.

Roth-Gordon, Jennifer, and Antonio José Bacelar da Silva. 2013. "Double-Voicing in the Everyday Language of Brazilian Black Activism." In *The Persistence of Language: Constructing and Confronting the Past and Present in the Voices of Jane H. Hill*, edited by Shannon Bischoff, Deborah Cole, Amy Fountain, and Mizuki Miyashita, 383–406. Philadelphia: John Benjamins.

Rothberg, Michael. 2009. *Multidirectional Memory: Remembering the Holocaust in the Age of Decolonization.* Stanford, CA: Stanford University Press.

Sandoval, Chela. 1991. "US Third World Feminism: The Theory and Method of Oppositional Consciousness in the Postmodern World." *Genders*, no. 10: 1–24.

Sansone, Livio. 2003. *Blackness without Ethnicity: Constructing Race in Brazil.* New York: Palgrave Macmillan.

Santana, Olívia. 2018. "Nesta reta final, vamos juntas e juntos escolher para Assembleia Legislativa da Bahia a primeira deputada estadual negra da Bahia." Facebook, video, October 5, 2018.

Santos, Frei David. 2018. "Prefácio." In *Heteroidentificação e cotas raciais: Dúvidas, metodologias e procedimentos*, edited by Gleidson Renato Martins Dias and Paulo Roberto Faber Tavares Jr., 5–9. Canoas, Brazil: IFRS Campus Canoas.

Santos, Jocélio Teles dos. 2005. *O Poder da Cultura e a Cultura no Poder: Disputa Simbólica da Herança Cultural Negra no Brasil.* Salvador: EDUFBA.

Santos, Renato. 2010. "New Social Activism: University Entry Courses for Black and Poor Students." In *Brazil's New Racial Politics*, edited by Bernd Reiter and Gladys L. Mitchell, 197–214. Boulder, CO: Lynne Rienner.

Santos, Sales Augusto dos. 2000. *A ausência de uma bancada suprapartidária afro-brasileira no Congresso Nacional (Legislatura 1995–1998).* 2 vols. Brasília: Centro de Estudos Afro-Asiaticos.

———. 2006. "Who Is Black in Brazil? A Timely or a False Question in Brazilian

Race Relations in the Era of Affirmative Action?" *Latin American Perspectives* 33 (4): 30–48.

———. 2021a. "Comissões de heteroidentificação étnico-racial: *Lócus* de constrangimento ou de controle social de uma política pública?" *O social em questão*, no. 50: 11–62.

———. 2021b. "Mapa das comissões de heteroidentificação étnico-racial das universidades federais brasileiras." *Revista da ABPN* 13 (36): 365–415.

Savarese, Maurício. 2019. "Brazil's New President Makes It Harder to Define Indigenous Lands." *Global News*, 2019. https://globalnews.ca/news/4808295/jair-bolsonaro-funai-indigenous-farm-brazil/.

Schucman, Lia Vainer, and Mônica Mendes Gonçalves. 2017. "O discurso da mestiçagem a serviço da branquitude: Antônio Risério e as contradições de um racismo 'anti'racialista." Alma Preta, December 19, 2017. https://almapreta.com/sessao/cotidiano/o-discurso-da-mesticagem-a-servico-da-branquitude-antonio-riserio-e-as-contradicoes-de-um-racismo-anti-racialista.

Schwarcz, Lilia Moritz. 2017. *Lima Barreto: Triste visionário*. São Paulo: Companhia das Letras.

Schwartzman, Luisa Farah. 2009. "Seeing like Citizens: Unofficial Understandings of Official Racial Categories in a Brazilian University." *Journal of Latin American Studies* 41 (2): 221–250. https://doi.org/10.1017/S0022216X09005550.

Segato, Rita Laura. 1998. "The Color-Blind Subject of Myth; Or, Where to Find Africa in the Nation." *Annual Review of Anthropology*, no. 27: 129–151.

———. 2007. *La nación e sus otros: Raza, etnicidad y diversidad religiosa en tiempos de políticas de la identidad*. Buenos Aires: Prometeo.

Seidler, Victor J. 1994. *Recovering the Self: Morality and Social Theory*. New York: Routledge.

Sheriff, Robin E. 2001. *Dreaming Equality: Color, Race, and Racism in Urban Brazil*. New Brunswick, NJ: Rutgers University Press.

Silva, Antonio José Bacelar da. 2014. "Dialogism as Antiracist Education: Engaging with Competing Racial Ideologies in Brazil." *Anthropology and Education Quarterly* 45 (4): 319–336. https://doi.org/10.1111/aeq.12073.

Silva, Antonio José Bacelar da, and Erika Robb Larkins. 2019. "The Bolsonaro Election, Antiblackness, and Changing Race Relations in Brazil." *Journal of Latin American and Caribbean Anthropology* 24 (4): 893–913. https://doi.org/10.1111/jlca.12438.

Silva, Denise Ferreira da. 1998. "Facts of Blackness: Brazil Is Not (Quite) the United States . . . and Racial Politics in Brazil?" *Social Identities* 4 (2): 201–234.

———. 2007. *Toward a Global Idea of Race*. Minneapolis: University of Minnesota Press.

Silva, Graziella Moraes, and Marcelo Paixão. 2014. "Mixed and Unequal: New Perspectives on Brazilian Ethnoracial Relations." In *Pigmentocracies: Ethnicity, Race, and Color in Latin America*, edited by Edward Telles and the Project on Ethnicity and Race in Latin America, 172–217. Chapel Hill: University of North Carolina Press.

Silverstein, Michael. 2011. "The 'Message' in the (Political) Battle." *Language and Communication* 31 (3): 203–216. https://doi.org/10.1016/j.langcom.2011.03.004.

Smith, Andrea. 2016. "Heteropatriarchy and the Three Pillars of White Supremacy: Rethinking Women of Color Organizing." In *Color of Violence: The INCITE!*

Anthology, edited by INCITE! Women of Color against Violence, 66–73. Durham, NC: Duke University Press.

Smith, Christen A. 2016. *Afro-paradise: Blackness, Violence, and Performance in Brazil*. Urbana: University of Illinois Press.

Soares, Glaucio Ary Dillon, and Nelson do Valle Silva. 1987. "Urbanization, Race, and Class in Brazilian Politics." *Latin American Research Review* 22 (2): 155–176.

Sodré, Muniz. 1999. *Claros e escuros: Identidade, povo e mídia no Brasil*. Petrópolis, Brazil: Editora Vozes.

Souza, Jessé. 1997. *Multiculturalismo e racismo: Uma comparação Brasil–Estados Unidos*. Brasília: Paralelo 15.

Speed, Shannon. 2005. "Dangerous Discourses: Human Rights and Multiculturalism in Neoliberal Mexico." *Political and Legal Anthropology Review* 28 (1): 29–51.

Spivak, Gayatri Chakravorty. 1988. "Can the Subaltern Speak?" In *Marxism and the Interpretation of Culture*, edited by Cary Nelson and Lawrence Grossberg, 271–316. Urbana: University of Illinois Press.

State of Bahia, Secretaria do Planejamento. 2020. *Panorama socioeconômico da população negra da Bahia*. Salvador, Brazil: SEI.

Tavolaro, Lilia Gonçalves Magalhães. 2006. "Race and Quotas, 'Race' in Quotes: The Struggle over Racial Meanings in Two Brazilian Public Universities." PhD diss., New School for Social Research.

Teles dos Santos, Jocélio. 2005. *O poder da cultura e a cultura no poder: Disputa simbólica da herança cultural negra no Brasil*. Salvador: EDUFBA.

Teles, Gilberto Mendonça. 1973. *Vanguarda européia e modernismo brasileiro: Apresentação crítica dos principais manifestos, prefácios e conferências vanguardistas, de 1857 até hoje*. 2. ed. Petrópolis: Editora Vozes.

Jones-de Oliveira, Kimberly F. 2003. "The politics of culture or the culture of politics: Afro-Brazilian mobilization, 1920–1968." *Journal of Third World Studies* 22 (1): 103–120.

Telles, Edward E. 2004. *Race in Another America: The Significance of Skin Color in Brazil*. Princeton, NJ: Princeton University Press.

Telles, Edward E., and Tianna Paschel. 2014. "Who Is Black, White, or Mixed Race? How Skin Color, Status, and Nation Shape Racial Classification in Latin America." *American Journal of Sociology* 120 (3): 864–907. https://doi.org/10.1086/679252.

Tosta, Antonio Luciano de Andrade. 2011. "Modern and postcolonial? Oswald de Andrade's "antropofagia" and the politics of labeling." *Romance Notes* 51 (2): 217–226. https://doi.org/10.1353/rmc.2011.0011.

Treviño González, Mónica. 2005. "Race, Hegemony, and Mobilisation: What Roles for the State and for Civil Society? The Transformation of Racial Politics in Brazil." PhD diss., McGill University.

Twine, France Winddance. 1997. "Mapping the Terrain of Brazilian Racism." *Race and Class* 38 (3): 49–62.

———. 1998. *Racism in a Racial Democracy: The Maintenance of White Supremacy in Brazil*. New Brunswick, NJ: Rutgers University Press.

Urciuoli, Bonnie. 2011. "Discussion Essay: Semiotic Properties of Racializing Discourses." *Journal of Linguistic Anthropology* 21 (S1): E113–E122. https://doi.org/10.1111/j.1548-1395.2011.01100.x.

Valente, Ana Lúcia E. F. 1986. *Política e relações raciais: Os negros e as eleições paulistas de 1982*. São Paulo: FFLCH-USP.

Valentino, Nicholas A., Vincent L. Hutchings, and Ismail K. White. 2002. "Cues That Matter: How Political Ads Prime Racial Attitudes during Campaigns." *American Political Science Review* 96 (1): 75–90.

Vargas, João H. Costa. 2004. "Hyperconsciousness of Race and Its Negation: The Dialectic of White Supremacy in Brazil." *Identities* 11 (4): 443–470.

———. 2006. "Black Radical Becoming: The Politics of Identification in Permanent Transformation." *Critical Sociology* 32 (2–3): 475–499.

———. 2012. "Gendered Antiblackness and the Impossible Brazilian Project: Emerging Critical Black Brazilian Studies." *Cultural Dynamics* 24 (1): 3–11. https://doi.org /10.1177/0921374012452808.

———. 2018. *The Denial of Antiblackness: Multiracial Redemption and Black Suffering.* Minneapolis: University of Minnesota Press.

Vaz, Lívia Maria Santana e Sant'Anna. 2018. "As comissões de verificação e o direito à (dever de) protecão contra a falsidade de autodeclarações raciais." In *Heteroidentificação e cotas raciais: Dúvidas, metodologias e procedimentos*, edited by Gleidson Renato Martins Dias and Paulo Roberto Faber Tavares Jr., 32–79. Canoas, Brazil: IFRS Campus Canoas.

Volosinov, V. N. 1986. *Marxism and the Philosophy of Language.* Cambridge, MA: Harvard University Press.

Weinstein, Barbara. 2015. *The Color of Modernity: São Paulo and the Making of Race and Nation in Brazil.* Durham, NC: Duke University Press.

Wirtz, Kristina. 2011. "Cuban Performances of Blackness as the Timeless Past Still Among Us." *Journal of Linguistic Anthropology* 21: E11–E34. http://dx.doi.org/10 .1111/j.1548-1395.2011.01095.x.

Woolard, Kathryn A. 2004. "Codeswitching." In *A Companion to Linguistic Anthropology*, edited by Alessandro Duranti, 73–94. Malden, MA: Blackwell.

Wortham, Stanton Emerson Fisher. 2001. *Narratives in Action: A Strategy for Research and Analysis.* New York: Teachers College Press.

Zakabi, Rosana, and Leoleli Camargo. 2007. "Eles são gêmeos idênticos, mas, segundo a UnB este é branco e este é negro." *Veja*, June 6, 2007, 82–88.

Index

Page number in *italics* represents figure.

About the Author

ANTONIO JOSÉ BACELAR DA SILVA has a PhD in linguistic and sociocultural anthropology and is an assistant professor in the Center for Latin American Studies at the University of Arizona.